CHICAGO PUBLIC LIBRARY
HAROLD WASHINGTON LIBRARY

D0891888

R0033030432

Infancy and Epistemology

DISCARD

Infancy and Epistemology:

An Evaluation of Piaget's Theory

Edited by

George Butterworth

Lecturer in Psychology,
University of Southampton

ST. MARTIN'S PRESS · New York

© The Harvester Press Limited, 1982

All rights reserved. For information, write:
St Martin's Press, Inc., 175 Fifth Avenue, New York, NY 10010
Printed in Great Britain
First published in the United States of America in 1982

ISBN 0-312-41588-5

Library of Congress Cataloging in Publication Data

Main entry under title:
Infancy and epistemology.
   Includes bibliographies.
    1. Cognition in children. 2. Infant psychology.
    3. Knowledge, theory of. 4. Piaget, Jean, 1896–
    I. Butterworth, George.
BF720.C63153   1982   155.4'22   81-18555
ISBN 0-312-41588-5   AACR2

REF
BF
720
.C63
I53
1982

Contents

Preface

One effect of the recent explosion of research on perception and cognition in babies has been to change the contemporary sterotype from that of the 'incompetent' to the 'competent' infant. However, the implications of this reappraisal extend far beyond the simple reversal of a popular misconception. The study of human infancy confronts the psychologist with assumptions that usually remain unexamined or even unacknowledged, but which are basic to the discipline. The epistemological questions raised by the experimental psychology of childhood, pioneered by Jean Piaget, attracted many of the younger contributors to this book into the field. To us, it seems that the study of babies has the potential to reconnect experimental psychology with its epistemological roots and our aim is to take one further step in this direction. The intention, in our various contributions, has been to identify some of the conditions for a synthesis between biological, psychological and philosophical approaches to the origins and acquisition of knowledge.

Doubtless there are lacunae in our discussions and whole areas of relevant research have been omitted (mainly for reasons of space) but all the chapters address, from one perspective or another, Piaget's basic assumptions about the origins of knowledge in infancy. The chapters have been arranged in three groups.

Part I 'The theoretical background' brings together three chapters which concentrate on theoretical assumptions basic to Piaget's genetic epistemology. In the first chapter, Russell sets out Piaget's presuppositions on the nature of perception in infancy and its relation to conceptual development. Piaget, in an attempt to reconcile the contradiction between nativism and empiricism, retained the assumption (common to both nativists and empiricists) that veridical perception must rely upon some process of supplementation or construction. Given this basic assumption, the developmental issue concerns the source of this supplementation or structuring. It was usual for nativists to invoke innate knowledge, whereas the empiricists appealed to 'past experience' acquired through physical contact with objects. Piaget's particular solution was to reject the doctrine of innate ideas, but to continue to supplement sensory data through the mechanism of 'circular reaction' with the consequence that his is a 'representationalist realist' or 'mediated' theory of sensory perception, in which experience acquires structure as a consequence of the invariant properties of action.

Costall's chapter, on J. J. Gibson's theory of visual perception, establishes a theoretical contrast with Piaget. This comprises a thorough, theoretical review of the principles of J. J. Gibson's theory of 'direct perception' to provide a background to many of the phenomena reported in Part II of this book. Gibson rejected the traditional empiricist hypothesis of the unreliability of vision (to which Piaget also subscribed) and claimed that there are higher order structures in ambient light which directly specify the objective properties of our environment. In J. J. Gibson's view, many of the developmental problems which Piaget requires the infant to solve, such as the tutoring of vision by touch, or the establishment of intersensory coordination, either dissolve or are radically simplified within a theory of direct perception. As Costall puts it, a theory of direct perception avoids foisting more developmental problems on the infant than are strictly necessary.

Nor does a Gibsonian account of the *process* of sensory perception simply push developmental problems backward into evolutionary biology. Rather, the value of this approach is to demonstrate that traditional accounts, which stress the limitations and unreliability of sensory experience, may simply be misconceived. To *misconceive* the *nature* of objective perception raises developmental problems equally for evolutionary and cognitive developmental theorists. The practical importance of a correct starting point for our theories is that the human infant spends many months, with limited mobility, when access to the world is primarily in terms of sensory experience. The distal senses of looking and listening may be as important to the foundations of knowing as are the 'circular reactions' and proximal experience on which Piaget lays such stress.

For J. J. Gibson, perceptual development entails the education of attention to available information, but it does not presuppose the existence of explicit knowledge. As Costall explains, action also plays a fundamental role in Gibson's theorizing, although in a different way to Piaget's constructivist account—rather than action giving rise to structure in sensory stimulation, its role is to make use of the 'affordances' of things specified by sensory stimulation. Action is controlled by the invariant properties of reality.

The third chapter of the introductory section sets the debate about infant competence into a biological context. Here Kathleen Gibson relates the developmental evidence to what is known of neuro-ontogenesis. As she shows, many recent discoveries can be accommodated within a biological framework in which mid-brain and cortical centres fulfil developmentally different control functions. Mid-brain centres appear more closely linked to 'direct' perceptual functions of the kind J. J. Gibson described whereas cortical processes seem more concerned with the 'mediated' perception which concerns Piaget.

In summary, the chapters in Part I provide the theoretical framework for the remainder of the book, and each subsequent chapter elaborates the specific details about the topics under consideration.

In Part II 'Precursors of knowledge in perception and action' the focus is on some specific topics where empirical studies have yielded results incompatible with Piaget's theory of sensorimotor development. *Two* chapters examine phenomena in the neonatal period: facial imitation and cross-modal coding, discussed by Andrew Meltzoff and pre-structured visual perception as in the new born baby's response to looming, discussed by William Ball and Eliane Vurpillot. The third chapter in this section, by George Butterworth, considers the possibility that there may exist information in sensory stimulation to enable the infant to distinguish self from environment and to perceive object permanence and identity *before* conceptual knowledge has been acquired. These chapters make detailed and carefully qualified arguments but in each case, it seems reasonable to conclude that there is evidence for objective perception prior to the development of the constructive processes considered necessary by Piaget.

The main conclusion of the studies reported in Part II is that there appears to exist a pre-established harmony between sensory perception and action. The evidence on infants suggests that J. J. Gibson's theory of direct perception may offer a more satisfactory framework for understanding the nature of infant sensory pre-adaptation and the mutuality of infant and environment than the more limited account inherent in Piaget's assumptions of 'adualistic confusion'. Although Piaget was correct to argue that perception and knowledge constitute different levels of understanding, he may have been wrong to rule out direct sensory experience as a means of gaining access to information which may form one of the foundations of knowing.

Whatever its point of origin however, there still remains the problem of accounting for developmental change and the acquisition of knowledge. This question is addressed in Part III 'The development of representation'. Here the strength of the genetic method pioneered by Piaget becomes apparent as the authors trace the systematic transformations of complex sensorimotor systems from the level of 'direct' perception, through perception 'mediated' by stored representations and the beginnings of predictive knowledge. Bullinger describes the systematic differentiation of the control system for head and eye movements, as an example of this approach in the realm of motor development. Mounoud and Vinter describe the qualitative transitions that occur in imitation and auditory-visual coordination between the neonatal period and the end of the first year of life, to yield a modified theory of representation in the Piagetian tradition. The book ends with a chapter on the developmental transition to language at the end of human infancy. Although Piaget did not address the problem of language acquisition himself, there have been various accounts from a Piagetian stand point. Lock and Brown consider the significance of the evidence on infant perceptual competence for theories such as these. They offer a new approach in which structures implicit in sensory experience are made explicit through social interaction, eventually to establish syntactic structures.

In summary, the third section of the book reinforces Piaget's insistence on the qualitative transformations of early cognitive processes as the basis for development and re-emphasizes the continuity between structures of knowledge and their foundations in human biology.

It was Baldwin's insight and Piaget's lifetime labour to demonstrate that the study of development can constitute both method and theory in psychology; the structure of mind can be unravelled by observing its ontogeny. Like any theory, Piaget's stands or falls on his assumption about the starting point for development; the original nature of mind. The genetic method allows these assumptions to be tested before the infant has acquired knowledge and such observations, reported in various chapters, have done most to shake Piaget's purely constructivist theory of perception, thought and language. Pre-adaptation of the baby to the physical and social environment is much more coherent than Piaget had supposed but it should come as no surprise to the experimental developmental psychologist, who is accustomed to thinking in evolutionary terms, that the infant should be so finely attuned to the environment of evolutionary adaptedness. On the contrary, much of this research demonstrates that the genetic method really does what Piaget said, it offers a key to the psychology of knowledge within the discipline of an evolutionary framework.

So the point of this book is not to overthrow Piaget's theory in favour of J. J. Gibson's. Gibson's insights on the nature of perception were as profound as Piaget's on the question of development. Rather, the purpose is to move forward to a new synthesis. It is sad that these eminent men should have died before the volume was completed, perhaps it will be read as a tribute to them both.

George Butterworth
Southampton, June 1981

PART I
THE THEORETICAL BACKGROUND

1 Piaget's Theory of Sensorimotor Development: Outlines, Assumptions and Problems

JAMES RUSSELL

INTRODUCTION

Organisms which survive within particular environments do so through the possession of two basic functions, organization and adaptation. However benign the environment no organism can survive unless the relations between its organs, within an organ between cells and within a cell between chemical systems are integrated within a flexible, hierarchical structure—organization. Likewise, however perfectly balanced and smoothly regulated the organic elements within the total system, the organism will succumb if it is not adapted to that particular environment—even Olympic champions can only survive on planets more or less like the Earth.

But organisms do more than employ the environment for nutrition and bodily comfort: they manipulate it, interact with it and even try to understand it. Behaviour, and thus intelligence, is also to some degree successful by virtue of organizational and adaptive functions; indeed it is virtually impossible to say where 'biological' functions end and 'behavioural' functions begin. But what of human rationality—up to and including the higher reaches of logico-mathematical thinking—is this also a derivative of basic biological functions? If it is anything at all Piaget's theory of intelligence is a brilliantly elaborated affirmative answer to this question. From his earliest teens Piaget had been attempting to show the continuity between biological and intellectual life, but it was not until he wrote *The Origin of Intelligence in the Child* (hereafter referred to as *Origin*) in 1937 that such a programme began to be realised. The thesis of this book, which I am now going to critically discuss, is that in the human infant we can witness the transition from biological to intellectual functions, so that human infancy should be regarded, in J. H. Flavell's phrase, as 'the crucible of cognitive development'. Piaget gives the account of sensorimotor development in six stages but this is only for convenience: the essential message is one of continuity.

Biology and Intelligence

At the outset Piaget describes the functional invariants common to biological and intellectual life, calling the adaptive element of rationality 'the accord of thought with things' and the organizational element 'the accord of thought with itself' (Piaget, 1953, p.8). Piaget calls the intellectual manifestation of organization the *regulating function* and claims, adopting his usual Kantian terminology, that behaviour reflecting biological functions will constitute certain logical 'categories'. Each category consists of a pair of elements, with the first from the regulating function containing Totality and Relationship. All 'behaviour patterns and consciousness' consist of interdependent elements within a Totality, which is to imply that actions and thoughts consist of organized elements and are to that extent complete entities in contrast to reflexes of mental images. Moreover, for a totality to be organized its elements must form a definite system of Relationship to each other: in the total act of prehension, for example, success is dependent upon arm extension being related to finger spread and these to trunk orientation, just as the arithmetical notion of addition is correlative to that of subtraction. Piaget's own empirical example is Köhler's demonstration that chickens' colour perception is relational, just as others have argued (for example, Lawrenson and Bryant, 1972) that young children's stimulus coding is relational.[1]

A 'dynamic' expression of Totality and Relationship is what Piaget calls Ideal and Value. These form the second regulating category. This means that although an item of intelligent behaviour constitutes a whole as a static abstraction, when it is viewed as something within the stream of the agent's motivated behaviour the whole involves the *completion* of a 'goal state–means–end' sequence. Action completes a circle by joining the goal state to the end or ideal, so that a state of organism–environment disequilibrium (broken circle) becomes one of *equilibrium*. The values are the means whereby the goal is achieved and are thus the dynamic equivalents of relations within totalities; for instance, the infant's hand and the rattle form a completed whole wherein the grasping is both the means and the relating element.

Moving now to the biological invariant of adaptation, Piaget describes this as being reflected in intellectual functions in two ways: via the *implicative* function of *assimilation* and via the *explicative* function of *accommodation*. Each of these functions have two categories. Just as physical survival necessitates the literal assimilation of environmental material—food, sunlight, oxygen—so intelligent behaviour and thought involves making some aspect of the world part of our existing mental life-assimilation. This results in the two categories of Quality × Class (qualitative classifications) and Quantitive rapport × Number (quantitative relations). In the first of these, when the infant shakes a rattle he is assimilating it into the class of 'things to shake' and ascribing to it the quality of 'shakeability'; he is literally implicating or enfolding rattles within a mental category. As to the second assimilatory category of qualitative relation we might give the example of an infant who can discriminate his mother from his father because the mother has longer hair (quantitative), or because she talks more softly to him. In that everything which involves quantitative differences potentially involves also units of quantitification, this will later be elaborated as the notion of number.

But the concrete world is not infinitely malleable and assimilable and therefore actions have to be modified in the light of what obtains in reality: blankets and rattles, for example, cannot be shaken in the same way, indeed blankets present the infant with a very different range of assimilatory possibilities than do rattles. And so we have the complementary process of accommodation, whereby actions, and later concepts, are modified in accordance with concrete reality, with things, and thus develop, unfold, become explicated. Therefore the categories thus produced are those which concern things and events, the categories which deal with objects in space and of causal relations between them (Object × Space and Causality × Time). Piaget's actual account here is excessively gnomic, but what he appears to intend is that assimilatory activity is constrained by concrete things and their spatial and causal relations in a way that suggests they have an objectivity which qualities and quantitative relations lack. For we do, in a sense, *project* qualities, classes, relations and number onto the world through our assimilatory activity.

But what, you may well ask, has any of this to do with a baby's sensorimotor development? According to Piaget it has everything to do with it simply because sensorimotor development *is* the process whereby, what he calls the 'categories of reason' are constructed through action. These categories are not innate structures, they are not formed by the habitual linking of unitary sensations, they are not molded through rewards and success, and they do not represent a separate faculty with its own *sui generis* laws of development. Indeed Piaget takes great pains to show precisely how these four theories (nativism, associationism, pragmatism and vitalism) fail and how a fifth account which regards development as the interplay of complementary processes of assimilation and accommodation is the only remaining contender.

So before Piaget gets down to reporting empirical findings he presents a framework for describing the essential continuity of biology and knowledge. Organization is both psychologically and physiologically 'the internal aspect of adaptation' (*Piaget*, 1953, p.12), the set of mental functions which makes any intelligent action possible. Adaptation is 'organization grappling with the actions of the environment', the interaction between a structuring intelligence and the world. On the psychological level Piaget refers to organization as 'rational activity' and adaptation as 'experience'.

The Stages

Piaget's task is now to describe, indeed to explain, the progression of his own three infants—as representatives of infanthood—from helpless neonates into small children who can do such things as invent new means for specific ends, represent invisible events, think through possible event sequences, and so on. Additionally, his aim is to achieve this with the minimum of explanatory terminology and by assuming very little in the way of native capacity. He has at his disposal a kind of learning theory in terms of assimilation–accommodation interaction, as well as the notion of organization understood as the tendency towards wholeness, which is partly motivational and partly reflecting the general tendency of all mental activity towards equilibrium between individual actions and between actions and the environment.

The metatheories which Piaget rejects respectively assume cognitive development to begin with a cognitive framework being applied to the world (nativism), with perceptual input (associationism), with the reinforcement of random movements (pragmatism), or with a kind of primitive striving (vitalism). For Piaget, intelligent life begins with directed action. Action is not initially intelligent, but is elicited and reflective: a stimulus to the palm elicits hand clenching, to the side of the cheek head turning, to the lips sucking, and so on. Piaget is also at pains to show that one rarely encounters anything like a pure reflex in the human neonate, in the sense of something that springs out as a complete, stereotyped package after a very specific kind of stimulation. Yet although there is a little flexibility there is insufficient to say that assimilation and accommodation can be differentiated as separate processes. So in order to describe the transition from reflexive to adaptive action he introduces two more items into his theoretical baggage: *scheme*[2] and *circular reaction*. Schema (of which Piaget's term is a derivative) is a term originally used by Kant to denote the application of categories of reason in experience, and by J. M. Baldwin (Baldwin, 1906a; Russell, 1978), to refer to early infant actions that are determined by current interests or drives (for example, the 'schematic meaning' of a rattle might be as something to suck). For Piaget a scheme is like a concept except that it is on the plane of action—striking, sucking, grasping etc. Even reflexive movement expresses a form of sterotyped scheme, but one so sterotyped that the analogy with the verbal concept breaks down. Circular reaction meant for Baldwin (Baldwin, 1906b; Russell, 1978) the deliberate repetition of an action which produces pleasant stimulation, which *overproduces* actions and thus creates a pool of actions to be used in accommodation. Piaget's usage is somewhat more determinate than Baldwin's, at least in the early weeks of life.

What is essential to the reflex is its finite and irreversible nature: the sequence is stimulus → movement. The movement will only be produced again given another stimulus of the same kind, and so a reflex-governed organism is powerless to produce the movement 'for itself'. But in the circular reaction we have a circular relationship between environment and movement whose essential feature is the organism's ability to *reproduce* the result originally produced by the environment by, as it were, going back to the beginning, to the original conditions of stimulation. For example, sucking is reflexive when it is elicited by the infant's finger *happening* to brush past the lips; it is part of a circular reaction when the infant is able to *continue* the sucking beyond the reflexive elicitation by putting his fingers into his mouth in a directed fashion. The notion of the circular reaction is meant to encompass the infant's abilities to reproduce actions—to continue them beyond stimulation conditions—and is thus the launching-pad of intentionality.

In the circular reaction we can view assimilation and accommodation as separate entities:

there is assimilation to the extent that it constitutes a functional use prolonging the assimilation reflex ... to suck thumb or tongue is to assimilate these objects to the very activity of sucking. But the circular reaction is accommodation to the extent that it realises a new co-ordination not given in the hereditary reflex mechanism. (Piaget, 1953, p.61)

Here is one of Piaget's observations which illustrates and requires no environmental trigger.

At 0;2 [14] and at 0;2 [16] I note how definitely the spontaneous grasping of the sheet reveals the circular reaction—groping at first then regular rythmical activity (scratching, grasping, holding and letting go), and finally progressive loss of interest (Obs. 53).

It should be noted that the circular reaction fulfils the regulating function described above and thus the categories of Totality (a self-completed action) and Ideal (goal-directedness). It also expresses the implicative function of assimilation and thereby the categories of Quality × Class (e.g., thumbs are categorized as suckable) and Quantitative rapport × Number (sucking can be more or less intense). Also the explicative function of accommodation is expressed: the Object × Space category (the thumb is more than a mere eliciting stimulus but now on the way to being cognized as a thing to be acted on whose spatial relations to other objects are manipulatable) and the Causality × Time category (the infant as agent causes the movement, the thumb causes a sensation and the former precedes the latter).

Piaget's explanation throughout puts the weight on the active process of assimilation; and this in contrast to Baldwin for whom accommodation is the active principle (Baldwin, 1902; Russell, 1978). The scheme and the circular reaction are both aspects of assimilatory activity, whereas accommodation is the *result* of them rather than their motivating, organising force. So in describing the second stage of sensorimotor development (Primary Circular Reactions:roughly two to four months) Piaget tries to characterize all the infant's cognitive acquisitions without departing from his assimilation terminology: the application of a scheme to a new situation or object is 'generalizing' assimilation; the application of a scheme to a familiar situation or object is 'recognitory' assimilation; the repetition of a scheme is 'reproductive' assimilation. When schemes become enriched by being applicable within more than one modality at once (for example, grasping what is being seen) Piaget talks of 'reciprocal' assimilation *between schemes* of hand movement and of looking. Therefore, assimilation is not only the organizing and motive force whereby the infant constructs reality, but is also the mechanism whereby the schemes themselves fuse and become differentiated. (Piaget is careful to dissociate assimilation from *association*.) Schemes do not only play an adaptive role, because the gradual progression of differentiation and integration between schemes, which is worked out in wonderfully convincing detail by Piaget, is the development of an 'internal' process of mental *organization*. But viewed adaptively assimilation is the motive force which determines the nature of experience, and whenever it overreaches itself accommodation is necessitated and is the result.

Assimilation is certainly an elastic concept. Indeed Piaget states that it can be regarded as taking place both 'from the point of view of consciousness and of behaviour' (Piaget, 1953, p.140). As regards consciousness *images* (of a thing-to-suck, to look at, grasp, etc.) are assimilated to schemes. But from the viewpoint of the circular reaction the act of assimilation is behavioural: 'the performed act leaves a vacuum which, in order to be filled, leads to the repetition of the same act' (*Ibid.* p.142); but the responding leads to unforseen results and thus the next performance is changed slightly, that is, accommodated.

This latter phenomenon—the modification of a circular reaction in order to reproduce a fortuitous effect on the world—is the essential feature of Secondary Circular Reactions which make their appearance during roughly the fourth month of life. They signal the arrival of true intentionality because the infant in this third state is capable of understanding that a chance effect of a circular reaction is the result of his own activity, and then going on to reproduce this effect—or attempting to. For the Primary Circular Reaction, things are, as Piaget calls it, the 'aliment', or the nourishing agent, of an essentially autistic act done for its own sake—sucking, vision, or prehension. For the Secondary Circular Reactions, on the other hand, things are the aliments for a movement that is directed, the grasping *of* something.

Let us consider just one example of this because it neatly illustrates the significance Piaget wishes to give these acquisitions. In Observation 107 Piages describes how a five-month-old Lucienne, when in her bassinet, confronts some spools suspended above her by means of elastic bands:

. . .She usually uses them in order to suck them, but sometimes she swings them while shaking herself when they are there. She manages to touch but not yet grasp them. Having shaken them fortuitously she then breaks off to shake herself a moment while looking at them (shakes of the leg and trunk), then she resumes her attempts at grasping.

Why has she broken off in order to shake herself for a few seconds? . . . Everything transpires as though the subject, endowed for a moment with reflection and internal language, said to herself something like this:

'Yes, I see that this object could be swung but this is not what I am looking for.'

But lacking language, it is by working the scheme that Lucienne would have thought that, before resuming her attempts to grasp. In this hypothesis the short interlude of swinging is a kind of motor recognition.' (*Ibid.*p.186).

Just before Piaget states that secondary schemes constitute:

the first outline of what will become 'classes' or concepts in reflective intelligence: perceiving an object as something 'to shake', 'to rub', etc. This is, in effect, the functional equivalent of the operation of classification peculiar to conceptual thought (*Ibid.* p.183).

He also states that the recognitory assimilation in the previous example, indeed generalizing assimilation also, can be regarded as a pre-conceptual form of meaning, and this because the act of making an element (sensory image) into part of a scheme by whatever kind of assimilation is tantamount to ascribing to it a significance *as* a something. So here again we have a parallel with verbal-conceptual abilities: the 'signifier' is the asimilatory act or verbal expression, the 'signified' is the perceived object or concept. The act/expression parallel is relatively straightforward, but the perceived object/concept parallel requires some justification; for are not things and concepts very distinct kinds of entity? Piaget's assumption is that they are not—indeed his whole theory depends on their being epistemologically equivalent. His point is that our knowledge of objects is itself the result of *intellectual construction*, 'the product of geometric, kinematic, causal etc. elaborations, in short, the product of a series of acts of intelligence' (*Ibid.* p.190). Knowledge of things is not the result of a direct perception of qualities whose coherence is more or less 'real'; rather it is the result of the kind of active organization and adaptation described above. This view is greatly elaborated in Vol. 2 of the infancy trilogy called, without metaphorical intent *The Child's* Construction *of Reality* (my emphasis). The commonsense view which regards the object as real in itself quite apart from intellectual construction, Piaget explains as a kind of throw-back to 'infantile realism'. It is difficult to determine exactly what Piaget means by this—perhaps it could mean the infant's apparent belief that objects have real causal powers which only have to be triggered off by his touching them (described in Vol. 2). Perhaps a better parallel would be with the intellectual realism of childish thought where a child might describe his dreams as real entities which come in through his window or out of his pillow, where he might draw an object from all angles at once, or where he might believe that thoughts and words are somehow in things (Piaget, 1929). Therefore, realist epistemologies are basically symptoms of the fact that even intelligent adults may not be fully liberated from primitive egocentric modes of thinking. Although Piaget's talk of 'qualities of the object . . . collected by the mind in a unique bundle' (*Piaget*, 1953, p.191) may have a seventeenth-century idealist ring to it, these are not qualities passively recorded but qualities actively assimilated to prior schemes.

By the fourth stage—the Co-ordination of Secondary Schemes

after about eight months of life—the process of scheme differentiation and integration has continued to such an extent that one scheme
can serve as the means for the realisation of another. A frequently
quoted example of this is Observation 122 where Laurent *sets aside*
(scheme one) his father's hand in order to *grasp* (scheme two) a
matchbox.

I will not present this and the final two stages in any great detail
because once the essential machinery of the theory has been understood further progress seems to occur almost as a matter of logical
inevitability. We are still, of course, dealing with circular reactions,
but in stage four the end or goal is really a separate entity which
is 'posited' without ever having been attained before-hand in
that situation. The goal of the circular reaction in the early weeks
of life was merely the prolongation of an effect *once it had been
achieved.*

Let us consider some stage four examples of the foreshadowing of
conceptual by sensorimotor intelligence. As especially interesting
case is that of negation. Piaget is by no means the only theorist to
have located the origins of negation in sensorimotor development.
Freud (1925) traced negation to the infant's spitting out of unwanted
food and his acts of excretion. Baldwin (1906a) originated negation,
qua class exclusion ('limitation'), in the infant's earliest selective
action such as grasping a rattle and ignoring a ball. Piaget's account
is closer in intention to that of Freud than that of Baldwin: he is
interested not merely in the negative face of class delineation but in
the act of negating a *proposition*, of assigning falsehood to it rather
than truth. For Piaget as for Freud such assignment is an act before it
is a judgement. We have an instance of this in the infant's removal of
obstacles in order to apprehend an object. Here the obstacle is
assimilated to the scheme of the objective, but at once schematized
itself as being negatively related to the fulfilment of that scheme.
There is an initial sensorimotor entertainment of the proposition
followed immediately by the rejection of it. Piaget justifies this
treatment of the negative by agreeing with Kant, Bergson and others
that a negative judgement is a kind of second-order judgement—a
judgement *passed on* a judgement. So if we adopt an assimilatory
perspective it is possible to view this sensorimotor procedure as both
affirmatory (assimilation) and negating (via removal) and thus as an
instance of the sensorimotor 'logic' of negation.

Psycholinguistic research has suggested that indeed the function of
the negative form *is* to negate a previously assumed positive proposition, and that when a negative sentence does not have this function it
is more difficult to process (Greene, 1979). Donaldson (1970) and

De Villiers and Flusberg (1975) have produced evidence that young children find descriptions of negative referents very difficult to complete; though Watson's (1979) data suggests that this effect can be modified. Children below about eight years of age find the discrimination between necessary and contingent sentences far more difficult when their forms are negative than when complex relative clauses are involved (Russell, 1980 (b)). Also Piaget himself, in his more recent work on the relation between performing a task and understanding the principles involved in success (Piaget, 1978), reports that younger children typically ignore negative elements in a task, such as the necessity for removing something. In general it does not appear that we need quarrel with what Piaget has to say about negation being a second-order judgement and therefore difficult, but the status which he wishes to give obstacle removal as an instance of sensorimotor negation is open to question, as we shall be discussing later.

Piaget characterizes the schemes of the fourth stage as being essentially mobile in the sense of grouping and re-grouping in relations of the kind found in conceptual–verbal intelligence. 'In effect', he says, 'the subordination of means to ends is the equivalent, on the plane of practical intelligence, of the subordination of premises to conclusions, on the plane of logical intelligence' (*Piaget*), 1953, p.238). To express the same thing in terms of Piaget's biological framework described above, the categories of reason (rooted in the regulating function out of the biological principle of organization) of Totality × Relationship and of Ideal × Value are now emerging in observable logical behaviour. The value of the object is now clearly dissociable from the action taken upon it because a hand, for example, can be valued negatively as an obstacle, positively as a useful intermediary, or positively as an end in itself.

In stage five—Tertiary Circular Reactions after about the twelfth month of life—the infant is still preoccupied with means and ends but this time the schemes he applies as means need not be familiar ones but may be specially invented for the purpose. These new means are discovered on the spot by 'active experimentation'. But how does this creativity, or 'fecundity' as Piaget calls it, arise? It is, Piaget would answer, central to the very notion of assimilation. But specifically the bridge from stage four to five is by way of the infant's systematic exploration of new objects by old schemes as an end in itself. Here the infant tries to 'understand' the nature of a new object by employing the scheme as the 'instrument of comprehension'. Presumably this fuels the development of actions conceived as sets of trials in the exploration of alternatives within a given context, from which it is a relatively short step to the development of alternative schemes for a given purpose, and thus 'fecundity'.

The cases which Piaget considers here are grouped under the different intermediaries used in the attainment of objectives—supports, sticks and strings. For example, an infant may be faced with the problem of retrieving a distant object given only a stick and given that the only stick-based schemes he possesses are ones connected with waving, throwing and striking. A new tailor-made scheme is required of tapping by progressive steps, which the infant must develop out of one of the familiar schemes.

To return to Piaget's sensorimotor/conceptual parallel, the distinction between the application of familiar schemes or the invention of new ones in the solution of a means–end problem, on the one hand, and the circular reactions themselves (primary, secondary, tertiary) on the other, is 'analogous to that which can be made on the plane of verbal or reflective intelligence between reason and judgements, reasons being a combination of judgements [circular reactions] of which some serve as means and others as ends' (*Ibid*. p.267).

It may be evident that as we pass through the stages less and less reference needs to be made to the process of accommodation. This is because action becomes progressively more determined by schemes which are, as it were, 'in the infant's head'. Of course there still *is* accommodation to things as they are—this is a logical necessity of successful action—but accommodation is treated more as the consequence of successful assimilation than as a regulative process in its own right. Successful accommodation is the outcome of a progressively complex assimilation. In the development of new means, for example, accommodation is directed by two forms of assimilation: of the 'initial' schemes which construct the means and the goal, and the 'derived' schemes—the finer grain of the assimilation process—which give meaning to the results of each individual assimilatory action (*Ibid*. p.296).

Stage six—the Invention of New Means through Mental Combination—arrives about half way through the second year of life. It is constituted by the infant's ability to 'think through' a sequences of actions of the kind encountered in the previous stages, without needing to act them out. Previous workers (Hobhouse, 1929; Köhler, 1921) have proved examples of such 'insightful' behaviour in apes, but Piaget was the first to attempt an explanation of its genesis in human beings. In Observation 181 he describes how Jacqueline (at 1;8) is faced with the problem of opening a door whilst carrying a blade of grass in each hand. She realises that if she merely places the grasses on the floor the draft of the door will chase them away, so she carefully places them out of the range of the door's movement. She does not have to witness the consequence.

Piaget does not set about explaining internalization positively by saying what new mental process the infant now undergoes— although here and in the later volumes he does describe how mental imagery supports this deduction. Instead he indicates what the infant *no longer requires* for intelligent action: the support of props in the concrete world. He reiterates that all schematic behaviour is 'internal' from the outset, and that therefore one should not even speak of the 'internalization of actual experiences' (Piaget, 1953, p.348). The elaboration of schemes out of reflexes, which has just been traced, is itself mental and thus internal. It so happens that after about eighteen months of age the schematic machinery of differentiation, integration, co-ordination, reciprocal assimilation etc. has no further need of what Piaget call 'external alimentation'.

Some skeptical points

The *Origin* is a masterpiece of close and—given the necessary degree of abstraction—lucid argument. It is rigorously consistent and all-inclusive and therefore carries, on its own terms, enormous conviction. The problem, or nest of problems, which I now wish to discuss concerns the nature of these 'terms', that is, the kind of assumptions that Piaget makes about the nature of mental development and the nature of knowledge.

In the light of these assumptions it is worth considering that Piaget's theory of intelligence was already very well developed before he ever came to the study of infancy. Through philosophical argument and much empirical work with children of school age he had already constructed the basic architecture of the system; so he saw his task (Piaget, 1952) as discovering the origin of mental processes in infancy for whose nature he had already developed a theory. Thus the 'categories of reason' are nothing other than Piaget's *own* explanatory categories. He was, in a sense, applying his own highly integrated and differentiated schemes to what he witnessed in his own children. This is not objectionable in itself: the 'application' has resulted in major discoveries which have since been substantially replicated in the essentials (White, 1969), and it has generated a series of fairly clear hypotheses, such as those concerning the egocentric nature of the infant's spatial universe and object knowledge which have also been, with substantial qualifications, supported (Bremner and Bryant, 1977; Harris, 1974). The point at issue is whether the principles upon which Piaget constructs his explanatory scheme are sound.

At all costs—and for philosophical reasons—Piaget wishes to avoid on the one hand what he calls the 'apriorism' which posits innate pre-organized cognitive structures, and on the other hand the empiricism which construes the mind as a recording instrument and explains the fact of organization by such principles as habit and association. He attempts to extract what is fruitful from each and eschew what is objectionable. In establishing his categories of reason Piaget borrows from apriorism the notion of self-organization (later called autoregulation) whilst rejecting the structural nativism and whilst making self-organization a *functional* principle common to all organic life. From empiricism he takes the notion of reality-monitoring whilst rejecting the notion of the organism as a passive receiver of stimulation: phenomena are recorded but only by virtue of prior action schemes which are modified by environmental contingencies in accommodation. This latter is also a functional, indeed a pragmatic principle, and is borrowed, with modifications, from Baldwin, who had one foot in the pragmatist camp.

Piaget had already carried out a similar exercize (the resolution of rationalism and empiricism) for conceptual intelligence in his previous works on childhood and had, of course, come up with roughly the same set of principles—assimilation, accommodation, regulation. For it is partly by virtue of this movement from philosophical principle to empirical hypothesis that Piaget is able to show what he takes to be the *foreshadowing* of conceptual intelligence by sensorimotor processes. He was faced with the same problem on both the conceptual and the sensorimotor level and solved it by the same set of principles. This suggests that there was the hidden assumption that both levels *could* be explained by positing the same set of principles.

This movement from the philosophical to the empirical should not, I believe, be objected to; it is one aspect of the genetic epistemological method and can be justified philosophically (Russell, 1979). My skepticism really concerns the nature of Piaget's attempt to extract the best of apriorism and empiricism and eschew the worst, and his resultant argument that the roots of conceptual intelligence are to be found in action schemes. There are, as we shall see, other ways of avoiding the unwanted consequences of apriorism and empiricism which do not necessitate the assimilation theory.

'The 'empiricist' face of Piaget's resolution is the assumption (not, I think, 'observation') that all the infant brings into the world behaviourally is a set of reflexes. He additionally assumes that the modalities are unco-ordinated. Piaget's empiricism consists of the rejection of any organizing principles or structures *prior to* assimilatory activity.

The 'nativist' face of Piaget's resolution consists of the notion of regulation and in the self-generated, organizing, and motivational aspects of the assimilation concept. The infant is biologically determined to regulate its own activity and also to assimilate data to schemes. The modalities are co-ordinated by the infant's own activity via reciprocal assimilation which is a native, functional principle.

The consequence of Piaget's revised empiricism-cum-nativism is that the human infant is, as it were, left an awful lot to do by himself. On the one hand no prior adaptation to the concrete world as a specific kind of environment is allowed beyond the reflexes. Although we have anatomical pre-adaptation (feet not flippers, lungs not gills, etc.) Piaget is reluctant to allow any pre-adaptation in the brain to a world of perduring three-dimensional objects with weight and solidity which interact in determinate ways, and to a world of people as a very special class of objects. Everything has to be achieved by regulation and by assimilatory activity, both of which result in the differentiation and integration of schemes.

Whether or not one happens to regard this kind of account as inherently implausible there are both philosophical and empirical objections to be raised. As will be evident from the previous review, Piaget is staunchly anti-realist in that he regards every item of concrete knowledge as an intellectual construction. The empiricist aspect of this is the proposal that things are, for the adult as well as for the infant, bundles of sensory data which have a coherence not because they possess this coherence in themselves but because the organism has organized perceptions through action on certain principles. Of course, accommodation has a role to play so the nature of these organizations are constrained within limits 'given' by the concrete world. But accommodation is a limit-setter to, rather than a determinant of, scheme elaboration. As mentioned above, there is a contrast here with Baldwin who regarded accommodation rather than assimilation as the determinant of cognitive change and claimed that the real world imposed itself upon the infant and energized change through its 'refractory' nature (Baldwin, 1906a).

The nativist aspect of this anti-realism arises out of Piaget's proposal that the infant's behaviour expresses certain biological universals of organization which, as we have seen, resulted in the six categories of reason. Piaget is nowhere more Kantian than in this aspect of his theory. On one interpretation of the *Critique of Pure Reason* (what Strawson (1966) has called the 'unacceptable face of the *Critique*') the Kantian categories can be construed as innate cognitive structures. On the basis of this Kant was able—indeed *had*—to argue that nature was mind-made. This, as Strawson tries to demonstrate, resulted in the 'disastrous' theory of two worlds, the 'phenomenal' world of experience and the 'noumenal world' of absolute reality which we have to posit but can never know. All species of idealism whether rationalist (Plato), empiricist (Berkeley), transcendental (Kant) or dialectical (Hegel) have the consequence that reality is 'mind-stuff'. They are then faced with the problem that if this is the case what does objectivity consist of and what is the source of our concepts? Platonic Ideas, God, the Noumenon, Geist and other solutions to the problem of objectivity have all been tried, and although they may have differing degrees of success with *conceptually* mediated knowledge, they all fail to account for the objectivity which is pre-conceptual and behavioural and which we are concerned with here.

Although in the *Origin*, as well as elsewhere (Piaget, 1956, p.3), Piaget is quick to reject Kantian apriorism, one is justified in suspecting that Piaget's categories of reason, though not construed as innate, involve Piaget in similar difficulties to those encountered by Kant (at least in one 'face' of the *Critique*). In Piaget, as in Kant, objectivity arises out of the application of categories through some kind of schematizing process. And although Piaget's categories are not innate structures but develop out of a self–world interaction, this aspect of Piaget's nativism makes the result of this interaction *inevitable*—an inevitability which is a function of the native human constitution. That is to say, the path from reflexes to categories of reason is wholly determined by regulative, assimilatory processes: the infant, as Piaget himself puts it, *constructs* reality. So although the Piagetian categories cannot be construed as innate they have to be regarded as the result of the infant's having certain innate functions. On Piaget's theory the infant is 'active', right enough, but this is an activity that is biologically canalized towards the categories of reason.

If, then, concrete reality is an intellectual construction out of action schemes Piagetian theory must encounter the problem of objectivity as do all forms of idealism. Needless to say Piaget himself foresees this as a possible difficulty and tackles it head-on in the closing pages of the book. He writes:

The principle problem to be resolved for an interpretation based on assimilation as well as for every theory of intelligence entailing the biological activity of the subject himself is, it seems to us, the following: If the same process of assimilation of the universe to the organism occurs from the physiological to the rational plane, how is it possible to explain why the subject comes to understand external reality to be sufficiently 'objective' and to place himself in it? (Piaget, 1953, p.412).

He also hints at the, almost inevitable, critical point that he is setting the problem of egocentricity for *himself* as well as for the child—with the result that he has to expand so much theoretical energy in explaining how the 'grouping' of actions and concepts via manipulation and social interaction results in the dissolution of egocentricity and the acquisition of objectivity in later childhood.

In addressing this problem Piaget admits that accommodation is not the answer because accommodation is little more than his term for the successful assimilation of reality to a scheme, or as he puts it 'such an explanation would be tantamount to either answering the question by the question itself, or else to saying that assimilation of things to the subject loses in importance in proportion as intelligence develops' (*Ibid.* p.412–3). And yet Piaget's answer is in terms of the process of *assimilation* itself. What produces objectivity is the fact of reciprocal assimilation, or the co-ordination of scheme with scheme. Thus, grasping an object may be integrated with seeing it, just as seeing in the sense of passive observation becomes differentiated from seeing as a preliminary to grasping. Thus it is the growing complexity of assimilatory processes, their gradual development into coherent systems by the synthesis of modalities, that 'makes possible the gradual objectivization of intelligence itself' (*Ibid.*, p.413).

Yet the solution, just like the problem, has a Kantian flavour to it. Piaget seeks to explain objectivity in terms of the process whereby visibility is correlated with touchability and with audibility in schematic action. Kant pointed out that only objects have the 'synthetic unity' (that is, things are seen where they are felt etc.) necessary for the application of categories. But Kant did not believe that this somehow solves the problem of objectivity—it is merely an assumption on which the solution is based. For what is Piaget's solution based on beyond the fact that things do, as it happens, possess this sensorial unity and that therefore assimilatory activity must encounter such regularities as it develops. There is no warrant for going further to claim that it is the gradual complexity of assimilation *itself* which constructs this synthesis, because this synthesis is a quality of things.

Can we therefore say instead that *by his assimilatory activity* the infant discovers the synthetic unity of objects and thereby the notion of objectivity? No, for a number of reasons, but mainly because this would render the assimilation process, as Piaget intends it, redundant; and because it involves no account of how the infant differentiates self-produced from world-produced sequences of perceptual input (see below). So, perhaps it is fair to claim after all that by giving the infant the task of constructing reality through his own activity Piaget is sentencing him to egocentricity. Not surprisingly in his account of childish thought Piaget's attempted solution to the problem of egocentricity on the conceptual plane by way of progressive grouping of operations is exactly parallel to the solution in infancy in terms of the progressive integration and differentiation of schemes via regulated activity. David Hamlyn (1978) has discussed the problems faced by such an account in the explanation of conceptual intelligence, notably that 'regulation' of *concepts* must involve norms of correctness and truth.

As Piaget is primarily a psychologist these objections to his modified nativism-cum-empiricism must be carried out into the empirical field. The kind of empiricism which Piaget produces as a counterweight to nativism leads him to underestimate the degree to which the human infant's brain is pre-adapted. Meltzoff (this volume) will be discussing the evidence that is now emerging for the supramodal nature of perception in early infancy—in contrast to Piagetian theory which assumes modal distinctiveness. Perhaps one of the most significant demonstrations of this has been Meltzoff and Moore's (1977) study of the imitation of facial gestures by neonates, that is, a visual datum being reproduced kinaesthetically. The psychophysicist Lawrence Marks (1978) argues on the basis of literary as well as experimental evidence that the 'unity of the senses' is hard fact rather than theory. Colwyn Trevarthen (1977) has suggested that there is a far greater degree of pre-adaptation in the infant's early looking and reaching than has previously been assumed.

As regards the latter it is possible to question the developmental significance of these patterns of 'pre-looking', 'pre-reaching' and so on. Yet although they *could* prove to be the behavioural equivalents of foetal gills and tail, (that is, they may not be developmental 'bridges') the very fact of such precocious organization forces us to accept that the brain, as an organ, is capable of such organization *prior* to any assimilatory activity. Similarly, although it is possible to overstate the degree to which sensorimotor development by differentiation and integration is an endogenous process, and although there are difficulties in the way of claiming that the 'object concept' is the result of brain-governed changes (see Russell, 1978, Sections 3.1 and 4.4), to neglect brain development as a direct determinant of sensorimotor development is to condemn ourselves to deal with this biological phenomenon only on the level of abstract terminology. It is simply unacceptable to do as Piaget does: on the one hand to claim that:

If the co-ordination of vision and prehension were a matter of pure physio-logical maturation of the nervous system, the *differences in dates of acqui-sitions* as revealed by three such normal children as Jacqueline, Lucienne and Laurent could not be understood (Piaget, 1953, p.108, my italics)

whilst doing mere lip service to brain development elsewhere (Piaget, 1970, p.719). It is one thing to claim that the acquisition of sensori-motor *knowledge* such as that of object existence, causality, space and time cannot, for essentially philosophical reasons, be a matter of maturation (for example, of memory capacity) alone because a literal interaction between subject and environment is necessary for such knowledge. Here, surely, Piaget is correct. It is quite another thing to claim that sensorimotor developments such as the integration of kinaesthetic and visual information cannot be essentially a matur-ational matter.

Does the theory of active assimiliation resolve nativism and empiricism?

The essential novelty of Piaget's account—though shared to some degree with the vitalism which he rejects—is his conception of the human infant as *actively* regulating its interaction with the world. In fact it is precisely this active element which classical rationalism and empiricism neglected. This notion is perhaps Piaget's greatest legacy to the psychology of infant development, so much so that it has become something of a shibboleth within the field. Correlative to it is Piaget's downgrading of perceptual experience, his treatment of it as a distorting tendency or as wholly determined by assimilatory activity. Only action is potentially intelligent according to Piaget; intelligence is the equilibrated set of interiorized actions; perception lacks the five qualities which characterize intelligence; as the child develops his operational activity becomes more complex in order to emancipate intelligence from perception. And as a consequence of his view that perception is part of the general process of the construc-tion of schemes Piaget became the first to argue for what is now known as a 'constructivist' (c.f. Neisser, 1976) as opposed to a 'realist' theory of perception (Gibson, 1966).

Piaget's theory of the relation of 'perception' and 'intelligence' can be questioned not only because it may lead to the underestimation of the primitively logical nature of early perceptual skills (Bryant, 1974) but because (Piaget's (1969) fourteen differentiating features be-tween perception and intelligence notwithstanding!) it produces a systematic underestimation of the extent to which action may be dependent upon perception as well as vice versa.

Baldwin wrote of the act of assimilation as being like the casting of a net, and Piaget's usage is similar in this instance: the act of casting is somehow primary to what is caught. Perceptions are the aliments of action, the nutritional elements, and although their features become progressively more important to the infant, this is only insofar as he wants his action to succeed. From the point at which circular reactions have evolved out of reflexive action Piaget's assumption is that acting is the expression of a need-to-function (c.f. the *Function-lust* of K. Bühler), and that the perceptible world has the status of the raw material. It is partly the inevitable mismatch between scheme and sensory data that necessitates accommodation and partly the progressive integration of schemes and thus modalities that ensures that a solipsistic universe is not the result.

But are there not difficulties in the way of assuming that action determines the collection of perceptual data in this way, that such data are merely the fish in the net? Is it not the case that all directed action must be taken on the basis of, not merely what sensory data happen to be present, but the way that such data are seen, heard or felt *as*? Before the infant brings the rattle to his mouth to suck it, or before he reaches out to grasp it, there must be some perceptual apprehension, however primitive, of the data *as*, respectably, suckable and graspable. I think that this can be called 'perception'. The actions which then ensue, ensue on the basis of these modes of perception *as*.

Piaget's reaction to such a description would probably be that we have here misinterpreted the nature of the scheme. As quoted above the scheme, for Piaget, is not merely the action but the 'internal' process of cognitively framing sensory data for which the 'external' fact of action on things is the alimentation. What else, Piaget would argue, is perceiving *as* other than assimilation? But if this is a species of assimilation what are we to make of the *act* of sucking, grasping, etc.? This must also be assimilation, but is it not something quite different from the initial, as we might call it, 'perceptual assimilation'? It is action taken on the basis of perceptual assimilation, which will, of course, determine the next phase of perceptual assimilation. But in running perceptual and active assimilation together we end up with a concept so broad and indiscriminate that it seems capable of explaining almost any *possible* developmental phenomenon and therefore hardly any *actual* phenomena.

One might propose that perceptual assimilation is a function of active assimilation rather than vice versa. But *could* it be this way round? If intelligent action really does begin with action itself then grasping for grasping's sake, for example, would have to result in the notion that some perceptual images are more 'graspable' than others. The empirical difficulty of such a view is that we would therefore have to conceive of the infant initially grasping in a wholly indiscriminate fashion, that is, mostly thin air—and neonates simply do not behave like this. A logical difficulty with such a view is that grasping completely without regard to sensory context should properly be treated as something akin to hand flexion rather than incipiently directed action. The fact is that even the most casual observation of the human neonate tells us that there is a primary unity between sensory datum and action. Piaget labels this 'reflexive' as if it should be regarded as the model of the knee jerk, and therefore as something that has to be *overcome*, something from which the infant has to break free by making action progressively more *independent* of eliciting conditions. But perhaps what is commonly regarded as the reflexive stage is better seen as evidence of the primitive unity of the perception → action sequence: the infant does not then have to make action independent of perception, but rather comes to integrate the progressive strength and flexibility of its actions to the progressive informativeness of its perceptual input. No one would deny that these two processes are interdependent— obviously they feed off each other; but what one can deny is the proposal that the former determines the latter. I think that it is reasonable to suggest that the progressive enrichment of the perceptual field may even lead the way, that perception may 'teach' action. This may well not be the case, of course, but it is a more defensible position than that perceptual assimilation is the outcome of active assimilation. Other chapters in this volume illustrate the form this enrichment might take.

Action is also important in an even more crucial sense: as a necessary condition for the objectivization of perceptions as being of something external to the self. There are two possible ways of viewing these—perhaps they are, in fact, two aspects of the same fundamental process. Firstly, we can assume that the infant has what Baldwin called 'functional interests', that is, he is primed to want to grasp, suck, track images etc. The motivational features of the infant's cognitive life are subsumed under the umbrella of 'assimilation' (see Wolff, 1960) in Piaget's theory. Also, given that the infant is relatively incompetent at fulfilling these interests he will on occasions fail. Baldwin called the inevitable failure 'embarrassment'—a necessary mismatch between striving and the 'datum'. Without this embarrassment it is difficult to envisage how an objective world would ever come to be cognized. This is emphatically *not* the same process as accommodation: it does not have to lead to the adaptive modification of the action, but what it must lead to is a resultant consciousness of perceptual data as not being infinitely assimilable. Secondly, by acting the infant will produce sequences of perception that are action-dependent (for example, he turns to the left and the visual image of a table lamp moves to the right), which can be discriminated from world-governed sequences (for example, mother moves the lamp off the table). It was Kant again, who, in the Second Analogy section of the *Critique*, showed how such a discrimination was necessary to the experience of an objective world.[3].

So we can agree with Piaget that the acquisitions studied in the second volume of the infancy trilogy (object existence, causality, space and time) cannot be explained by positing brain-governed changes alone. Though a necessary condition of knowledge acquisition, improvements in theory capacity, perceptual differentiation and integration etc. do not by themselves provide the infant with any basis for cognizing perceptual data as being *of* anything. But none of this justifies the view that assimilation, as construed by Piaget, is the master developmental process on the grounds that assimilation is essentially about action.

The consequence of the present line of argument which:

(a) takes a more realist view of the concrete world;
(b) accepts that the human infant's action and perception is extensively pre-adapted;
(c) regards much of sensorimotor differentiation and integration as brain-governed;
(d) makes perceptual processes primary to motor; and
(e) attempts to unpack the notion of assimilation into its perceptual, motoric and motivational elements

is to implant a degree of skepticism about the parallels which Piaget draws between sensorimotor and conceptual intelligence. It is solely by virtue of the assimilation concept that this parallel, of which I have provided many examples above, has such explanatory power within Piaget's theory. For if we conceive of the human infant as active and structuring to *that* extent then to that extent we will also be able to view him as truly intelligent, as being, in fact, like the adult or older child who purposely manipulates judgements in reasoning. By virtue of that assumption we are able to regard the infant's removal of an obstacle to get something he wants as relating premises to conclusions and negating propositions. (Although Piaget writes in the *Origin* of this being an 'analogy' the architecture of the theory necessitates its being a good deal more than this.)

However if we dissociate the perceptual from the motoric from the motivational aspects of assimilation and if we regard things as more than intellectual constructions, if indeed we regard perception not as merely the internal aspect of assimilation but as constituting the field of the infant's consciousness, we can still regard such procedures as primitively intelligent in some way but need not give them even the most primitive *judgemental* status. The perception of the matchbox, in Observation 122, as graspable and of the hand as removable in the context of wanting the matchbox leads the infant to remove the hand and grasp the matchbox. There is no reason why we should refrain from calling this means–end behaviour: what can be questioned in the purported intimacy of the relationship between means–end behaviour and logicality. In means–end behaviour of this kind, given the perceptual and motivational context as described, a certain form of action follows *because the world is organized: infant–adult's hand–matcbox*.

Although the degree to which concepts and logical systems are culturally relative is highly controversial (see Warren, 1979), the fact that concepts change between the age of language acquisition and adolescence certainly is not. But directed action does not evolve and change in the way that concepts do: it becomes more successful in terms of what the infant wants to do. For concepts, on the other hand, the notion of success is in the system itself not as something *vis-à-vis* the judging subject and the world. When conclusions 'follow' they do so because of the rules of the system in which the premises are embedded; when actions 'follow' given a concrete situation and a motivated agent who perceives the world in a certain way they do so because of mental states and thing states coming together in a certain way.

So it is only defensible to talk of construction when such degrees of freedom do exist and when the determinant of the response is not a mental state (a perceptual–motivational state of the infant). Moreover in the conceptual case we have something (a judgement) *made on the basis of* what obtains in the concrete world and which is true by virtue of this. But the perception of a matchbox as graspable etc. is not 'made' nor is it on the basis of anything: it is the immediate apprehension of sensory data in a certain way.

So it is only within an account which regards perception of things as the product of intellectual constructions that such an analogy holds between patterns of successful action and patterns of logic. This analogy is not a mere spin-off from the main course of Piaget's argument in the *Origin*: it is wholly determined from the point at which he derived categories of reason out of biological and then action functions. But if we adopt a realist epistemology we view successful action in a different light: not as the manipulation of intellectual constructions, but as action upon objects jointly determined by a perceptual–motivational state of the subject and by what obtains in the world. Of course the eight-month-old infant does not see the object as real to the same extent as we do, but this need only be translated as 'the infant's intellectual construction of the object is less elaborated than the adult's which is in turn less elaborated than that of the physicist which will in turn be less elaborated than that of the physicist in the twenty-first century, within Piaget's epistemology. Outside of this epistemology, both eight-month-old infant and psychologist father see real objects, but in the former case they have less objectivity than for the latter. Moreover, within the human conceptual system the father's knowledge of the matchbox's existence (given some conditions about his being sane and alert) is not relative: it is the kind of thing that we mean when we say 'He knows for certain that there is a matchbox in front of him'. Of course he cannot see the object from all sides at once whilst feeling it all over etc., but to say that we can only claim certain knowledge of a thing when we are receiving all the perceptual input that there could be at once[4] is to make the same kind of insistence as the solipsist who claims we can never *really* know another's mental states. The whole-hearted constructivist and the solipsist both fail to recognize, in different ways, that the validation of claims to know is something that must take place within a system of judgements which contains criteria for truth and that once validated under their own terms cannot be questioned. The matchbox of the physicist is not a 'higher' form of intellectual construction of the object. It is something entirely different: an attempt to describe the material nature of the matchbox and explain its behaviour.

Finally, none of these skeptical points should be taken as implying that Piaget has *overestimated* the infant's knowledge of the concrete world and of the relation of his actions to it. We can certainly characterize the infant's behaviour as evincing pre-conceptual knowledge that (say) he has to x to obtain y, as we might regard the result of operant shaping as resulting in a form of 'epistemic behaviour' (Russell, 1980(c)) that x leads to y. To call both cases 'epistemic' behaviour is not to suggest a *parallel* between them in terms of the kind of behaviour that they are, but, negatively, to disclaim an explanation of the behaviour in terms of S–R schedules, and, positively, to imply that, as the behaviour takes place because of the subject knowing something about the world, the explanation should make reference to such things as 'cognitive states', 'plans', 'consciousness', 'purpose' and cognate terms. The divergence from Piaget here is about the way in which this knowledge is *partial*. However, the perceptual–motivational account of directed action of Bindra (1978) diverges from Piagetian theory far more radically because its explanatory constructs *are* scheduled behavioural units: S–S, however, rather than S–R.

CONCLUSION

I doubt that there are a set of stand-up-knock-down arguments for realism beyond the statement that it is the only alternative open to us, and I think it is rather late in the day to debate the relative merits of constructivist versus realist epistemology. My case is simply that Piaget's theory of sensorimotor development depends utterly on his constructivist epistemology. It is important also to note that this is not merely the psychological assumption that the brain constructs models of reality from fleeting and degenerate input (the field of artificial intelligence is predicated on this assumption), or that we must go 'beyond the information given'. The brain may well frame hypotheses and models on the basis of inadequate evidence, but this cannot mean that what we *know* of the world is some kind of ever-evolving set of scientific hypotheses (Anscombe, 1974).

In the *Origin* Piaget brilliantly illustrates the inadequacies of nativism and empiricism as theories of sensorimotor development, and provides his own, essentially Kantian, assimilation theory as the best contender. But over forty years on it has come about that these two dogmas bave been replaced by this third wherein unreflective acknowledgement is given to 'interaction', 'the active infant', 'infancy as the period within which basic cognitive structures are formed', and so on. Of course dogmas have great heuristic value but they have this partly because they cannot be systematically questioned.

Notes

1 In fact two-year-old and three-year-old children are equally capable of coding *absolute* stimulus values in the kind of situation used by Lawrenson and Bryant. (Russell, 1980a).

2 Although early translations of Piaget used the term 'schema' the correct translation should be 'scheme'. See Furth (1969).

3 Baldwin has something similar in mind here, perhaps running the two cases together:

We are justified, I think, in saying that consciousness has a very different colouring in two such cases for example as these: the one in which an appetite has led to a train of movement sensations after which the object of the appetite is obtained; and the other in which there is the perception of the movement of a ball through a series of positions, as it bounds about the room . . . . It has been argued with emphasis that the active processes, those constituting on developing the interest, are or may be those which determine the object as such to the thinker (Baldwin, 1906a, pp.48–9).

4   The signified of a perception—that is to say, the object itself—is therefore essentially intellectual.

No one has ever 'seen' a mountain or even an inkwell from all sides at once in simultaneous view of their different aspects from above and below, from East and West, from within and without, etc. (Piaget, 1953, p.190).

References

Anscombe, E. (1974) 'Comment on Professor R. L. Gregory's paper', in Brown, S. C. (ed.) *Philosophy of Psychology*, Macmillan, London.

Baldwin, J. M. (1902) *Development and Evolution*, Macmillan, Basingstoke.

Baldwin, J. M. (1906a) *Thought and Things, Vol. 1 Functional Logic*, Swan & Sonnenschein, London.

Baldwin, J. M. (1906b) *Mental Development in the Child and in the Race*, Macmillan, Basingstoke.

Bindra, D. (1978) 'How adaptive behaviour is produced: a perceptual– motivational alternative to response-reinforcement', *The Behavioural and Brain Sciences*, 1, 41–93.

Bremner, J. G. and Bryant, P. E. (1977) 'Place versus response as the basis of spatial errors made by young children', *Journal of Experimental Child Psychology*, 23, 162–71.

Bryant, P. E. (1974) *Perception and Understanding in Young Children*, Methuen, London.

De Villiers, J. G. and Flusberg, H. B. T. (1975) 'Some facts one simply cannot deny', *Journal of Child Language*, 2, 279–86.

Donaldson, M. (1970) 'Developmental aspects of performance with negatives', in Flores d'Areais, G. B., and Levet, W. J. M. (eds) *Advances in Psycholinguistics: Research Papers*, North Holland, Amsterdam.

Freud, S. (1925) 'Negation', in Strachey, J. (ed.) *Standard Edition of the Complete Works of Sigmund Freud, Vol. XIX*, Hogarth Press, London.

Furth, H. (1969) *Piaget and Knowledge*, Prentice-Hall, New York.

Greene, J. M. (1970) 'Syntactic form and semantic function', *Quarterly Journal of Experimental Psychology*, 22, 14–27.

Gibson, J. J. (1966) *The Senses Considered as Perceptual Systems*, Houghton, Boston.

Hamlyn, D. W. (1978) *Experience and the Growth of Understanding*, Routledge & Kegan Paul, London.

Harris, P. L. (1974) 'Perseverative search at a visibly empty space in young infants', *Journal of Experimental Child Psychology*, 18, 535–42.

Hobhouse, L. T. (1929) 'Comparative psychology', *Encyclopaedia Britanica*.

Köhler, W. (1921) 'Zur psychologie des schimpansen', *Psycholische Forschung*, 1, 22–37.

Lawrenson, W. and Bryant, P. E. (1972) 'Absolute and relative codes in young children', *Journal of Child Psychology and Psychiatry*, 13, 25–35.

Marks, L. (1978) *The Unity of the Senses*, Academic Press, London.

Meltzoff, A. N. and Moore, M. K. (1977) 'Imitation of facial and manual gestures by human neonates', *Science*, 198, 75–8.

Neisser, U. (1976) *Cognition and Reality*, W. H. Freeman, San Francisco.

Piaget, J. (1929) *The Child's Conception of the World*, Routledge & Kegan Paul, London.

Piaget, J. (1952) 'Autobiography', in Boring E. G. *et al.* (eds) *History of Psychology in Autobiography*, Vol. 4., Clark University Press, Massachusetts, Worcester.

Piaget, J. (1953) *The Origin of Intelligence in the Child*, Routledge & Kegan Paul, London.

Piaget, J. (1956) *The Child's Conception of Space*. Routledge & Kegan Paul, London.

Piaget, J. (1969) *The Mechanisms of Perception*, Routledge & Kegan Paul, London.

Piaget, J. (1970) 'Piaget's theory', in Mussen P. (ed.) *Carmichael's Manual of Child Psychology*. Vol. 1, John Wiley, Chichester.

Piaget, J. (1978) *Success and Understanding*. Routledge & Kegan Paul, London.

Russell, J. (1978) *The Acquisition of Knowledge*, Macmillan, Basingstoke.

Russell, J. (1979) 'The status of genetic epistemology', *Journal for the Theory of Social Behaviour*, 9, 53–70.

Russell, J. (1980a) 'Pre-schooler's success at coding absolute stimulus values', *Journal of Genetic Psychology* (in press).

Russell, J. (1980b) 'Discrimination between necessarily and contingently true judgements in children' (unpublished data).

Russell, J. (1980c) 'Epistemic behaviour and operant conditioning' (unpublished manuscript). 1980(c)

Strawson, P. F. (1966) *The Bounds of Sense*, Methuen, London.

Trevarthen, C. (1977) 'Basic patterns of psychogenic change in infancy', in Nathan H. (ed.) *Proceedings of the OECD Conference on Dips in Learning, St. Paul de Vence, March, 1975*, OECD, Paris.

Warren, N. (1979) 'Universality and plasticity, ontogency and phylogeny: the resonance between culture and cognitive development', in Sants, H. J. (ed.),

Developmental Psychology and Society, Macmillan, Basingstoke.

Watson, J. M. (1979) 'Referential description by children in a negative form', *British Journal of Psychology*, 70, 199–204.

Wolff, P. H. (1960) *The Developmental Psychology of Jean Piaget and Psychoanalysis*, International Universities' Press, New York.

White, B. L. (1969) 'Piaget's theory of sensorimotor development', in Elkin, D. and Flavell, J. H. (eds) *Studies in Cognitive Development*, Oxford University Press, London.

2 On How so much Information Controls so much Behaviour: James Gibson's Theory of Direct Perception

ALAN COSTALL

Upon the whole I am inclined to think that the greater part, if not all, of those difficulties which have hitherto amused philosophers, and blocked up the way to knowledge, are entirely owing to ourselves. That we have first raised a dust, and then complain that we cannot see.
(George Berkeley)

Epistemological Dualism and the Psychology of Perception

Psychology prides itself on having thrown off an unpromising past in philosophy to make its mark in the world of science, and tends to be wary of any in its ranks caught looking back. Yet when psychology first established itself as an independent discipline, there was little intention of breaking all ties with philosophy. William James, for example, was well aware that the new psychology was far from self-sufficient:

When we talk of 'psychology as a natural science', we must not assume that that means a sort of psychology that stands at last on solid ground. It means just the reverse; it means a psychology particularly fragile, and into which the waters of metaphysical criticism leak at every joint, a psychology all of whose elementary assumptions and data must be reconsidered in wider connections and translated into other terms. It is, in short, a phrase of diffidence, and not of arrogance. (James, 1892, pp.467–8)

The official history of psychology might describe the late nineteenth century as the period of our brave strike for freedom, but it seems clear that if we had failed to move we would have soon been pushed. Frege's influential arguments against psychologism stressed the irrelevance of psychology in the matters of philosophy (Sober, 1978), and the departure of psychology was necessary for philosophy's own search for a kind of identity as a conceptual as opposed to empirical investigation. As a result, the door was quickly closed behind psychology, and has, on later occasions, been slammed in its face, with accusations of amateurism, 'hasty epistemologizing', or confusion concerning what it was really about (for example, Hintikka, 1975; Hamlyn, 1961, 1969). In the face of this kind of rejection, and the rather curious pleas of arch-empiricists within psychology for philosophical neutrality, the task of examining and repairing the foundations has been largely neglected.

Many of the central concepts of psychology stem from a scientific cosmology introduced at the time of the Renaissance, yet remain largely unchallenged. The prevailing conception of nature is essentially that of Galileo's doctrine of dynamics: 'an irreducible brute matter, or material, spread throughout space in a flux of configurations . . . senseless, valueless, purposeless' (Whitehead, 1926, p.22). Within this scheme, mind came to be viewed as a passive container, a convenient repository for all those properties of the world which somehow failed to figure in this mechanical philosophy. The remaining problem, of course, concerned the place of mind itself:

The mechanical theory of nature which has dominated modern science seems bound to state the relations of minds to matter and of matter to minds in terms of mechanical processes which by their nature secure no place for mind and so-called mental processes. . . . In general, the connections between the experiencing individual and the things experienced—conceived in their physical reality—were reduced to a passive conditioning of states of consciousness.

Into such a mind was carried . . . whatever in nature could not be stated in terms of matter in motion. . . . The result of this was to force upon the mind the presentation of the world of actual experience with all its characters, except, perhaps, the so-called primary characters of things. Mind had, therefore, a representational world that was supposed to answer to the physical world, and the connection between this world and the physical world remained a mystery. (Mead, 1938, pp.359–60.)

The problem of perception, as traditionally conceived, has been to explain how communication is possible between the realms of the physical and the mental, between, to paraphrase D. H. Lawrence, the dry and sterile little world and the abstracted mind which inhabits it (Willey, 1973, p.36). Although a number of writers, in philosophy, phenomenology, and radical behaviourism, have questioned the validity of such an enterprise, James Gibson has been the first within the main stream of experimental psychology to have embarked upon a sustained and radical reformulation of the philosophical framework of perceptual theory. Unfortunately, his claim to have found psychological support for realism (e.g., Gibson, 1967a)—a claim which is either obviously wrong or highly obscure (cf. Blackmore, 1979; Hintikka, 1975; Austin, 1962)—has distracted attention away from the true value and unity of his work over the last thirty years, the identification of some of the conditions for a psychology of perception free of the rigid dualisms of traditional epistemology (see Tibbetts, 1972).

He takes the view that we have often been too busy seeking solutions to stop and question the problems themselves. His strategy, therefore, is based on their elimination, rather than resolution, for, he argues, once the appropriate terms for describing perception are employed, the classical puzzles simply disappear. His relevance to infancy research, of course, is in helping psychologists to avoid foisting more problems onto babies than either babies or psychologists really need.

The Psychophysical Approach to Perception

An attempt to bridge the gulf between the material world and perceptual experience came early in the history of experimental psychology, by way of psychophysical monism. The project of psychophysics was to employ classical scientific method against the materialist orientation of the nineteenth-century thought, against the scientific cosmology which had led to the dualist schism in science and western culture in general (Arguelles, 1972). As a start, in 1860, Fechner set out to show that sensation was not only within the pale of scientific measurement but entered into 'functionally dependent relations' with physical stimulation. The possibility of extending the project to 'higher mental activity' was, he stressed, a matter of opinion, although he himself could foresee no boundaries:

> Indeed, I feel that the experience of harmony and melody, which undoubt-edly have a higher character than single tones, is based on the ratio of the vibrations that themselves underlie the separate sensations, and that these ratios can change only in exact relationship to the manner in which the single tones are sounded together or follow one another. Thus, harmony and melody suggest to me only a higher relation, and not one lacking a special relationship of dependency between the higher mental sphere and its physi-cal basis. Indeed everything seems to agree with this suggestion so easily pursued and extended. (Fechner, 1966, p.13)

Fechner's optimism ran counter to the widely held view that whilst sensation considered as the direct effect of sensory excitation is immediately dependent upon the physical stimulus, perception itself transcends its physical basis, relying upon some kind of mental contribution from the perceiver. This is the view which still domin-ates current perceptual theory, and is encountered in nearly all of the textbooks:

In the fading twilight of a room we can begin to realize that what we know about the objects that furnish it is not supplied directly by the senses. Rather there is an interplay between the evidence from our eyes and the knowledge, both acquired and and innate, that we have in our brains. And we use this knowledge to make sense of the nerve signals from our retinas. (Oatley, 1978, p.10)

At first, the Gestalt movement threatened the small amount of ground covered in the progress of psychophysics. In their reaction to atomistic psychology, the Gestaltists questioned the phenomenological validity of sensations as units of experience, and also the 'constancy hypothesis', the notion that local stimulation has a constant result regardless of other excitations. Their objection was not solely to space atomism, the analysis of spatial configurations into their constituent parts, but especially to time atomism, the tachistoscopic dissection of consciousness into time fragments as a means of understanding its structure (Katz, 1951). Their general rejection of both atomism in psychology and the assumption of fixed psychophysical correspondence gave way, however, to a specific challenge to an analysis based upon sensations. The alleged self-evidence of sensation, they argued, is not founded on the testimony of consciousness, but on a widely held prejudice (c.f. Merleau-Ponty, 1962, pp.3–12).

The Gestaltists' own theory of isomorphism (which came close to Fechner's proposed 'inner-pychophysics') held that the structural characteristics of consciousness are in every instance related to corresponding brain processes. However, the correlation only becomes apparent, they argued, once a molecular interpretation of consciousness and physiological processes is rejected, for it is in their molar properties that the correspondences were supposed to lie: 'And if this is so, our two realms, instead of being separated by an impassable gulf, are brought as closely together as possible with the consequence that we can use our observations of the behavioural environment and of behaviour as data for the concrete elaboration of physiological hypotheses' (Koffka, 1935, p.56). These assumed molar brain processes were seldom investigated directly, therefore, but inferred either from the general properties of physical forms, or from psychological studies of the effects of variations in stimulation.

Paradoxically, their research strategy eventually led the Gestaltists to reinstate the constancy hypothesis, though in the form of perceptual or global psychophysics in contrast to the earlier, sensory psychophysics of the Structuralists:

When Korte investigated the dependence of the phi-phenomenon upon brightness, separation, etc., a new form of psychophysics began to emerge, in which the experience was a full event, rather than a fragmentary 'sensation', and in which the stimulus variables manipulated were not necessarily ones which seemed intuitively similar to, or attributively responsible for, the quality of response. In general, Gestaltists hoped to restore stimulus-response correlations by treating entire configurations as the stimuli, and entire phenomenal events as the responses; in the process, the simple associational formulae of perceptual learning were discarded. (Hochberg, 1957a, p.74)

A synthesis seemed to have finally emerged from the Gestalt reaction to the so-called atomistic psychology of the structuralists (c.f. Katz, 1951, p.3). The important contributions to this new psychophysics of perception included the work by Michotte on phenomenal causality and permanence (Michotte, 1962, 1963); the studies by Johansson (1950, for example) on the perception of movement configurations, by Heider on social events (Heider, 1944; Heider and Simmel, 1944), by Wallach (1948) on neutral colour, and, of course, Gibson's psychophysical approach to the classical problem of the visual perception of space.

Gibson's Psychophysical Theory of Perception
Gibson's contributions to the study of perception span a remarkably long period, from before the 1930s to the most recent statement of his theoretical position, *The Ecological Approach to Perception* (Gibson, 1979). He has not only introduced a radically fresh approach to the traditional problems of perception, but has subsequently revised his own earlier theoretical position in an essential way. However, a central and enduring theme of his work over the years has been frankly epistemological, the attempt to challenge the prevailing view that the objectivity of experience is the product of some kind of mental contribution from the perceiver: 'the old idea that a perception is determined partly from the outside and partly from the inside' (Gibson, 1970, p.79).

His initial, psychophysical theory of perception was outlined in the late 1940s but more fully elaborated in the following decade (1947, 1948, 1950, 1959). The aim was to show that the stimulus–response formula could be repaired without any need for patching up with assumptions of mediational processes. Given a whole tradition of perceptual theory since Berkeley based on the conviction that visual stimulation is inherently ambiguous, the problem of visual space perception would, on the face of it, seem a singularly unpromising point of departure:

The 18th century scholars understood that the eye can obtain an image of an object but cannot sense the external object at a distance—the object 'itself'. The paradox was that the latter is nevertheless apprehended. There arose among philosophers a dispute, now centuries old, over whether and how we can believe in an external world. If objects with solidity and distance were creations or constructions of the mind, then it could be inferred, for example, that they were mental objects. Physical objects either did not exist or, if they did, were unknowable. If they were nevertheless known, the explanation must be supernatural. A vast amount of intellectual effort and ingenuity has been devoted to this type of controversy or to some means of escaping from the dilemma on which it is founded. And the dilemma itself appears to rest, in part at least, on the conviction that such properties as distance and solidity cannot be sensed and that apprehension of them poses a unique and special problem. If a sensory basis for such properties could be discovered in the retinal image, however, the dilemma might collapse and the whole intellectual superstructure would fall with it. (Gibson, 1950, p.13)

He considered the perception of space as a fundamental problem, an essential starting point without a solution for which other problems must remain unclear (*Ibid*. p.viii).

Part of Gibson's programme was to 'reassert the constancy hypothesis on the basis of a broader conception of stimulation' (Ibid, p.62), to establish a psychophysics of the visual perception of space. He first came to question the privileged status of the traditional atomistic concepts of sensation and specific nerve energies within psychology and sensory physiology when he discovered that adaptation, after effects, and contrast occur in the perception of curvature and orientation. Previously, such effects had been supposed to be peculiar to secondary qualities like colour and temperature:

To the extent to which color and line perceptions behave in a similar way, to that extent at least are the perceptual mechanisms similar. And any similarity in the mechanisms underlying two such different kinds of perception is provocative of thought. Color has usually been regarded as 'sensory' while line has frequently been considered 'perceptual'. Color is a 'subjective' experience while line is 'objective'. The former is a 'secondary quality', the latter is a 'primary quality'. Any interpretation of the facts presented would at least tend to break down rather than to more firmly establish the above distinction. (Gibson, 1933, p.29)

By the 1950s, he had abandoned the conception of elementary units of consciousness in favour of the notion of dimensions of variation of experience (Gibson, 1948, p.159), and relegated sensation from its previously central position in perceptual theory to an incidental role as an experience associated with an atypical, passive mode of relating to the world—the visual field (Gibson, 1950, p.43).

An unprejudiced examination of what is actually perceived, 'carried out without preconceptions and without reference to theories as to how vision might occur' (*Ibid.* p.26), he argued, does not reveal elementary sensory experiences corresponding to the abstract geometrical concepts of space, time, points, or instants, but a world which is extended, textured, coloured, surfaced, and meaningful (*Ibid.* p.60). These variables of experience, according to the psychophysical hypothesis, must correspond to the variables of the energy flux at the receptors: 'Not only the qualities of objects but also their very object-character, substantiality, solidity etc., are taken to be discoverable in stimulation. Objects are, as it were, 'sensed' (Gibson, 1959, p.460).

But Gibson's attempt to reinstate the constancy hypothesis, to relate perception to proximal stimulation, was only part of his project towards a psychophysics of perception. His psychophysical hypothesis and his 'radical reformulation' (Gibson, 1950, p.60) of the problem of stimulation can be properly understood only in the light of the epistemological purpose of the theory. His purpose was not merely to restore the constancy hypothesis and thus eliminate the need for postulating any internal processes of organization (compare, for example, Hochberg, 1974, p.17). For unlike the Gestaltists, Gibson's concern was, and remains, not with the problem of psychophysical dualism, but primarily with the problem of the epistemological dualism between perceptual experience and the objective world. It was not enough, therefore, to demonstrate that perception is, after all, a function of proximal stimulation, that the coherence and structure of experience does not require any process of organization since 'order exists in stimulation as well as experience' (Gibson, 1950, p.187). It was also necessary to show that stimulation is, in turn, a function of the objective environment:

The theory goes beyond the relation of perception to stimulation. . . . It considers also the relation of stimulation to the external environment. The hypothesis is that . . . neglected but discoverable stimulus variables are generally quite specific to the features of the outer world which are important to the animal in question. The classical variables of stimulation, of course, do not indicate the relevant objects and events of the environment with any reliability; hence they are termed 'cues'. But if the variables of higher order can be shown to specify the world, although not to represent or replicate it, an explanation is possible for perception as defined—the business of keeping in touch with the world. (Gibson, 1959, p.457–8)

Gibson presented his theory, therefore, as a sequence of stages which involve the tracing of an unbroken chain of causation from the world through stimulation to perception. This involved not only a phenomenological analysis of perception, but a consideration of the sources of stimulation. For the latter task, he proposed a new kind of physics concerned with those entities of the world which we can perceive with our unaided senses. The function of such an enterprise was not to mine a whole new seam of esoteric facts about the world, but to take stock of those properties of our terrestrial habitat which are (literally) before our eyes, and which structure the ambient energy present in our surroundings:

It is sometimes said that present day physics has 'reduced' the world to insubstantial particles or fields. Hence the mystery of how we perceive substantial objects is not only profound, it is insoluble. This nonsense is only plausible because the physics appropriate for the study of the perception of surfaces remains undeveloped. (*Ibid.* p.470).

Gibson's treatment of the problem of visual space represented a profound departure from traditional analyses based upon the abstract terminology of geometrical optics. His basic idea was to conceive of space not as a vast, structureless container of an object or array of objects, but as a continuous, textured surface, or an array of such surfaces (c.f. Bower, 1974, Chapter 4). Space is a surface, and things rest, or come to rest, on this ground surface. Therefore, he argued, it is not objects themselves but their background which gives rise to the spatial character of the visual world, and which must be considered in the analysis of stimulation: 'instead of investigating the differences in stimulation between two objects, the experimenter is led to investigate the variations in stimulation corresponding to a continuous background' (Gibson, 1950, p.6).

The 'Ground Theory' provided the basis for Gibson's introduction of his broader conception of stimulation. Firstly, he considered stimulation in terms of variables rather than isolated units, and these variables in turn were considered to be of higher-order rather than local and punctate, involving successive order and simultaneous patterning, for example, ratios, proportions, gradients, and transformations (*Ibid.* p.154). Secondly, he stressed that these higher-order variables should be thought of as correlates, rather than copies or replicas of the distal stimulus: 'the question is not how much [the retinal image] resembles the visual world but whether it contains enough variations to account for all the features of the visual world' (*Ibid.* p.62). Thirdly, the variables of stimulation are constrained by the lay-out of the world itself; for example, the texture elements of surfaces tend to be of even scatter, and objects tend to be in contact with the ground instead of floating in a void (*Ibid.* p.177).

In his autobiography, Gibson explained that he had no patience with the attempts to patch up the stimulus–response formula by invoking mediational processes: 'in behaviour theory as well as psychophysics you either find causal relations or you do not' (Gibson, 1976b, p.132). In his 1950 book he believed that he had completed the repair of the old stimulus–response formula, or at least indicated the way to proceed. He identified a number of higher-order variables of stimulation, such as texture gradients and motion perspective, which might uniquely specify the objective properties of the world. Such variables, he argued, were precise correlates of continuous physical distance, and not mere cues or probable indicators, and therefore in no need of any kind of mental process of supplementation. In particular, he suggested that certain higher-order variables remain invariant, and correspond to the unchanging and stable properties of the world (Gibson, 1950, pp. 152–4); if so, the constancy of experience would not depend upon any process of mental compensation or construction, and might constitute a direct response to stimulation.[1]

The point of Gibson's psychophysical formulation was to show that stimulation can provide an adequate account of the objectivity of experience, that there was no need to postulate a representational world answering to the physical world, leaving the perplexing problem of the connection between these two worlds. The supposed inadequacies of stimulation were, he claimed, mistaken—having been based upon an atomistic conception of stimulation, the assumption that sensations provide the raw material for perception, and the failure to consider the constraints placed upon stimulation by the world in which we live.

In the 1950s, therefore, Gibson's theory was based upon the argument that stimulation can provide a sufficient causal explanation of perception. For Gibson, the significance of such a psychophysical theory for epistemology was clear. Since it avoided the need to invoke a mental, representational world mediating our contact with reality, the classical epistemological puzzle of perception simply disappeared: 'The objectivity of experience is not a paradox of philosophy, but a fact of stimulation' (*Ibid.* p.186).

The Senses Considered as Perceptual Systems
Stimulus–response accounts of perception have some plausibility within the confines of the laboratory—where the subject agrees, as it were, to lend his eyes to the experimenter (Merleau-Ponty, 1963, p.45). Critics of Gibson's psychophysical theory, however, seldom questioned the traditional experimental paradigms, nor the mecha-

nistic assumptions which gave rise to them. Indeed, the stimulus–
response formulation provided the starting point, at least, for their
own theories. They were concerned, rather, with Gibson's failure to
acknowledge that perception is active—'active', that is, in the
peculiar sense that the stimulus is processed in some covert fashion
by the perceiver. Gibson, however, remained largely unimpressed by
the evidence brought to bear upon him:

> All the observations and experiments of past generations . . . seem to make it
> perfectly evident that the observer contributes meaning to his experience,
> that he supplements the data, and that significance accrues to sensation. . . .
> Psychologists are accustomed to use stimulus situations with impoverished,
> ambiguous, or conflicting information. They have been devised in the hope
> of revealing the constructive process taken to characterize all perception. In
> these special situations there must indeed occur a special process. It could
> appropriately be called guessing. But I would distinguish perceiving from
> guessing, and suggest that we investigate the first and try to understand the
> second by means of corollaries about deficient information. (Gibson, 1963,
> p.11)

Nevertheless, since the early 1960s, Gibson was engaged in a
sustained and explicit revision of his theoretical position. He abandoned the psychophysical framework of his theory. His new
approach was framed in terms of the control of behaviour through
the active adjustment to, and detection of, information available in
ambient energy. Strangely enough, the catch-phrase of many of his
critics, that perception is 'an effort after meaning', now provides an
apt, if somewhat brief, description of Gibson's own theory. The
important difference lies, however, in his initial and unshaken
conviction that the world is not some huge kind of projective test,
and his new conviction that the stimulus–response formula is not
even partly right, but totally inappropriate.

The direction of Gibson's new approach was outlined in a series of
important papers published in the early 1960s (Gibson, 1960, 1961,
1962, 1963). It arose very much as a reaction to some crucial
inconsistencies within his initial theory. His analysis of motion
perspective (Gibson, 1950, 1958; Gibson, Olum and Rosenblatt,
1955), for example, sat very uneasily within the psychophysical
framework of the theory. The flow of optical texture, which, Gibson
argued, specified both the layout of the environment and the observer's path of locomotion, does not count as a stimulus in any
conventional sense of the term (Gibson, 1960; Mace, 1977). His
introduction of the concept of attention to the theory was also
problematic. It was intended to account for the failure of the stimulus
to have an effect on any one occasion (Gibson, 1958, pp.465–8), yet

within a stimulus–response story attention could only appear as 'an act of mind upon the deliverances of the senses' (Gibson, 1963, p.12), as a *deus ex machina.*

It is, however, when the subject is free of the clutches (and clamps) of the experimenter that the terminology of stimulus and response is most obviously strained. The difficulties are abundantly clear in Gibson's classic study on active touch:

Active touch is an exploratory rather than a merely receptive sense. When a person touches something with his fingers he produces the stimulation as it were. More exactly, variations in skin stimulation are caused by variations in motor activity. What happens at his fingers depends on the movements he makes—and also, of course, on the object that he touches. Such movements are not the ordinary kind usually thought of as responses. They do not modify the environment but only the stimuli coming from the environment. Presumably they enhance some features of the potential stimulation and reduce others. They are exploratory instead of performatory. (Gibson, 1962, p.477)

The psychophysical account provides not merely a distorted picture, but one subject to a disastrous reversal, in which responses seem to give rise to stimuli, yet themselves lack any obvious cause. Although Gibson retained the term stimulus in a qualified way in his second book, *The Senses Considered as Perceptual Systems* (1966), he came to see that the term can only lead to confusion outside of its home in physiology (Gibson, 1979)[2] and finally believed that a systems approach can provide a profound alternative both to the mentalism of traditional theories and the mechanistic assumptions of psychophysics.

The concept of the niche of the organism is central to Gibson's new, ecological approach (Gibson, 1966, 1979). It is a relational or dialectical concept. Unlike that of habitat, which indicates a physical locality, the concept of niche refers as much to a way of life as to the environment which supports it.

The inseparability of the concept of perception and the concept of environment was, of course, a central theme of Gibson's earliest book (1950). Indeed, as Gibson noted (1966, p.187), this important insight was outlined even earlier, by Fritz Heider in 1926:

Not all parts of the environment are of equal significance for our action. We do not have to know how the particles of the air move, but the fact that a chair stands here and a table there is important and can determine our behaviour. . . . We live only in one particular level of this world; we have no relationship to many of the facts or events of our surroundings, they are not 'real' for us. In order to gain more understanding of the significance for behaviour of the structures in the environment, we must start with a discussion of the solid units among which we live. (Heider, 1959, p.8)

In the jargon of systems theory, an organism is an 'open system' which cannot be comprehended in isolation. The unit of study must be the animal in its environment. But the organism does not 'fit' into its environment as a piece into a puzzle; 'it is not "in" the environment as coins are in a box' (Dewey, 1922, p.272). It cannot be situated solely in terms of location and scale, but as an acting, living being. A predator, for example, may share the same habitat as its prey, but 'occupies' a different niche. Similarly, the niche of a nocturnal animal differs from those of its diurnal neighbours. They lead different sorts of lives. The really important insight of the ecological approach—still less than entirely explicit in Gibson's own writings—is that the concept of perception is inseparable not only from the concept of environment but from the concept of action (see Shaw and Bransford, 1977).

Gibson's ecological approach to perception was most fully developed in relation to vision (Gibson, 1979), although it was also extended to the other senses and their inter-relationships (Gibson, 1966). Perception was no longer considered as a one-way chain of causation, from object to 'percept'—nor, for the most part at least, as a stage on the way to action—(Gibson, 1972, 1979, p.56). He argued that the external senses should be considered as active, exploratory, intimately interconnected, systems, rather than as passive, mutually exclusive channels; they should be categorized not in terms of anatomy, but by their function as modes of external attention: looking, listening, touching, smelling and tasting. They serve, as he put it, to pick-up available information.

Gibson's new concept of information is central to his revised theory, and has been articulated in most detail in the case of visual information (Gibson, 1961). Gibson's earlier tenet, that proximal stimulation is univocally related to its source by virtue of physical laws is retained in the later concept of information. Information specifies the objective properties of the world. But Gibson did not consider information as a stimulus; it is not a cause of perception. It is obtained not imposed: 'The world is specified in the structure of the light that reaches us, but it is entirely up to us to perceive it. . . . Perceiving is an act, not a response, an act of attention, not a triggered impression, an achievement, not a reflex' (Gibson, 1979, pp.63 and 149).

The concept of information stemmed from Gibson's new analysis of the optical basis for visual perception. In 1961, Gibson outlined a 'proto-discipline' of ecological optics (c.f. Gibson, 1959, pp.472–5), which he further developed in his last two books (1966, 1979, see also 1972, 1974); he also indicated the lines along which related disciplines, corresponding to the other senses—for example ecological acoustics—might proceed (Gibson, 1966). In his ecological optics, the retinal image no longer provides the starting point for his analysis. Indeed, the organism itself figures only indirectly in his account, by defining the salient structures of the environment. Once again, however, Gibson concluded that surfaces are 'where most of the action is' (Gibson, 1979, p.23). Classical optics, he pointed out, not only failed to recognize that radiant light becomes directionally structured by the structures of the environment, but failed to explore the interesting possibility that the structure of the resulting ambient optical array might prove quite specific to its source. For such structure, univocally related to the environment itself, would constitute information potentially utilizable by a sentient organism—and (to be more parochial) would at last provide psychologists with the basis of an adequate theory of the objectivity of perception. Perception, Gibson stressed, is not, as classical optics had assumed, of light *per se*, but of things by means of light (Gibson, 1970, p.75).

In a normal terrestrial environment, radiant light will necessarily become structured, and the ambient optic array surrounding and converging upon any given location will be unique, as will the changing array converging to a moving location. Gibson's claim is that such structure contains an inexhaustible amount of information.

He suggested that the analysis of the informational resources of light can, and should, proceed without any reference to the sentient organism in question (c.f. Mace, 1977, p.52; Warren, 1978, p.11). The arguments for the proposed autonomy and priority of ecological optics are based on two observations: that the environment existed before the perceptual systems evolved and provided the conditions for their evolution; and that identical information can be picked up by radically different kinds of receptor systems.

The proposal that ecological optics is (both logically and strategically) distinct from, and prior to, the psychological questions of perception is plainly wrong for a number of reasons. Firstly, the organism does, in fact, figure in ecological optics from the outset (albeit indirectly), in defining the relevant structures of the environment. Secondly, as Gibson himself emphasized, the organism's body itself structures and is specified in the optic array. Thirdly, in terms of research efficiency, there is little point in attempting to itemize available sources of information in relation to situations in which perception is known to be unreliable—not because information is absent necessarily, but because even if it is present it is evidently ineffective. In any case, the arguments for the autonomy of ecological optics are based on the assumption that a niche is a pre-existing slot into which the organism must fit. Yet a niche is negotiated. Organisms must find a place for themselves in a heavily populated world— sometimes, as for migratory species, at great trouble and expense.

In practice, Gibson's approach to ecological optics has been informed by psychological considerations. Demonstrations of the unreliability of 'peep-hole' vision, notably the Ames room and the trapezoidal window, convinced him that the optic array converging upon a single location can only prove a weak or impoverished source of effective information (compare Gibson, 1950; Kennedy, 1974). But he regarded such conditions of perceiving the world as so special as to verge upon the mythical:

> The main fallacy ... is the generalization from peephole observation to ordinary observation, the assumption that because the perspective structure of an optic array does not specify the surface layout nothing in the array can specify the layout. The hypothesis of invariant structure that underlies the perspective structure and emerges clearly when there is a shift in the point of observation goes unrecognized. The fact is that when an observer uses two eyes and certainly when one looks from various points of view the abnormal room and the abnormal window are perceived for what they are, and the anomalies cease. (Gibson, 1979, p.168.)

In view of the psychological evidence for the ambiguity of a frozen or static array, Gibson concluded that we should concentrate upon the flow of the optical array surrounding a moving point of observation in order to discover the richness of available and potentially usable information. (This richness is enhanced, of course, by disparity information, yet, as Haber has remarked (1978, p.36), Gibson devoted little attention to the fact that a static (intact) individual simultaneously occupies two station points.) The structure in the flowing array is subject to a variety of changes—it is enlarged, compressed, or even wiped out—and within this flowing structure there also exist elements of non-change; the invariant structure specifies the stable and unchanging properties of the environment and part of the changing structure is propriospecific, that is it is informative about the path of locomotion itself. (See Lee, 1980, for an important extension of these ideas.) The case of a stationary point of observation can also be nicely accommodated within this scheme, as long as it is not conceived as an isolated point in space (or time); a static array is quite specific, after all—to rest.

The crucial issue within Gibson's ecological programme is not simply whether information exists but whether it exists and is utilized. Ecological optics gets its point and its direction from the consideration of the informational opportunities and requirements of the organism in question. Gibson's analysis is obviously centred upon the problems of human perception. The detailed successes and failures of the research programme have been reviewed in a number of recent publications (Gibson, 1979; Warren, 1978; Mace, 1977; Hochberg, 1974). There have been some notable successes though, of course, constructivists are free to meet any such advances by partial and local retreat. But his specific proposals should not distract us from his central point. And that is not, as many take it, merely a methodological caution, that we had better clarify and examine what we mean by information before embarking upon the explanation of information processing by the perceiver, whether at the level of psychology or physiology. It is concerned with the criteria of objective knowledge. His point is that the constructivist theorist of perception who insists upon the possibility of objective knowledge and explains it in terms of prior knowledge, or who belatedly smuggles in realist principles, simply begs this issue—and the theorist who gives up the epistemological ghost entirely, in the face of the objective evidence of physics, physiology, or psychology, is plainly just confused (c.f. Katz and Frost, 1979).

Perception and Action: The Theory of Affordances

The idea of niche is central to Gibson's ecological approach. As I argued earlier, this idea implies the inseparability not only of the concepts of perception and environment but also of action. Before closing this chapter I will briefly examine Gibson's proposals for the relation between perception and action. My purpose is to show that these provide the foundation for an action-based theory of perception differing radically from the familiar constructivist alternatives.

In fact, in his final writings, Gibson would seem to have offered two quite distinct formulations of the relation between perception and action, one largely grounded within a functionalist, systems theory, framework, the other stemming from the Gestaltist notion of physiognomy, of meaning as directly perceived rather than derived (see Blocker, 1969).

His first formulation is concerned with the issue of how information controls (or comes to control) behaviour. It is based upon the important insight that the perceptual systems are not only interdependent, but themselves constitute a sub-system within a total functioning organism, an insight, as Gibson (1971, p.6) noted, earlier glimpsed by Koffka: 'If communication between the sensory and the motor system exists . . . then these two systems become part-systems of a larger system, the final equilibrium being an equilibrium of this larger system' (1935, p.316). In this view, perception is an aspect of our total functioning, not a preliminary state on the way to action but concurrent with activity. To consider perception in terms of the control of behaviour is to concentrate upon perception as an aspect of our active engagement in the world, and not at the level of reflective awareness. To this systems approach, Gibson brought to bear his concept of information, for even the organism itself is not a closed system:

Locomotion and manipulation are neither triggered nor commanded but controlled. They are constrained, guided, or steered, and only in this sense are they ruled or governed. And they are controlled not by the brain but by information . . . . Control lies in the animal–environment system. Control is by the animal in its world, the animal itself having subsystems for perceiving the environment and concurrently for getting about in it and manipulating it. (Gibson, 1979, p.225)

This approach to perception, in terms of the control of behaviour, whilst admittedly schematic, does provide an important corrective to a prevailing epistemological assumption within the theory of perception, that our relation to the world is exclusively that of a disembodied, detached spectator.[3]

The essential details of Gibson's systems approach to the relation of perception and action were outlined in his second book (Gibson, 1966). In his later writings, however, he embarked upon what seems to be an alternative formulation, the theory of affordances (Gibson, 1977, 1979), which obscures and in some important respects even runs counter to advances made within his systems treatment of perception.

The theory of affordances returns to an issue discussed by Gibson in his first book (1950, Chapter 11), the distinction between our perception of the physical layout of the world and our perception of the significance of things for our actions. The theory of affordances is based upon the claim that visual information is available to specify what an object affords: we can see that it is graspable, for example, or can be eaten, or walked upon. In this development of the Gestaltist notion of physiognomy, however, Gibson took care to avoid the kind of extreme subjectivism entailed by Koffka's notion of the behavioural environment, or the ethological concept of Umwelt.

The term affordances refers to what the environment offers the animal, and was coined by Gibson to emphasize that these must be defined with that animal in mind. The floor of a house, for instance, may not afford locomotion to an elephant, whilst a leaf may do so for an insect, but not for ourselves. Nevertheless, Gibson's point is that affordances themselves are real; they are objective properties of objects, or more precisely, invariant groupings of properties. For humans, a surface which affords walking must be level, solid, rigid, not frictionless but not too rough, and so on. These surface properties, in turn, structure light in a unique way. Thus, Gibson argues, all of these properties are specified in the ambient optic array. Gibson's crucial proposal in the theory of affordances is that we typically, and primarily, attend to the higher-order invariant information which specifies what objects afford for our actions, rather than the lower-order information which specifies its isolated properties. We simply can see that a surface affords walking.

The problem for the theory of affordances is that surfaces are not 'where all the action is', nor are they all that matters for action. A floor, for example, may prove to be wafer thin (remember Koffka's example of the horseman riding across the frozen Lake Constance). Gibson's response to this difficulty has been to slacken his strict sense of information, and, in effect, revert to a position close to Brunswik's probabilistic functionalism (c.f. Hochberg, 1957b). The surface properties of objects do not, he admitted, guarantee their internal structure, but they do happen to serve as a reliable guide: a firm green apple is hardly ever worm-ridden or made of wax; a carpet usually has a healthy, substantial floor beneath. Nevertheless, there is room for doubt. For the fact remains, that although the structure of the optic array may be quite specific to the surface characteristics of an object, it is not univocally related to its internal constitution.[4]

Now it is true that we are not obsessively circumspect in our dealings with objects. On the other hand, we certainly can tell whether a floor is sound or rotten, though not, to be sure, as merely contemplative spectators. Gibson's mistake in the theory of affordances was to ignore his own good advice. Visual information is not exclusive and sufficient in the control of all of our actions in the world; the visual system is not autonomous (Gibson, 1966). Furthermore, the perceptual systems are a part-system of a larger system; perception is often concurrent with our activities, rather than a preliminary phase. The point is, surely, that we perceive that a surface affords walking in the very activity. Although visual information is itself insufficient in this case, since a further requirement is that the object is substantial (not merely superficially promising), this further property is specified in the information available to the other perceptual systems, including the haptic and auditory systems (the 'give' of the floor, ominous creaks, and so on). And this information which controls and guides our locomotion becomes available during the act of walking. This, of course, does not imply that locomotion involves separate periods of looking, then stepping, then cautious probing with our feet; here perception and action are not distinct phases but simultaneous aspects of our total functioning—a point which is perfectly explicit in Gibson's earlier writings (for example Gibson, 1966, p.274), as in the work of others, such as Dewey and Mead, before him.

Gibson's theory is often taken to imply the primacy of perception over action since it finds no place for action either in terms of the construction of reality (in Piaget's sense, for example), or as the basis of an internal comparator along the lines suggested by von Holst or Held. His critics (and sometimes, it seems, even Gibson himself) failed to recognize the fundamental role of action in his theory. In Gibson's second book, there is an obvious emphasis on the active nature of perception, though based on a rather rigid dualism between investigative and performatory behaviour. But his later work goes further, however, and points to a more intimate and radical connection between perception and action: they are aspects of the unitary functioning of a total system, the animal in its world.

As I have tried to show in this section, the theory of affordances can not only be reconciled with Gibson's formulation of perception in terms of the control of behaviour, but can be seen as a crucial development of this approach. For the essential point of the theory of affordances is that our primary way of coming to know objects is in our practical dealings with them. As Gibson (1979, p.134) put it:

Phenomenal objects are not built up of qualities; it is the other way around. The affordance of an object is what the infant begins by noticing. The meaning is observed before the substance and surface, the color and form, are seen as such.

Engagement in the world is prior to reflective awareness. And this, for Gibson, is both the developmental and epistemological point.

Notes

1 See Bohm (1965) for a discussion of the relation between Piaget's and Gibson's use of the concept of invariant, and also Gibson's comments (1950, p.153n.) on Cassirer (1944).
2 Compare Merleau-Ponty (1963, esp. p.45). The early mechanism—

vitalism controversy within embryological theory provides some interesting parallels to the current disputes within psychology (von Bertalanffy, 1933).
3 It is revealing to look again at Berkeley's writing on perception in the light of these proposals (c.f. Morgan, 1977).
4 Except, perhaps, when the object is undergoing certain kinds of mechanical disturbance, such as compression or collison.

References

Arguelles, J. A. (1972) *Charles Henry and the Formation of a Psychophysical Aesthetic*, University of Chicago Press, Chicago.

Austin, J. L. (1962) *Sense and Sensibilia*, Oxford University Press, London.

Bertalanffy, L. von. (1933) *Modern Theories of Development* (trans. Woodger, J. H.), Oxford University Press, London.

Blackmore, J. (1979) 'On the inverted uses of the terms 'realism' and 'idealism' among scientists and historians of science', *British Journal of the Philosophy of Science*, 30, 125–34.

Blocker, H. (1969) 'Physiognomic perception', *Philosophy and Phenomenological Research*, 29, 377–90.

Bohm, D. (1965) *Special Theory of Relativity*, Benjamin, New York.

Bower, T. G. R. (1974) *Development in Infancy*, W. H. Freeman, San Francisco.

Cassirer, E. (1944) 'The concept of group and the theory of perception', *Philosophy and Phenomenological Research*, 5, 1–35.

Dewey, J. (1896) 'The reflex arc concept in psychology', *Psychological Review*, 3, 357–70.

Dewey, J. (1922) *Human Nature and Conduct*, Henry Holt, New York.

Fechner, G. (1966) *Elements of Psychophysics Vol. 1* (trans. Adler, H. E.), Holt, Rinehart & Winston, New York.

Gibson, J. J. (1933) 'Adaptation, aftereffect, and contrast in the perception of curved lines', *Journal of Experimental Psychology*, 16, 1–31.

Gibson, J. J. (ed.) (1947) *Motion Picture Testing and Research*, U. S. Government Printing Office, Washington.

Gibson, J. J. (1948) 'Studying perceptual phenomena', in Andrews T. G. (ed.) *Methods in Psychology*, John Wiley, New York, pp.158–88.

Gibson, J. J. (1950) *The Perception of the Visual World*, Houghton Mifflin, Boston.

Gibson, J. J. (1958) 'Visually controlled locomotion and visual orientation in animals', *British Journal of Psychology*, 49, 183–94.

Gibson, J. J. (1959) 'Perception as a function of stimulation', in Koch, S. (ed.) *Psychology: A Study of a Science Vol. 1*, McGraw-Hill, New York, pp.456–501.

Gibson, J. J. (1960) 'The concept of the stimulus in psychology', *American Psychologist*, 15, 694–703.

Gibson, J. J. (1961) 'Ecological optics', *Vision Research*, 1, 253–62.

Gibson, J. J. (1962) 'Observations on active touch', *Psychological Review*, 69, 477–491.

Gibson, J. J. (1963) 'The useful dimensions of sensitivity', *American Psychologist*, 18, 1–15.

Gibson, J. J. (1966) *The Senses Considered as Perceptual Systems*, Houghton Mifflin, Boston.

Gibson, J. J. (1967a) 'New reasons for realism', *Synthese*, 17, 162–72.

Gibson, J. J. (1967b) 'Autobiography', in Boring, E. G. and Linzey, G. (eds.) *A History of Psychology in Autobiography Vol. 5*, Appleton-Century-Crofts, New York, pp.127–43.

Gibson, J. J. (1970), 'On theories for visual space perception: A letter to Johansson', *Scandinavian Journal of Psychology*, 11, 75–9.

Gibson, J. J. (1971) 'The legacies of Koffka's principles', *Journal of the History of the Behavioral Sciences*, 7, 3–9.

Gibson, J. J. (1972) 'A theory of direct perception', in Royce, J. R. and Rozeboom, W. W. (eds.) *The Psychology of Knowing*, Gordon & Breach, New York, pp.215–40.

Gibson, J. J. (1974) 'A note on ecological optics', in Carterette, E. C. and Friedman, M. P. (eds.) *Handbook of Perception Vol. 1*, Academic Press, New York, pp.309–12.

Gibson, J. J. (1977) 'The theory of affordances', in Shaw, R. and Bransford, J. (eds.) *Perceiving, Acting and Knowing*, Lawrence Erlsbaum Associates, Hillsdale, N. J., pp.67–82.

Gibson, J. J. (1979) *The Ecological Approach to Visual Perception*, Houghton Mifflin, Boston.

Gibson, J. J., Olum, P. and Rosenblatt, F. (1955) 'Parallax and perspective during aircraft landings', *American Journal of Psychology*, 68, 372–85.

Haber, R. N. (1978) 'Visual perception', *Annual Review of Psychology*, 29, 19–78.

Hamlyn, D. W. (1961) *Sensation and Perception: A History of the Philosophy of Perception*, Routledge & Kegan Paul, London.

Hamlyn, D. W. (1969) *The Psychology of Perception: A Philosophical Examination of Gestalt Theory and Derivative Theories of Perception*, Routledge & Kegan Paul, London.

Heider, F. (1944) 'Social perception and phenomenal causality', *Psychological Review*, 51, 358–74.

Heider, F. (1959) 'On perception and event structure, and the psychological environment: Selected papers by Fritz Heider', *Psychological Issues*, 1(3), Monograph 3.

Heider, F. and Simmel, M. (1944) 'A study of apparent behaviour', *American Journal of Psychology*, 57, 243–259.

Hintikka, J. (1975) 'Information, causality and the logic of perception', in Hintikka J. (ed.) *The Intentions of Intentionality Boston*, D. Reidel, Holland, pp.59–75.

Hochberg, J. (1957a) 'Effects of the Gestalt revolution: The Cornell Symposium on Perception', *Psychological Review*, 64, 73–84.

Hochberg, J. (1957b) 'Review of Egon Brunswik *Perception and the Repre-

sentative Design of Psychological Experiments', *American Journal of Psychology*, 70, 480–5.

Hochberg, J. (1974) 'Higher-order stimuli and inter-response coupling in the perception of the visual world', in MacLeod, R. B. and Pick, H. L. (eds.) *Perception: Essays in Honor of James J. Gibson*, Cornell University Press, Ithaca, pp.17–39.

James, W. (1892) *Psychology: Briefer Course*, Macmillan, London.

Johansson, G. (1950) *Configurations in Event Perception*, Almkvist & Wiksell, Uppsala.

Katz, D. (1951) *Gestalt Psychology*, Methuen, London.

Katz, S. and Frost, G. (1979) 'The origins of knowledge in two theories of brain: The cognitive paradox revealed', *Behaviorism*, 7, 35–44.

Kennedy, J. M. (1974) *A Psychology of Picture Perception*, Jossey-Bass, San Francisco.

Koffka, K. (1935) *Principles of Gestalt Psychology*, Harcourt, Brace & World, New York.

Lee, D. N. (1980) 'The optic flow field: The foundation of vision', *Philosophical Transactions of the Royal Society London, Series B*, (in press).

Mace, W. M. (1977) 'James J. Gibson's strategy for perceiving: Ask not what's inside your head, but what your head's inside of', in Shaw, R. and Bransford J. (eds.) *Perceiving, Acting, and Knowing*, Lawrence Erlbaum Associates, Hillsdale, N. J. pp.43–65.

Mead, G. H. (1938) *The Philosophy of the Act*, University of Chicago Press, Chicago.

Merleau-Ponty, M. (1962) *Phenomenology of Perception* (trans. Smith, C.), Routledge & Kegan Paul, London.

Merleau-Ponty, M. (1963) *The Structure of Behavior*, (trans Fisher, A. L.), Beacon Press, Boston.

Michotte, A. (1962) *Causalité, permanence et realitè phenomenales*, Publications Universitaires, Louvain.

Michotte, A. (1963) *The Perception of Causality* (trans. Miles, T. R. and Miles, E.) Methuen, London.

Morgan, M. J. (1977) *Molyneux's Question: Vision, Touch and the Philosophy of Perception*, Cambridge University Press, Cambridge.

Oatley, K. (1978) *Cognitive Psychology: Perception: Part Two*, The Open University Press, Milton Keynes.

Shaw, R. and Bransford, J. (eds.) *Perceiving, Acting, and Knowing*, Lawrence Erlbaum Associates, Hillsdale, N.J.

Sober, E. (1978) 'Psychologism', *Journal for the Theory of Social Behaviour* 8, 165–92.

Tibbetts, P. (1972) 'Perceptual theory and epistemological dualism: Some examples from experimental psychology', *Psychological Record*, 22, 401–11.

Wallach, H. (1948) 'Brightness constancy and the nature of achromatic colours,' *Journal of Experimental Psychology*, 38, 310–24.

Warren, R. (1978) 'The ecological nature of perceptual systems', in Carter, E. C. and Friedman, M. P. (eds.) *Handbook of Perception, Vol. 10, Perceptual*

Ecology, Academic Press, New York, pp.3–18.

Whitehead, A. N. (1926) *Science and the Modern World.* Cambridge University Press, Cambridge.

Willey, B. (1973) *Nineteenth-Century Studies: Coleridge to Mathew Arnold*, Penguin, Harmondsworth.

3 Comparative Neuro-Ontogeny: Its Implications for the Development of Human Intelligence

KATHLEEN R. GIBSON

Introduction

Ontogenetic studies can clarify behavioural processes by delineating the gradual differentiation and construction of complex adult behaviours from their simpler embryonic and infantile origins (Baldwin, 1894; Bekoff, 1978; Butterworth, 1981; Parker, 1977; Tinbergen, 1961).

Extension of this method into the phylogenetic realm through studies of comparative behavioural ontogeny may provide even greater insights into behavioural mechanisms than can be gained from the study of behavioural ontogeny in a single species. Recent studies of primate behaviour from a Piagetian perspective, for instance, indicate that the ontogenetic processes resulting in intelligence are similar in diverse primate species (Chevalier-Skolnikoff, 1977, 1978; Matthieu, 1978; Parker, 1973, 1976, 1977; Redshaw, 1978). The more intelligent species achieve their greater intelligence not by altering early developmental processes, but by adding later stages of intelligence to the end of the developmental cycle (Parker and Gibson, 1979).

This terminal addition results in an apparent recapitulation of the phylogeny of intelligence during ontogeny. It suggests that early intellectual development is canalized in similar directions in all primate species including the human and that certain fundamental behavioural processes may be prerequisite to the appearance of intelligence in any species.

Despite the demonstrated utility of ontogenetic methods in unraveling the nature of intelligence, there have been few attempts to utilize them as a method of delineating the neural functions which mediate intelligence or other complex behaviours (Bronson, 1974, 1981; Gibson, 1970, 1977, 1978a, 1978b). Though meagre in number, these indicate that parallels between behaviour and maturation of brain structure at differing ages within a single species, can aid in elucidation of neural function.

Further, if intelligence develops similarly and by means of terminal addition in all species, then cross-species similarity of neurological development should also exist. In all taxa, brain regions should develop in the same sequence. Those structures playing the greatest role in the mediation of higher intelligence should mature last. Some evidence that this is the case has been presented elsewhere (Gibson, 1970, 1977, 1978a; Parker and Gibson, 1979). This paper explores this concept in greater depth and suggests that the neurological control of behaviour in the human infant may be best understood if placed within the framework of comparative neuro-ontogeny and comparative animal behaviour.

Parameters of Brain Maturation
Neuro-ontogenetic data are derived from a variety of anatomical, physiological, and chemical techniques. The majority of extent data which can be used for cross-species comparisons come from studies of myelination. Myelination refers to the acquisition of a lipoprotein sheath by nerve fibres during development. Myelinated fibres transmit impulses more quickly and have shorter refractory periods, lower thresholds to stimulation and greater specificity than non-myelinated fibres (Bishop and Smith, 1964).

Myelination is a late developmental process occurring subsequent to the major proliferation of dendrites and axons and to the onset of synaptic function and impulse transmission (Caley and Maxwell, 1971; Jacobson, 1978). Since myelination and onset of synaptic function do not coincide in time, other maturational parameters such as dendritic or electrical maturation will also be mentioned.

In general, brain structures myelinate in the order in which they mature with respect to other parameters (Jacobson, 1978). This phenomenon is particulary pronounced in the cerebral cortex. In humans, cortical areas and layers myelinate in exactly the same sequence in which they mature with respect to cell density, dendritic and axonal processes, and cell Nissl substance (Conel, 1937–67).

Definitive correlations can be found between myelination and the development of behaviour in humans and other vertebrates (Gibson 1970, 1977; Langworthy, 1928, 1929, 1933). Myelination itself must play a very strong contributory role, as it demonstrably influences behaviour. For instance, demyelinating diseases such as multiple sclerosis produce marked behavioural changes.

With these considerations in mind, myelination is used here as an index of the relative rates and sequences of maturation of specific brains, neural tracts and regions.

Species Variations in Levels of Brain and Behavioural Maturation at Birth

Species vary greatly in their maturational state at birth. Altricial mammals including tree shrews, the majority of insectivores and carnivores, some rodents (for example, mice, rats and squirrels) and some lagomorphs (for example, rabbits) are noted for their behavioural and physical immaturity at birth. They are born without body hair, with eyes and ears closed, with poor body temperature regulation and poor locomotor ability. Sensory systems and reflexes are immature. They remain in nests or other stationary places while the parents forage (Ewer, 1968; Portman, 1967).

Pre-cocial mammals including whales, dolphins, elephants, arteriodactyls and perissodactyls, some rodents (for example, guinea pigs) and some lagomorphs (for example, European hares) are relatively mature at birth. They are born with body hair, open eyes and ears, and well-regulated body temperatures. Sensory and locomotor systems are relatively mature. From birth they can keep up with a mobile group through their own locomotor efforts (Ewer, 1968; Portman, 1967).

The closest human relatives, the monkeys and apes, are pre-cocial in most birth parameters but locomotor systems are immature. This is probably best considered an adaptation to the primate habitat rather than a sign of altriciality (Portman, 1967). Primates can keep up with migratory groups from birth through their own muscular efforts, but they do so by clinging to the mother's fur.

Like altricial young, human infants cannot keep up with a mobile group through their own efforts. Although capable of supporting its own body weight at birth through grasping, the human infant, unlike the primate, cannot keep up with its group through this behaviour. It has no grasping foot, and its mother has no clingable fur. Other considerations, however, suggest that far from being altricial, the human infant is at least semi pre-cocial (Portman, 1967). The infant is born with body hair, with well-developed reflexes, and usually with relatively mature body temperature regulation. At birth, eyes and ears are functioning well. This physical maturity suggests that some human behaviours should be advanced at birth. Comparative studies of brain maturation lead to the same interpretation.

The single most critical parameter controlling early infantile behaviour, the developmental state of the brain at birth, varies markedly among mammalian species. Among placental mammals, neonatal brain weight may be as little as two per cent to as much as eighty per cent of the final adult brain weight (Portman, 1967; Sacher and Staffeldt, 1974). These differences in maturational state at birth correlate with the overall state of neonatal physiological and behavioural maturity found in any given species. In altricial forms, neonatal brain weight varies from two per cent to twenty per cent and averages about twelve per cent of final adult brain weight. By contrast, the neonatal brain size of precocial mammals varies from thirty per cent to eighty per cent or more of the final adult weight. State of myelination at birth varies from an almost adult state of myelination in the highly precocial guinea pig to no myelin at all in the highly altricial rat (Gibson, 1970). EEG activity supports the myelination data. In the guinea pig EEG activity has very nearly reached its adult form at birth. In altricial forms (pigeons, mice, cats, rats, dogs, rabbits), EEG activity begins at or subsequent to birth (Ellingson and Rose, 1970).

Monkeys and apes are pre-cocial in neural parameters. At birth their brains have achieved forty–seventy per cent or more of final adult brain weight. In the rhesus monkey myelination at birth is relatively advanced (Gibson, 1970, 1977). EEG activity begins prior to birth as in pre-cocial forms although it does not fully mature until two years of age or later (Ellingson and Rose, 1970).

Neonatal humans are intermediate between altricial and precocial forms. Newborn humans have achieved twenty-five per cent of their final adult brain weight. Myelination at birth is less advanced than in the monkeys, but much more so than in altricial cats, dogs, or rats (Gibson, 1970). In the human, EEG activity begins prior to birth as in pre-cocial forms, although, as in monkeys, it does not mature until years subsequent to birth (Ellingson and Rose, 1970).

Not only has the neonatal human brain achieved more of its final adult size and function than have the neonatal brains of altricial species, by absolute standards, it is a very large brain. At birth the human brain weighs approximately 400 g (Blinkov and Glezer, 1968). This is comparable in size to the adult chimpanzee brain and it is nearly four times as large as a brain of the adult rhesus monkey.

While much of this tissue may consist of neurons which are not yet functional (Jacobson, 1978), EEG studies cited above indicate that there is, nevertheless, considerable function in the neonatal human brain. Certainly, the human infant must possess at least as much functional neural tissue as the adults of small-brained species such as lizards or even primitive mammals and much more than the brains of altricial young. These data on neonatal brain weight and maturity are consistent with only one interpretation: the human infant should possess behaviours of considerable complexity (see the section on objections to the Piagetian framework on p. 66).

Post-natal Brian Maturation: Implications for Behaviour Maturation

To state that the brains of neonatal humans process complex behaviours is not equivalent to stating that the processing mechanisms are mature or even closely resemble those of adult brains. The neonatal human brain, though large, has achieved only twenty-five per cent of its final adult size; most of its functional capacity is yet to develop.

Little of this increase results from the addition of new neurons. Even in the highly altricial rat, the great majority of neurons are formed pre-natally. In both the rhesus monkey and the human, the percentage of neurons formed subsequent to birth is almost certainly negligible (Rakic, 1975).

Post-natal size increases result from growth of axons and axon collaterals, the formation of dendritic processes and spines, the myelination of axons and increases in numbers of glial cells. Most of these developmental events result in increased neuronal interconnectivity and neuronal interactions.

Detailed examination of maturation of specific brain regions indicates that fibre tracts and brain areas mature in the same general sequence in all mammals including humans. Myelination, in all species studied occurs in the sequence: cervical spinal cord, caudal brain stem, cranial brain stem, thalamus and striatum, limbic system, and neocortex (Gibson, 1970).

Physiological data supports the myelination sequence. In the human, spontaneous EEG activity is registered in the pons at 70 fetal days, in the limbic system at 129 fetal days and in the cortex at 170 days. Movements in response to direct electrical stimulation are recorded in the human from the lower brain stem at two fetal months, from the tegmentum at four months, from the diencephalon at five months, from the pallidum at five to eight months, from the striatum at eight fetal months and from the cortex at three postnatal months (Bergström, 1969).

The sequence outlined above primarily applies to the beginning of myelination and to the initiation of physiological function in each region. It does not necessarily apply to the achievement of an adult maturation level which may take years (Conel, 1939–67; Gibson, 1970; Yakovlev and Lecours, 1967).

The brain is characterized by an extraordinary degree of interconnectivity both within and between regions and although early maturing, sub-cortical structures cannot reach full functional maturity until the cortex itself is mature (Purpura, 1977). Consequently, in order to comprehend the contribution of postnatal brain maturation to behavioural maturation, it is necessary to understand cortical anatomy, function and development.

Cortical Anatomy and Function

The human cortex consists of four primary areas each of which serves a single modality: somatosensory, visual, auditory and motor; four secondary areas surrounding each of the primary areas and subserving the same modalities; and three association areas: parietal, temporal and frontal. Each primary area has reciprocal vertical interconnectivity with brain stem or spinal cord structures which process information in the same sensory or motor modality. Each association area interconnects with subcortical structures which process polysensory functions (see Fig. 3.1).

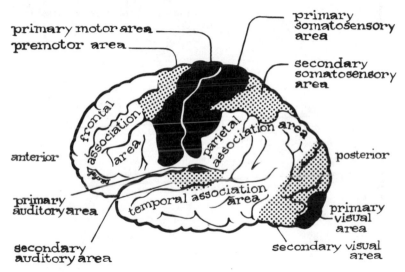

Fig. 3.1. Lateral view of human cerebral cortex demonstrating primary, secondary and association areas.

Primary areas interconnect with their respective secondary areas. Otherwise they have few cortico–cortical interconnections. Association areas, in contrast, have widespread intracortical connections both with each other and with secondary cortical areas.

Hence, the primary areas are anatomically designed to process specific motor and sensory functions and serve to expand and modify the function of specific sensory or motor structures of the brain stem. Association areas are far removed anatomically from direct sensory or motor processing areas. They are constructed to integrate multi-modal information and mediate more abstract thinking.

Each cortical area consists of six layers which are numbered from outside in as I–VI. Layers V and VI are cortical output areas which send projection fibres to the brain stem and spinal cord. The particular regions to which they project varies with the cortical area (visual cortex to visual subcortex, association cortex to polysensory areas of the brain stem, etc.). Layer IV and the lowest portions of layer III are the primary receptive layers for specific sensory afferents from the brain stem. Layer III emits the primary efferent fibres (association fibres) which travel to other cortical areas. Layer II is the primary recipient of these cortical association fibres. Layer I receives fibres from brain stem structures mediating multimodal information (see Fig. 3.2).

Hence, the lower cortical layers may be conceived as primarily controlling or modifying brain stem structures and layers I and IV as

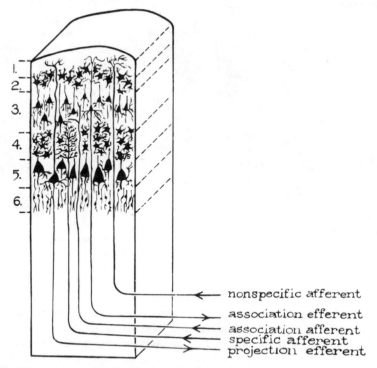

Fig. 3.2.   A cross-section through the cerebral cortex demonstrating cortical layers and efferent and afferent tracts.

primarily receiving and analyzing information from the brain stem. Layers III and II, in contrast, are involved in intracortical processing. Some functions of the neocortex which have critical import for human and primate behavioural development are *internalization, differentiation, construction* in simultaneous and sequential modes, and *mobility* (Gibson, 1977, 1978a, 1978b). In the neocortex each of these processes is applied to visual, auditory, somatosensory and motor data.

Internalization is the ability to evoke images or ideas of perceptual events in the absence of the relevant environmental stimuli. Differentiation refers to the ability to break global actions, perceptions or constructs into their component parts. Neuromuscular differentiation is evident, for instance, both in ontogeny and phylogeny as control of the digits progresses from a global whole hand control in which all five digits are moved simultaneously (characteristic of lower primates and human infants) to individualized control of specific digits. Perceptual differentiation occurs when individual members of a class of objects can be distinguished from each other: individual faces, individual chairs, etc.

Mobility is the ability to inhibit one response, percept, or concept and then move on to another. At its simplest level, lack of mobility is exhibited by reflex actions which cannot be inhibited. Another form of lack of mobility would include the persistance of a learned routine once it has lost its utility.

Construction refers to the ability to take separate individual perceptions, motor actions or constructs and join them together to make new wholes of a simultaneous or sequential nature. Examples of sequential construction include the formation of sentences by the sequential linkage of sounds, words, and concepts and the formation of a goal directed action plan by the sequential linkage of a series of subsidiary behaviours. Examples of simultaneous construction would be the formation of an object image, by mentally adding together all of its component parts (size, shape, color, position) and the formation of a three dimensional spatial 'map' of a geographic area by mentally adding together visual images from a series of walks or drives around the region.

Constructed behaviours must be distinguished from global or wholistic 'linked' behaviours in which, as in construction, two or more actions may occur together. In global behaviours, the linkage occurs in a particular invarient and undifferentiated simultaneous or sequential pattern.

Although differentiation and mobility may occur in the absence of construction, the converse is not true. Construction requires both constructional materials (differentiated percepts, actions or concepts) and the mobility that allows various combinations of these.

Limited differentiation and mobility may also be exhibited by animals which lack a cortex; it is doubtful that any construction exists in such species. In mammals, the well developed neocortex permits the construction of spatial and perceptual worlds, the recognition of objects by more than one property, and some flexibility in dealing with the environment and it may permit flexible combination and recombination of existing action patterns or mental schemes into new wholistic patterns in order to solve novel problems (Parker and Gibson, 1977).

The highly expanded human neocortex with its especially well developed frontal, parietal and temporal association areas provides for greater differentiation, mobility and constructional capacity than in any other species.

This should be contrasted with the rather simplistic view that the cortex is the seat of learning. Much learning does not require fully developed cortical capacities. Rather it involves development of a pre-existing behaviour as in the improvement of skills or in learning to make an existing response in one situation, but not in another (Bower, 1974). Simple habituation and conditioning, for instance, are exhibited by invertebrates who have no semblance of a cortex. The cortex comes into its own when very fine differentiations or complex constructions are required.

Functionally, all cortical areas probably play some role in differentiation and construction. Cortical functions differ from area to area according to the modality served and according to the complexity and nature of the resulting constructions. In general, the primary areas serve to localize stimulation in space and to differentiate fine, isolated sensory and motor stimuli within a single modality. Some inter and intramodal construction and differentiation of constructed forms and patterns occurs within the secondary areas. The association areas are the master constructors of the brain which attend to many multimodal stimuli at once and synthesize these stimuli into new constructed wholes. Each association area has a wide variety of functions ranging from the construction of early maturing concrete behaviours to the construction of highly abstract intellectual concepts. A detailed review of cortical function can be found in Luria (1966) and Gibson (1977).

Cortical Maturation
That the cortex functions neonatally is evidenced by the fact that cortically mediated EEG activity can be detected pre-natally (Berg-

ström, 1969) and epileptic fits of motor origin can be elicted pre-
natally (Caveness, 1960). Further, the behaviours of cortically dam-
aged infants can be differentiated on the basis of items such as muscle
tone, sleep-waking cycles and abnormal crying, and visual following
patterns (Brazelton, Scholl and Robez, 1966; Hill, Cogan and
Dodge, 1963; Robinson, 1969).

Although the cortex functions at birth, much physiological and
anatomical evidence indicates that its function is immature and
rudimentary. Evidence from animal studies indicates that as it
matures, the cortex, like other brain areas, may change in function
and in neural processing mechanisms. For instance, electrical stimulation of the motor cortex of the newborn macaque yields
primarily global movements such as sucking, but as the cortex
matures, stimulation yields more highly differentiated movements
for example of individual digits (Hines and Boynton, 1940). These
changing patterns coincide with changes in cortical anatomy during
maturation.

Cortical myelination can be studied with respect to long fibre
tracts interconnecting cortex and other neural areas and with respect
to fibres within the cortical areas. Detailed data on post-natal
myelination exist for the rat, monkey and human which each follow
the same pattern. The pattern of myelination is similar to other
cortical maturation parameters including neurogenesis, maturation
of chromaphile substance, axon formation and dendritic ramifica-
tion (Conel, 1939–67; Flechsig, 1920; Jacobsen, 1963; Gibson,
1970; Rakic, 1975; Yakovlev and Lecours, 1967).

In both monkey and human, myelination in fibre tracts begins
prior to birth in the projection tracts (tracts connecting cortex and
brain stem) associated with the primary areas. Projection tracts
emanating from the association areas myelinate subsequent to birth.
Some myelin is found in projection tracts underlying all cortical areas
by four weeks in the monkey (Gibson, 1970) and by four months in
the human (Flechsig, 1920).

The beginning of myelination in commissural tracts which interconnect the two cortical areas and in association tracts which
interconnect cortical areas of the same hemisphere is also subsequent
to birth. The first myelin is found in these intracortical tracts at two
post-natal weeks in the monkey and the second post-natal month in
the human (Gibson, 1970; Yakovlev and Lecours, 1967).

At birth, the layers of the human neocortex are still unmyelinated
and the cortex lacks adult dendritic proliferations and electrical
patterns. It will not completely mature in these parameters until
adolescence or later (Yakovlev and Lecours, 1967).

In the human as in the monkey and rat, the layers myelinate and mature according to other histological and physiological parameters in the order VI, V and I, IV, III and II. Within each layer neurons with long axons projecting to other areas mature first, small axonal local circuit neurons last (Jacobson, 1974).

In humans the first intracortical myelin appears in layer VI of the motor, premotor and somatosensory areas at one month of age. Primary auditory and visual areas have some myelin by three months. Secondary sensory areas receive myelin in layer VI between three and six months. Association areas have some myelin at six months.

Myelin is found in all six layers of the motor region by six months, in the premotor and primary somatosensory areas by fifteen months, and in the primary auditory and visual areas by twenty-four months. It is found in all six layers of the secondary areas between two and four years of age and in the association regions between four and six years of age. The most anterior portion of the frontal association area is not myelinated in all six layers until eight years of age (Conel, 1939–67).

Thus, primary areas are the earliest to begin myelinating (and presumably functioning) and association areas last. All neural areas, however, have a protracted period of maturation which has by no means been completed even at the latest stage of development reported here. Hence, association areas are functioning before primary areas are mature.

These maturational data suggest the following framework of human behavioural development. The earliest neonatal behaviours will primarily reflect brain stem processing mechanisms. The behaviours supported by these brain stem structures should be global, relatively undifferentiated, and relatively immobile. No constructive capacity should be present.

Gradually, as the infant develops, cortical processing will take over. The first cortical functions to manifest themselves behaviourally, probably within the first weeks or months of life, should be brain stem modulating effects provided by layers V and VI of the primary sensory and motor areas. These may appear as reflex inhibitions or as beginning differentiations of previously global activities. As the upper levels of the primary areas begin to mature, within modality sensory differentiations should become apparent.

Within modality constructions, such as construction of object concepts and simple intermodal spatial integrations depending on the secondary areas, should make their appearance subsequent to the beginning of within modality differentiations. During the latter half of the first year of life the association areas should begin functioning at first in a very rudimentary fashion. Eventually, functioning of these areas should be manifested by greater behavioural mobility and by simple concrete crossmodal construction: simple tool to use, beginning language functions such as naming, simple spatial constructs, and the ability to co-ordinate several motor actions in the pursuit of one goal.

Overall behavioural development should reflect increasing differentiation, mobility, construction, and abstraction of first perceptual and then conceptual wholes. New abilities should build upon and elaborate pre-existing ones.

Cognitive Development

Piaget

This conception of behavioural development may be correlated with theories of cognitive development as presented by Jean Piaget (1952, 1954, 1955, 1962). According to Piaget, during the first 18 months of life the behaviour of the human infant matures through a series of six sensorimotor stages. These begin with stage one 'The Reflex Stage', which extends from birth to one month and end with stage six 'Representation and the Invention of New Means Through Mental Combinations', beginning at 18 months. During this sensorimotor period the infant develops intelligence with respect to overt motor actions (Piaget, 1952).

Gradually, as the infant matures through the six developmental stages, he develops many complex behaviours including among others: the concept of three-dimensional space, the concept of an object as a permanent structure which exists even when it cannot be seen, vocal and gestural imitation, and simple tool using and object manipulative abilities. Most importantly, by the end of this period or about eighteen to twenty-four months of age, he can combine and recombine action schemes into a wide variety of novel simultaneous or sequential patterns in order to solve new manipulative problems never before encountered.

Piaget's descriptions of development focus heavily on process and mechanisms. All four of the cortical processes described in the preceding section: differentiation, mobility, construction and internalization are integral to Piaget's framework in all of his stages.

Analyses of Piaget's descriptions of development during the sensorimotor period and later stages, indicate that behavioural maturation as he described it correlates remarkably well with patterns of brain maturation. Specifically, Piaget's description conforms to the predicted subcortical control of the earliest neonatal behaviour, followed by cortical maturation in the following sequences: primary areas, secondary areas, association areas (Gibson, 1977, 1978a).

During stage one of the sensorimotor period, behaviours are as predicted from the sub-cortical model: global, immobile, poorly differentiated and non-constructed. The first evidence of differentiation and construction occurs within single sensory modalities. Only later do cross-sensory associations and internalizations begin.

Just as the cortical model predicts that new abilities will emerge by differentiating, abstracting and reconstructing existing perceptual and conceptual information, Piaget claims that:

Behaviour patterns characteristic of the different stages do not succeed each other in a linear way (those of a given stage disappearing at a time when those of the following one take form) but in the manner of the layers of a pyramid (upright and upside down), the new behaviour patterns simply being added to the old ones to complete, correct, or combine with them. (Piaget, 1952, p.329)

Detailed correlations between the emergence of specific sensorimotor abilities and the maturation of specific cortical areas have been presented elsewhere (Gibson, 1977), so the remainder of this section will illustrate two behaviours central to Piaget's scheme: development of the object concept, and of concepts of space. Then some specific behaviours thought to contradict Piaget's theories will be discussed.

According to Piaget, the infant manifests a mature object concept when he can solve invisible displacement tasks. Bower's (1974) interpretation of object concept developments seems most compatible with concepts of cortical development and is described below.

The neonate has no particular behaviour with respect to a vanished object. By eight weeks, the infant will visibly track a moving object until it disappears behind a screen and then visually anticipate its reemergence. At about the same age, if a stationary object is occluded by a screen and does not reappear when the screen is removed, the infant registers surprise.

Up to 20 weeks of age, however, the infant does not appear to recognize that a moving object which has become stationary or a stationary object which has become mobile can be the same object. In Bower's interpretation, the infant identifies moving objects according to their movement trajectory and stationary objects according to their position.

The ability to recognize that a mobile and a stationary object may actually be identical emerges at about twenty weeks of age when the infant has acquired the ability to recognize an object by the sum of its visual properties: place, movement, size, shape and colour. At this point change in a single parameter will not result in the infant considering it a new object.

The development of the object concept to this five month point clearly evidences emerging cortical function. Smooth visual tracking of a small moving object emerges in approximate synchrony with the initial myelination of lowest cortical layers of the primary visual cortext between one and three months of age. [see Bronson 1974]. As these layers are efferent and control brain stem structures, it is likely that they and not the later maturing layers are responsible for the emergence of smooth tracking.

Smooth visual tracking may be considered to require simple cortical constructional behaviours (that is, the adding together of a series of separately perceived spatial points in order to construct a concept of smooth movement). By five months, the infant has evidenced much more advanced constructional capacities. He can add together many properties of a single object: size, shape, colour, place and movement to emerge with a wholistic object concept. In adults the ability to construct an object concept from many visual attributes is lost with damage to the secondary visual areas. In the infant, myelination of the visual secondary area occurs sometime after three months of age and before six months. In other words, neural maturation occurs in synchrony with the ability to visually construct an object.

Even at five months of age, the object concept is far from mature. It is not until eighteen to twenty-four months of age that the infant can find an invisibly displaced object. In the succeeding eighteen months, the problem advances beyond that of constructing concepts of a single object to that of constructing concepts of spatial and causal relationships between two or more objects. According to Bower, the infant first learns that two objects cannot be in the same place at one time, then two objects can be in the same place if one is inside the other (inside concept). At approximately this same time (fifth stage) the infant also constructs the concept of the support: if one object rests on another and the supporting object moves, so will the one that rests upon it. Finally the concept of inside amalgamates with the concept of the support to form a construct that if a container moves, so will its contained object.

The complexity of this development may be evidenced by the fact that there is no animal other than human which in its natural state uses artificial containers to transport objects. In humans, this ability develops in concert with other object–object relationships such as simple tool use.

Both the fully developed object concept, its corollary the concept of the moveable container, and simple tool use probably require parietal association area function for their maturation. Lesions of this area in the adult produce in comprehension of container–contained relationships as well as of causal interactions between objects. For instance, patients may hold glasses of water upside down and cannot use simple tools such as toothbrushes.

Because the constructions required are fairly complex and hierarchical, cortical–cortical association layers and association fibres of the parietal areas are probably involved (not simply cortical efferent fibres to the brain stem). It is notable in this regard that the behaviours in question mature between eighteen and twenty-four months and the first myelin is acquired by layer III (from which cortical association fibres emerge) of the parietal association areas between fifteen and twenty-four months of age.

Hence, the development of the object concept correlates well with cortical development in the sequence: subcortical control, control by primary areas, control by secondary areas.

Piaget's descriptions of the development of spatial constructs also conform to these predictions. During stage one, the infant lacks co-ordination between sensory and motor schemes; behaviour is dominated by sucking, grasping and looking. Since these reactions are not co-ordinated, each leads to perception of stimuli of one sensory modality only. As a result, the infant perceives the world as separate visual, auditory, and tactile spaces. The tactile spaces are further broken down into oral and palmer spaces. These cannot be correlated with each other until five or six months of age, after the infant has managed to construct spatial concepts.

This descripton harmonizes with neural maturation data indicating that in the first months of life, each primary cortical area functions in isolation and can mediate only isolated spatial perceptions. Spatial integration of visual and somatosensory schemes as described by Piaget requires constructive capacities of secondary areas and of parietal association areas, and it develops in conjunction with beginning myelination of secondary visual and somatosensory areas between three and six months of age.

Objections to the Piagetian Framework

Although Piaget's description of the development of object and spatial concepts correlates well with patterns of cortical development, in one major way his description of neonatal behaviour is incompatible with neural data. Brain maturational data indicate that the neonate should possess a wide behavioural repertoire yet Piaget describes only a limited number of reflexes.

That the neonatal behavioural repertoire is much broader is now clear (Bower, 1972, 1974; Meltzoff 1981, this volume Ch4. A critical question is whether it is simply more extensive or whether it actually differs in quality from the reflexive, non-constructed behaviours described by Piaget and predicted from studies of cortical maturation.

A number of scholars believe that neonatal behaviour does differ qualitatively from that described by Piaget. In particular, behavioural evidence indicates that, visual, somatosensory and auditory spaces are unified rather than separate in the neonate (Bower; 1974). Visual–somatosensory unity is indicated by early infantile abilities to grasp visual objects, to manually 'protect' themselves against looming objects, to imitate facial gestures, and to note cross-modal equivalence between somatosensory and visual objects. These neonatal behaviours, however, need not imply cortical function and need not differ from the global non-differentiated kind reported by Piaget.

Briefly, as early as the second week of life an infant, if properly supported, can reach and grasp a visual object (Bower, Broughton and Moore, 1970b). Within the first week of life an infant can distinguish between a looming object headed directly toward his body and one on a near miss path (Ball and Vurpillot 1981 this volume Ch5, Bower, Broughton and Moore, 1970a). The former elicits protective hand responses; the latter does not.

Analysis of the visual reach and grasp indicates that both the action and the spatial perceptions involved differ fundamentally in the newborn from that of the six-month-old infant. Up to five months of age, the visual reach and grasp possesses all of the elements of a subcortically controlled behaviour. It is not until approximately six months of age that clear evidence of cortical control emerges.

At the youngest ages vision *elicits* the reach and grasp (Bower, 1974), the infant reaches toward the perceived object, then just as the hand approaches the object but prior to touching it, the whole hand closes around and grasps the object. The elements of the reach and grasp always occur in the same sequence and in the same wholistic patterns. If the object moves or if the initial reach begins on the wrong trajectory, the infant cannot correct his arm and hand trajectory in motion. He must complete his action and then return his arm to the starting position and begin again. There is no differentiation and no construction in this action (that is, there is no evidence of cortical control).

By twenty-six weeks of age, vision *guides* the reach and grasp (Bower, 1974; Butterworth, 1981). Once begun, the hand trajectory is no longer invariant. It can be corrected in motion. In other words, there is now mobility in action. A wrong trajectory can be inhibited and a new one begun during the reach.

By this time motor differentiation is also beginning; reach and grasp can occur separately, or the infant may touch rather than grasp.

In succeeding months, the ability to move each finger individually, not merely as part of a whole hand closure develops. During the second half of the first year, the motor elements begin to be joined together in varied combinations; for instance, the ability to first grasp and then reach, a motor construct essential for later tool use. Hence, beginning at five months and extending through the first year, cortical function manifests itself by first differentiating the reach and grasp, and later constructing new motor patterns from its elements.

The rationale for concluding that the earliest neonatal reach and grasp may be subcortically mediated extends beyond the simple fact that the behaviour does not evidence cortical processing capacities. Firm evidence indicates that the visually elicited (as opposed to guided) reach and grasp is subcortically mediated in other animals. Monkeys who have ablations of the visual cortex reach and grasp visually presented objects (Humphrey, 1970). A wide variety of lower vertebrates with rudimentary or non-existent cortices including amphibians and reptiles can reach and grasp by use of alternative anatomical organs: for example by tongue flicking or jaw lunging (Ingle, 1970). These tongue or jaw 'grasping' actions evidence similar processing capacities to the neonatal human. They are visually elicited, not visually guided. Once initiated, tongue flicking in amphibians, for instance, continues on its trajectory which cannot be changed in flight.

In these animals, the reach and grasp appears to be mediated by a mid-brain structure, the optim tectum (known as the superior colliculus in mammals including humans, see Fig. 3.3). In fish and amphibians, the optic tectum is considered the highest visual processing area. In human adults, its visual functions are overshadowed by the cortex. The superior colliculus, however, is a prime functional visual region in the human neonate (see Fig. 3.3 and Bronson, 1974).

The superior colliculus plays a role in spatial orientation especially with respect to moving visual objects. It mediates both the reach and grasp and the response to looming objects. Electrical stimulation of

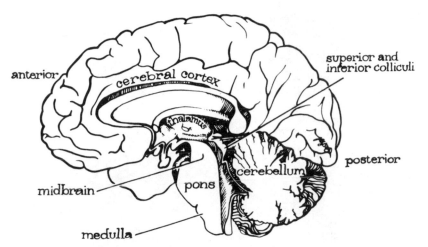

Fig. 3.3.   A mid-line view of the brain demonstrating the superior and inferior colliculi.

the colliculus produces head turning and visual following. Ablation results in loss of orienting reactions and loss of protective responses to looming objects in a wide variety of vertebrates (Casagrande, Harting, Hall, Diamond and Martin, 1972; Ingle, 1970, 1972; Sprague and Meickle, 1965).

Anatomically, the superior colliculus is admirably designed to mediate these visual-body orientation or visual-body avoidance reactions. Emerging from the colliculus are two sets of fibre tracts. One set travels to the cortex for further visual processing; the other descends to brain stem structures which control orienting movements of the head, neck and limbs. In all vertebrates, the superior colliculus (or optic tectum) is divided into two lamina. The outer lamina contains a precise map of the retina, the inner is multimodal and receives auditory and somatosensory information. It contains a precise map of the body (Gaither and Stein, 1979; Trevarthen, 1968), with points on the retina lying adjacent to corresponding body points. Within the tectum the most anterior or nasal points of the retina are adjacent to the most anterior point of the body, the most posterior or temporal are adjacent to the most posterior body points. Points corresponding to the superior and inferior retina lie in proximity to points representing the superior and inferior body respectively (see Fig. 3.4).

Hence, the superior colliculus is admirably disposed to mediate precise visual–somatosensory body-orienting reactions. In the col-

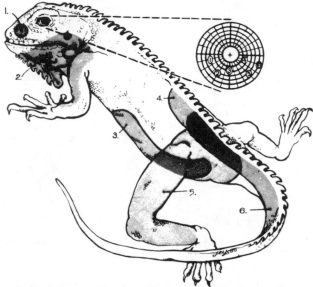

Fig. 3.4.   The superior colliculus of the iguana and other vertebrates maps both visual and somatosensory space. Spatial points on the retina correspond with spatial points on the body. Drawing adapted from Gaither and Stein (1979).

liculus, visual and somatosensory spaces are precisely linked. Direct output to motor areas exists and stimulation of either the outer visual or the inner somatosensory layer can result in the same movement. In this respect, the superior colliculus is in strong anatomical contrast to the cortex in which visual and somatosensory areas are widely separated and do not have access to the same output channels.

Other evidence indicates that in the neonate auditory and visual spaces are also closely linked. At birth the infant orients his eyes towards the source of a moderate sound (Wertheimer, 1961) and turns his eyes away from a loud sound (Butterworth and Castillo, 1977). These ear-eye co-ordinations appear to be analogous to visual grasping and protective reactions. They are probably mediated by similar mechanisms.

Just posterior to the optic tectum in lower vertebrates and to the superior colliculus in mammals is a twin structure: the auditory tectum or inferior colliculus. The inferior-colliculus is primarily concerned with auditory data. It sends projections to the superior colliculus and the two appear to utilize the same efferent tracts (Crosby, Humphrey and Lauer, 1962).

These data indicate that neonatal space is unified at birth, not separated. If spatial behaviours are analyzed according to behavioural and neural processes, however, Piaget's concepts emerge not so much wrong as incomplete.

These neonatal spatial behaviours are global, undifferentiated and unconstructed, just as Piaget claims. The spatial processes provided by the colliculus are not really those which Piaget addressed.

In the colliculus, visual and somatosensory spaces are linked. For Piaget, visual and somatosensory spaces are not linked, but differentiated and constructed. The body and each of its parts is mobile within space and the hand can be placed in varied spatial relationships with other objects. The hand or individual fingers, for instance, can be placed on top of, behind, under, alongside or grasp objects; offer them gravitational support, push, pull, squeeze, twist, rub them, etc. It can bring other objects into varied spatial relationships with each other. These are far more advanced than the mere reaching and grasping for a single object, which the neonate exhibits. They demand not only linkage of visual and somatosensory space but also conceptualization of the relationship of individual body parts to space and of individual objects in space to each other (that is, they demand cortical capacities of differentiation, mobility and construction).

Hence, rather than be discarded, Piaget's concept of body–spatial relationships should be modified. A stage prior to the beginnings of spatial conception must be postulated in which concepts of visual space are dominated by the superior colliculus and are linked to somatosensory and auditory spaces. These linked spaces must be differentiated for the infant to perceive separate visual and somatosensory spaces and to differentiate and construct within each spatial domain. This period corresponds to the first months of life and to the beginning of Piaget's descriptions. Once differentiation is attained and further cortical maturation has occurred, the infant can then begin to construct cross-modal spatial concepts and proceed through the later Piagetian stages.

Additional behaviours have been described in recent years which suggest that vision, somatosensation and motor skills may have even more complex neural linkages in the neonatal brain stem. Within the first three weeks of life, the human neonate can imitate simple facial expressions such as tongue protrusion, lip protrusion and mouth opening. Within the first month it can recognize object equivalence through cross-modal tactile and visual perceptions; see Meltzoff 1981, this volume Ch4. Previously, facial imitation was thought to appear only at the end of the first year of life (Piaget,

1952) and cross-modal recognition of object equivalence at four or five years.

It is most unlikely that these early infantile abilities are mediated by the cortex which at this age is still functioning in a very rudimentary manner. The possible sub-cortical control of these abilities has not yet been researched but a working hypothesis may be suggested that somewhere in the brain stem, tactile–visual 'maps' similar to the spatial maps of the superior colliculus may be coded. If so, these abilities would appear at an early age in a relatively global, undifferentiated form. Gradually, with cortical development, they would differentiate into new sequential or simultaneous imitational and perceptual constructs.

The behavioural aspect of this hypothesis should be readily researchable. If it proves correct, then it will indicate that in imitation and cross-modal perception of object equivalence as well as in grasping and reaching, a global behavioural form precedes the intelligent constructed form. It will again imply that Piaget's behavioural descriptions are not necessarily wrong, but that the behaviours described by Piaget are preceded in time by others that he missed.

Recapitulation in the Development of Brain and Behaviour

As compared to other animals, both sub-cortical and cortical components of the human brain have enlarged in primate and human evolution (Stephan, 1972). The neocortex, however, has demonstrated much greater enlargement than any other area of the brain. In reptiles the neocortex is tiny. In mammals, it overshadows all other brain regions in size. In absolute terms, the human neocortex is one of the largest and in proportion to body size, it exceeds that of any other mammal (Jerison, 1973).

As the neocortex has enlarged phylogenetically, it has developed extensive reciprocal vertical interconnections with the brain stem. Consequently, in evolution, the neocortex has not only added new functions of its own, it has of necessity, modified brain stem functions. This corticalization of function in evolution resembles that which occurs during neural ontogeny.

Within the neocortex, layers II and III were the last to evolve; they are also the latest to mature. In recent primate and hominid evolution, association areas have exhibited by far the greatest size increases (Passingham, 1975). These are the last cortical areas to mature.

When humans are compared to other primates, most of the recent cortical enlargement represents increases in cortical neuropil (that is, axons, dendrites and glial cells rather than increases in numbers of neurons themselves), see Holloway (1966). What increase in neuronal numbers has occurred has primarily been with respect to small celled local circuit neurons. These intracortical changes also resemble changes which occur during ontogeny. Cortical neuropil increases, not cortical neurons.

These parallels between the ontogeny of the human brain and its phylogeny indicate that in some respects, neural ontogeny recapitulates neural phylogeny (Bronson, 1981: Jacobson, 1978; Parker and Gibson, 1979). The latest post-natal stages of human brain development can be viewed as periods of terminal addition. Cortical neuropil not present in apes is added to the end of the developmental cycle especially in association areas (Parker and Gibson, 1979).

This recapitulation is not absolute, nor is it a 'law'. Those subcortical structures which have enlarged in recent phylogenetic history mature early. Rather, it is a recapitulation of neural processing mechanisms which is reflected by a transition from sub-cortical to cortical control during vertebrate phylogeny and in the early human neonatal period, followed by ever increasing control by the association areas in hominid evolution and in post-infantile development.

Since all vertebrate brains mature in a similar pattern, recapitulation implies that human neonatal processing mechanisms may resemble the sub-cortical neonatal processing mechanisms of other vertebrates and the neural processing mechanisms of adults of species which possess little in the way of a neocortex. The older the infant, the greater will be the divergence of human neural processing mechanisms from other animals. At the end of the developmental cycle, new abilities not found in apes will emerge.

Recapitulation, as postulated here, does not imply that all behaviours mature in the order in which they evolved. The human smile, the neonatal bipedal reflex, neonatal imitation, and infantile babbling are all examples of late evolving behaviours that mature early. Simple motor actions or global behaviours that have evolved late are probably processed by the same sub-cortical mechanisms that process previously evolved behaviours of the same nature. They will mature early in concert with the maturation of sub-cortical structures.

Recapitulation of neural processing mechanisms does not always result in behavioural recapitulation. It does when the evolution of a specific behaviour has resulted primarily from increasing cortical capacities for differentiation and construction. Since intelligence, as described by Piaget, results from these processes, the ontogeny of intelligence would be expected to recapitulate its phylogeny.

Evolutionary studies indicate that phylogentically human ances-
tors passed through the following stages: ancestral mammal-like
reptile → ancestral mammal → common ancestor of prosimians and
other primates → common ancestor of monkeys, apes and humans
→ common ancestor of apes and humans → ancestral human.
Behavioural data indicates that prosimians exhibit only the very
earliest stages of sensorimotor development. Monkeys display some
aspects of sensorimotor stages 5–6; and apes have reached the
pre-operational stage. By three to four years, intelligence above and
beyond that exhibited by apes developes in humans by terminal
addition (Parker and Gibson, 1979). Hence, comparative data suggests that maturation of human intelligence recapitulates its phylogeny.

Two behaviours described earlier also support the recapitulation
hypothesis: grasping and the object concept. In prosimians, all visual
grasping involves whole arm control. A prosimian reaches towards
an object and then grasps it, moving all digits at once. The reach and
the grasp are not differentiable. Monkeys have differentiated the
reach and the grasp and exhibit some independent control of the
thumb and index finger (Bishop, 1962). Still greater individual digit
control is displayed by our closest relatives, the apes. This pattern of
the evolution is nearly identical to the maturational processes described above; in both instances, differentiation of hand control
depends on the development of the neocortex.

While the phylogeny of the object concept has not been well
researched, that the common ancestor of monkeys, apes and humans
had reached stage 5 in the object concept series is suggested by the
fact that all monkeys which have been tested have reached at least
this level (Mathieu, Bouchard, Granger and Herscovitch, 1976;
Parker, 1977; Wise, Wise and Zimmermann, 1974). That the common ancestor of apes and humans had reached stage 6 is indicated by
this achievement in all living species of apes (Chevalier-Skolnikoff,
1976, 1978; Mathieu, 1978; Parker, 1976, Redshaw, 1978).

Achievement of an object concept, or lack thereof, in basal
reptiles, basal mammals and prosimians is based on behavioural
evidence. Amphibians and reptiles exhibit sub-cortically mediated
visual orienting and visual reaching and grasping reactions. They do
not possess the ability to move their eyes and do not engage in
eye-tracking movements. Hence, they cannot engage in stage 1 of the
object concept series, the visual tracking of a small moving object as
it first passes and then emerges from behind a screen. Furthermore,
most visually oriented reptiles do not pursue prey, but sit and wait
for it to appear, then grasp it with a quick lunging movement of the

tongue or jaws (Hamilton, 1973). If the prey should disappear, they simply wait for another. In consequence, the ability to follow a moving object which has disappeared has no utility in their lives.

Mammals possess eye tracking abilities. Generally, they do not sit and wait for food to appear. They actively search for it and in the case of animal prey, engage in at least limited pursuit. For them, the abilities to trace 'escaped' prey and to conceive of food items which exist, but are not visible, are a necessity. Unlike reptiles, most mammals also engage in some object exploration with mouths or other manipulators. This suggests that some level of the object concept probably existed in the common ancestor of modern mammals. Further research, however, is needed to clarify the probable level of object permanence in this ancestor.

Prosimians, however, can capture insects which are both stationary and in flight. This suggests very strongly the presence of stage 3 of the object concept series: the ability to recognize that a stationary object and one in flight are the same. Consequently, these behavioural data from reptiles, mammals, monkeys and apes lend support to the concept that the development of intelligence in general and specific behaviours, in particular, may recapitulate phylogeny.

The recapitulation of neural processing mechanisms has much greater implications for neonatal human behaviour that the simple concept that some behaviours may mature in the order in which they evolved. It implies that the human infant at some point in its development possesses all the neural processing capacities exhibited by other vertebrates. If, in other vertebrates, brain stem structures code for 'pre-wired' 'innate' behaviours, then they probably do so for human infants as well.

Canalization

Even in animals which possess a high degree of mental constructional ability, hence intelligence, that intelligence leads most members of the species to develop highly similar behaviours. In humans, language is the prime example of a highly intelligent species-specific behaviour; tool using and constructional activities are others.

Strong neuroanatomical resemblance also charactizes the brains of all adult members of any given species and indeed of all members of any vertebrate class. No matter the learning conditions, every normal mammal has a cortex, a pons and a medulla oblongata. Within a species neuroanatomical resemblances are remarkable, extending to details of external cortical structure and the internal organization of tracts and nuclei. Even dendritic morphology, one of the most plastic aspects of the brain, varies from individual to individual only in the number of branches and spines. The gross dendritic morphology of particular neuronal types exhibits little variability even in the face of strong environmental insult (Jacobson, 1978).

The neural maturational process which results in this strong neural and behavioural similarity requires proper genetic, hormonal, nutritional, social and cognitive inputs. Yet the brain itself exerts a major control over hormonal outputs. feeding behaviours and the types of social and cognitive experiences which an animal may seek for itself. When ancillary conditions are seriously defective, brain maturation and functions may proceed abnormally, but whether or not any given brain will experience optimum developmental conditions depends in part upon its own activity.

Recent theories indicate that the complex interactions which occur between neural and extraneural factors during development are best understood if brain maturation is viewed as a canalized epigenetic process (Fishbein, 1976; Wilson, 1978). In a canalized process, the genetic system is programmed to interact with the normal succession of environments (both internal and external) in a manner which assures that structures mature in a given sequence and reach a particular end point. The environment acts primarily to 'channel' genetically programmed development in the proper direction.

Canalized processes lead to strong structural, functional and behavioural similarity, but not identity, among conspecifics. They are buffered to withstand and adapt to the environmental fluctuations usually encountered in natural habitats although the extreme behavioural deprivations provided by some laboratory experiments may be expected to disrupt a canalized process and lead to structural and behavioural abnormality. Normal environmental variability should lead to individual differences in behaviour through learning.

Canalized systems are adaptations to the environmental situations encountered by a species during its evolutionary history. As canalized systems require specific environmental inputs at specific points in the developmental process, they will proceed more smoothly and certainly, if the genome programmes for behaviours which actively seek these environmental inputs (Parker, 1980). One might hypothesize therefore that evolution has not provided developing organisms with passive nervous systems which merely receive whatever input happens to infringe upon them; but with brains which actively search for optimum conditions (Gibson, 1978b). Such a hypothesis demands some form of 'innate' spontaneous stimulus-seeking behaviours, even if these 'innate' behaviours must be viewed as a product of both genetic and environmental history.

The time has come to cease asking whether genes or environment are essential to the development of a particular behaviour and to start asking what is the nature of the genetic and environmental interactions which occur; what specific environmental stimuli are required at any point in time, and what latitude of environmental variation is compatible with normal development?

Summary
Cross species comparisons of brain maturational data reveal several general principles of critical significance for the understanding of human neonatal behaviour patterns.

1   Species differ dramatically in their relative level of brain maturation at birth. This state of neonatal brain maturation correlates strongly with the behavioural capacity of the new-born. By mammalian standards, the human brain reveals an intermediate maturational state at birth. Since the adult human brain is very large, however, the actual amount of neural tissue possessed by the neonatal human is immense in comparison to other neonates. These data imply that human infants should possess a large behavioural repertoire including some behaviours of considerable complexity.
2   In all vertebrates, neural structures mature in the same sequence. This sequence mirrors the evolutionary sequence and suggests that in ontogeny neural processing mechanisms (though not necessarily specific behaviours) recapitulate phylogeny. The behaviours of the neonates of all species, including humans, possess similar brain stem mediated neural processing mechanisms. These are reflected in behaviours of a global and undifferentiated form which are readily susceptible to learning by conditioning. Advanced behaviours recently described for the human infant including visual reaching and grasping, auditory–eye movement co-ordination, neonatal imitation and neonatal cross-modal perceptions are probably brain-stem mediated and fit within this category of global undifferentiated behaviours.
3   In mammalian and human ontogeny, post-natal neural maturation is characterized by increasing cortical control. This is reflected by increasing differentiation of sensory and motor patterns, and by the ability to construct simultaneous and sequential perceptual and behavioural wholes by variably combining and recombining differentiated sensory and motor schemes. Piaget's descriptions of the development of neonatal behaviours pertain to developing neocortical control and to developing abilities to construct variable perceptual and motor patterns.

4   Recent theories suggest that neural development is canalized. That is, the genetic programme requires specific environmental inputs at specific points in the life cycle if normal neural maturation is to occur. In turn, the developing nervous system is programmed to help create its own environment in order to assure that these inputs occur.

Acknowledgements
For a number of years now, I have maintained a detailed working relationship with Dr Sue Parker. Conversations with her have been so critical to my own intellectual growth that it is often difficult for me to know where my ideas leave off and hers begin. Certainly many of the ideas presented here must be viewed as a product of our joint intellectual efforts.

I also wish to thank Ms. Janice Anne Jeys for the illustrations and Ms. Jackie Wright for typing the manuscript and offering editorial suggestions.

References

Baldwin, J. M. (1894) *Mental Development in the Child and in the Race*, Macmillan, New York.

Ball, W. and Vurpillot, E. (1981) Action and the Perception of Displacement in Infancy. In Butterworth, G. E. (ed.) *Infancy and Epistemology*, Harvester Press, Brighton, pp.115–36.

Bekoff, A. (1978) 'A neuroethological approach to the study of ontogeny of co-ordinated behavior', in Burghardt, G. M. (ed.) and Bekoff, M. *The Development of Behavior: Comparative and Evolutionary*, Garland, New York.

Bergström, R. M. (1959) 'Electrical parameters of the brain during ontogeny', in R. J. Robinson (ed.) *Brain and Early Behavior*, Academic Press, New York, pp. 15–84.

Bishop, A. (1962) 'Control of the hand in lower primates', in Buettner-Janusch, J. *Annals of the New York Academy of Sciences*, 102, 181–514.

Bishop, G. H. and Smith, J. M. (1964) 'The size of nerve fibres supplying the cerebral cortex', *Experimental Neurology*, 9, 483–501.

Blinkov, S. M. and Glezer. I. I. (1968) *The Human Brain in Figures and Tables*, Plenum Press, New York.

Bower, T. G. R. (1972) 'Object perception in infants', *Perception*, 1, 15–30.

Bower, T. G. R. (1974) *Development in Infancy*, W. H. Freeman, New York.

Bower, T. G. R., Broughton, J. M. and Moore, M. K. (1970a) 'Infant responses to approaching objects: an indicator of response to distal variables', *Perception and Psychophysics*, 9, 193–96.

Bower, T. G. R., Broughton, J. M. and Moore, M. K. (1970b) 'Demonstration of intention in the reaching behavior of neonate humans', *Nature*, 228, 679–81.

Brazelton, T., Scholl, M. D. and Robez, J. S. (1966) 'Visual responses in the newborn', *Pediatrics*, 37, 284–90.

Broekkamp, C. L. E., van Dongen, P. A. M. and van Rossum, J. M. (1977) 'Neostriatal involvement in reinforcement and motivation', in Cools, A. R., Lohman, A. H. M. and van den Bercken, J. H. L. (eds) *Psychobiology of the Striatum*, Elsevier/North Holland Biomedical Press, Amsterdam, pp. 61–72.

Bronson, G. (1974) 'The postnatal growth of visual capacity', *Child Development*, 45, 873–90.

Bronson, G. W. (1981) 'Structure, status and characteristics of the nervous system at birth', in Stratton, P. M. (ed.) *Psychobiology of the Human Newborn*, John Wiley, Chichester.

Butterworth, G. (1981) 'The origins of auditory–visual perception and visual proprioception in human development', in Pick, H. A. Jr. and Walk, R. (eds) *Perception and Experience Vol II*, Plenum, New York.

Butterworth, G. and Castillo, M. (1976) 'Coordination of auditory and visual space in new born human infants', *Perception 5*, 155–60.

Caley, D. W. and Maxwell, D. S. (1971) 'Ultrastructure of the developing cerebral cortex in the rat', in Sterman, M. B., McGinty, D. S. and Adinolfi, A. M. (eds) *Brain Development and Behavior*, Academic Press, New York, pp.91–106.

Casagrande, V. A., Harting, J. K., Hall, W. C., Diamond, I. T. and Martin, G. F. (1972) 'Superior colliculus in the tree shrew: a structural and functional subdivision into superficial and deep layers', *Science*, 177, 444–7.

Caveness, W. F. (1960) 'Ontogeny of focal seizures', in Jasper, H. H., Ward, A. A. and Pope, A. (eds) *Basic Mechanisms of the Epilepsies*, Little Brown, Boston, pp.517–34.

Chevalier-Skolnikoff, S. (1976) 'The ontogeny of primate intelligence and its implication for communicative potential: a preliminary report', *Annals of the New York Academy of Science*, 280, 173–216.

Chevalier-Skolnikoff, S. (1977) 'A Piagetian model for describing and comparing socialization in monkey, ape, and human infants', in Chevalier-Skolnikoff, S. and Poirer, F. E. (ed.) *Primate Biosocial Development*, Garland Press, New York.

Chevalier-Skolnikoff, S. (1978) 'Intellectual development of orangutan and human infants', *American Journal of Physical Anthropology*, 48, 386.

Conel, J. L. (1939–67) *The Postnatal Development of the Human Cerebral Cortex, Vols 1–8*, Harvard University Press, Cambridge. Mass.

Crosby, E., Humphrey, T. and Lauer, E. (1962) *Correlative Anatomy of the Nervous System*, Macmillan, New York.

Dustman, R., Snyder, E., Creel, D. and Beck, E. (1979) 'Ontogeny of the visual evoked response in the stump-tailed macaque', *Developmental Psychobiology*, 12, 161–7.

Ellingson, R. J., and Rose, G. H. (1970) 'Ontogenesis of the electroencephalogram', in Himwich, W. A. (ed.) *Developmental Neurobiology*, Charles Thomas, Springfield, Mass., pp. 441–74.

Ewer, R. F. (1968) *Ethology of Mammals*, Elek. Science, London.
Fishbein, H. D. (1976) *Evolution, Development and Children's Learning*, Goodyear, Pacific Palisades.
Flechsig, P. (1920) *Anatomie des menschlichen Gehirns and Ruckenmarks auf myelogenetischer Grundlage*, George Thomas, Leipzig.
Gaither, N. S. and Stein, B. E. (1979) 'Reptiles and mammals use similar sensory organizations in the midbrain', *Science*, 205, 595–7.
Gibson, K. R. (1970) 'Sequence of myelinization in the brain of *Macaca mulatta*', Ph.D dissertation, University of California, Berkeley.
Gibson, K. R. (1977) 'Brain structure and intelligence in macaques and human infants from a Piagetian perspective', in Chevalier-Skolnikoff, S. and Poirier, F. E. (eds) *Primate Biosocial Development*, Garland Press, New York, pp.113–57.
Gibson, K. R. (1978a) 'Cortical maturation, an antecedent of Piaget's behavioural stages', *The Behavioral and Brain Sciences*, 1, 188.
Gibson, K. R. (1978b) 'Sociobiology, brain maturation, and infantile filial attachment', *The Behavioral and Brain Sciences*, 1, 446–7
Hamilton, W. J. III. (1973) *Life's Color Codes*, McGraw-Hill, New York.
Hill, K., Cogan, D. and Dodge, P. (1963) 'Ocular signs associated with hydranencephally', *American Journal of Opthalmology*, 51, 267–75.
Hines, M. and Boynton, E. P. (1940) 'The maturation of "excitability" in the precentral gyrus of the young monkey (*Macaca mulatta*)', Carnegie Institute of Washington, Pub. 518 *Contributions to Embryology*, 28, 309–451.
Holloway, R. L. (1966) 'Cranial capacity, neural reorganization, and hominid evolution: a search for more suitable parameters', *American Anthropologist*, 63, 103–21.
Humphrey, N. K. (1970) 'What the frog's eye tells the monkey's brain', *Brain Behavior and Evolution*, 3, 324–37.
Ingle, D. (1970) 'Visuomotor functions of the frog optic tectum', *Brain Behavior and Evolution*, 3, 57–71.
Ingle, D. (1972) 'Two visual systems in the frog', *Science*, 181, 1053–55.
Jacobsen, S. (1963) 'Sequence of myelinization in the brain of the albino rat. A cerebral cortex, thalamus, and related structures', *Journal of Comparative Neurology*, 121, 5–29.
Jacobson, M. (1974) 'A plentitude of neurons', in Gottlieb, G. (ed.) *Aspects of Neurogenesis*, Vol. 2., Academic Press, New York, pp.151–66.
Jacobson, M. (1978) *Developmental Neurobiology*, Plenum Press, New York.
Jerison, H. J. (1973) *Evolution of the Brain and Intelligence*, Academic Press, New York.
Langworthy, O. L. (1928) 'The behavior of pouch young opossums correlated with the myelinzation of tracts in the nervous system', *Journal of Comparative Neurology*, 46, 201–40.
Langworthy, O. L. (1929) 'A correlated study of the development of reflex activity in fetal and young kittens and the myelinization of tracts in the

nervous system', *Carnegie Institute of Washington, Contributions to Embryology*, 20, 127–72.

Langworthy, O. L. (1933) 'Development of behavior patterns and myelinization of the nervous system in a human fetus and infant', *Carnegie Institute of Washington, Pub. 443, Contributions to Embryology*, 24, 1–53.

Lipsett, L. (1969) 'Learning capacities of the human infant', in Robinson, R. J. (ed.) *Brain and Early Behavior*, Academic Press, London.

Luria, A. R. (1966) *Higher Cortical Functions in Man*, Basic Books, New York.

Mathieu, M. (1978) 'Piagetian assessment of cognitive development in primates', paper presented at the Forty-seventh Annual Meeting of the American Anthropological Association, Los Angeles, 1978.

Mathieu, M., Bouchard, M., Granger, L. and Merscovitch, J. (1976) 'Piagetian object-permanence in *Cebus capucinus, Lagothrica flavicauda*, and *Pan troglodytes*', *Animal Behavior*, 24, 585–8.

Meltzoff, A. N. (1981) Imitation, intermidal co-ordination and representation in early infancy. In: Butterworth,G. E. (ed.) *Infancy and Epistemology*, Harvester Press, Brighton, pp.85–114.

Morris, R., Levine, M., Cherubini, E., Buchwald, N. and Hull, C. (1979) 'Intracellular analysis of the development of responses of caudate neurons to stimulation of cortex, thalamus and substantia nigra in the kitten', *Brain Research*, 173, 471–87.

O'Keefe, J. and Nadal, L. (1978) *The Hippocampus as a Cognitive Map*, Clarendon Press, Oxford.

Parker, S. T. (1973) 'Piaget's sensorimotor series in an infant macaque: the organization of non-stereotyped behavior in the evolution of intelligence' PhD thesis, University of California, Berkeley University Microfilms, Ann Arbor.

Parker, S. T. (1976) 'A comparative longitudinal study of the sensorimotor development in a macaque, a gorilla, and a human infant from a Piagetian perspective', paper presented at the Animal Behavior Society Conference, Boulder, Colorado, 1976.

Parker, S. T. (1977) 'Piaget's sensorimotor period series in an infant macaque: a model for comparing unsterotyped behavior and intelligence in human and nonhuman primates', in Chevalier-Skolnikoff, S. and Poirier, F. E. (eds) *Primate Biosocial Development*, Garland Press, New York.

Parker, S. T. (1980) 'The acquisition of inherited characteristics during ontogeny', unpublished manuscript.

Parker, S. T. and Gibson, K. R. (1977) 'Object manipulation, tool use, and sensorimotor intelligence as feeding adaptations in cebus monkeys and great apes', *Journal of Human Evolution*, 6, 623–41.

Parker, S. T. and Gibson, K. R. (1979) 'A developmental model for the evolution of language and intelligence in early hominids', *The Behavioral and Brain Sciences*, 2, 367–408.

Passingham, R. E. (1975) 'Changes in size and organization of cortical functions in man and other primates', *International Review of Neurobiology*, **16**, 233–99.

Piaget, J. (1952) *The Origins of Intelligence in Children*, Norton, W. W., New York.

Piaget, J. (1954) *The Construction of Reality in the Child*, Ballantine Books, New York.

Piaget, J. (1955) *The Language and thought of the Child*, World Publishing, New York.

Piaget, J. (1962) *Play Dreams and Imitation in Childhood*, Norton, W. W., New York.

Portman, A. (1967) *Zoologie aus vier Jahrzehnten*, Piper, R., Munich.

Purpura, P. P. (1972) 'Factors contribution to abnormal neuronal development in the cerebral cortex of the human infant', in Berenberg, S. R. (ed.) *Brain: Fetal and Infant*, M. Nijhoff Medical Division, The Hague, pp. 54–78.

Rakic, P. (1975) 'Timing of major ontogenetic events in the visual cortex of the rhesus monkey,' in Buchwald, N. and Brazier, M. (eds) *Brain Mechanisms in Mental Retardation, UCLA Forum in Medical Sciences No. 18*, UCLA, Los Angeles, pp.3–40.

Redshaw, M. (1978) 'Cognitive development in human and gorilla infants', *Journal of Human Evolution*, **7**, 133–41.

Robinson, R. J. (1969) 'Cerebral function in the newborn', in Robinson R. J. (ed.) *Brain and Early Behavior*, Academic Press, New York.

Sacher, G. A. and Staffeldt, E. F. (1974) 'Relation of gestation time to brain weight and placental mammals: implications of the theory of vertebrate growth', *American Naturalist*, **108**, 593–615.

Sprague, J. M. and Meickle, T. H. (1965) 'The role of the superior colliculus in visually guided behavior', *Experimental Neurology*, **11**, 115–46.

Stephan, H. (1972) 'Evolution of primate brains: a comparative anatomical investigation', in Tuttle, R. H. (ed.) *The Functional and Evolutionary Biology of Primates*, Aldine, Chicago.

Teuber, H. L. (1976) 'Complex functions of the basal gangliz in the initiation of movement', in Yahr, M. A. (ed.) *The Basal Ganglia*, Raven Press, New York.

Tinbergen, N. (1961) *The Study of Instinct*, Clarendon Press, Oxford.

Trevarthen, C. (1968) 'Two mechanisms of vision in primates', *Psychol. Forschung*, **31**, 299–337.

Wertheimer, M. (1961) 'Psychomotor co-ordination of auditory and visual space at birth', *Science*, **134**, 1692.

Wilson, R. S. (1978) Synchronies in mental development: an epigenetic perspective', *Science*, **202**, 939–48.

Wise, K., Wise, L. and Zimmerman, R. (1974) 'Piagetian object permanence in the infant rhesus monkey.' *Developmental psychology*, **10**, 429–37.

Yakovlev, P. and Lecours, A. R. (1967) 'Myelogenetic cycles of regional maturation of the brain', in Minkowski, A. (ed.), *Regional Development of the Brain in Early Life*, Davis, F. A., Philadelphia: pp. 3–70.

PART II
PRECURSORS OF KNOWLEDGE IN PERCEPTION AND ACTION

4. Imitation, Intermodal Co-ordination and Representation in Early Infancy

ANDREW N. MELTZOFF

Introduction

The old philosophical problem of how humans come to co-ordinate information from different perceptual modalities, such as touch and vision, lies at the heart of many theories of perception and cognition. William Molyneux posed the problem in perhaps its most celebrated form by means of the following thought experiment (Locke, 1690). He asked us to imagine a blind man who can recognize a sphere and a cube on the basis of touch. The objects are then placed in front of the blind man and he is suddenly made to see. The question is whether he can now recognize these objects on the basis of vision alone. To Molyneux, Locke (1690), Berkeley (1709), and others the answer was clear. A blind man who recovered his vision could not recognize these objects by sight alone, because visual and tactual sensations are not intrinsically related to one another. Only after the man gained some experience in simultaneously looking at and touching the objects, would he learn which visual impression corresponded to which tactual sensations. Put metaphorically, the view is that the visual tactual modalities do not at first 'speak the same language' and that some experience is necessary to compile a dictionary which can be used to 'translate' tactual impressions into visual ones and *vice versa*.

Developmental psychologists, too, have speculated about the initial relationship between our perceptual modalities but have chosen human infants instead of blind men as their subjects. Piaget, for example, shares Locke's and Berkeley's assumption that the perceptual modalities are initially separate and unco-ordinated. He envisions the neonate as experiencing 'several heterogeneous spaces all centred on the child's own body—buccal, tactile, auditory . . . but without objective co-ordination. These different spaces are then gradually co-ordinated . . ." (Piaget and Inhelder, 1969, p.15). For Piaget, the co-ordination of modalities is accomplished through a process other than the passive association suggested by Locke and

Berkeley; however, the fundamental assumption is still strikingly similar. Initially independent sensory channels must become co-ordinated before information can be transferred across them. This assumption is at the foundation of Piaget's theory of infant development and has ramifications for his accounts of two important topics: imitation and representation in infancy.

This chapter discusses recent experiments concerning intermodal co-ordination, imitation and representation in early infancy. The results do not support the view that man begins life with separate and unco-ordinated sensory systems. On the contrary, they suggest that human neonates have an innate ability to detect equivalences in information picked up through different perceptual modalities. Following the metaphor introduced earlier, it appears that the tactual and visual systems already 'speak the same language' at birth. These findings suggest modifications both in the philosophical debate about Molyneux's question and in psychological theories of infancy, especially accounts of the ontogenesis of imitation and mental representation.

Posing the Problem

One way of examining the relationship between perceptual modalities is to study the imitation of gestures by human infants. Consider the case in which an adult shows an infant a facial gesture, such as mouth opening. The infant can see this gesture, but he cannot see his own mouth. If the infant is young enough, he will never have seen a reflection of his mouth in a mirror. How could the infant possibly know how to match the gesture he sees with a gesture of his own that he cannot see himself perform? Successful facial imitation seems to demand some degree of intermodal co-ordination. The infant must match the gesture he *sees* with a gesture he can only *feel* himself perform. The young infant presented with the problem of facial imitation is thus in a situation analogous to Molyneux's recently-recovered blind man. Neither will have had the opportunity to learn the intermodal correspondences necessary to solve the task.

Imitation, then, is more than a social game. Imitative interactions afford the experimenter a rich opportunity for exploring the perceptual-cognitive organization of the infant. For imitation to occur, the event-to-be-imitated, the model, must first be perceived. The infant must then alter his motor behaviour so that it matches the model. Further, if infants are forced to defer their imitation until after the model has disappeared, their ability to act on the basis of some 'internal model' or representation of an absent event can be addressed. In short, imitation directly raises issues of perception, movement organization, intermodal co-ordination, and representation. Piaget, more than other theorists, has explored imitation from this cognitive perspective. Our own research on infant imitation is best introduced by considering his theory.

Imitation, Intermodal Co-ordination and Representation in Piagetian Theory

Piagetian theory provides a rich and highly influential perspective on the relation between imitation, intermodal co-ordination and representation in infancy. Piaget assumes that the sensory modalities are independent from one another at birth (Piaget, 1952, 1954). Building from this premise, he postulates that the gradual interco-ordination of the modalities underlies the development of infants' imitative capacities (Piaget, 1962). Imitation, in turn, is singled out as the direct developmental precurser to mental representation (Piaget, 1962; Piaget and Inhelder, 1969, 1971). Thus, the age and developmental sequencing of Piaget's stages of imitation are not arbitrary. They are deeply rooted in the logic of Piagetian theory and cannot be altered without altering the theory itself.

The essential details of Piaget's theory can be most easily understood, I think, by recasting his six stages of imitation into three major developmental levels (see Table 1). What I will refer to as 'level 1' is the imitation of gestures the infants can see (or hear) themselves perform. The imitation of manual gestures, such as hand opening and closing, is an example. Such gestures are supposed to be easily imitated because the infant can use the same modality to compare the model's behaviour with his own. For instance, when hand opening and closing is demonstrated, the infants can use vision to compare the model's actions and his own behaviour. Piaget argues that, during level 1, infants imitate by capitalizing on such *intramodal* matches.[1]

What I call Piaget's 'level 2' is the imitation of gestures the infant cannot see himself perform, for example the imitation of facial gestures such as mouth opening. This type of imitation is said to be difficult because intramodal comparisons between the model and the imitative response are impossible. Unlike manual imitation, facial imitation seems to require the infant to perform an *intermodal match*. The infant must copy the gesture he sees with a body movement of his own that he can feel but cannot see.

For Piaget, then, developments in the first two levels of imitation are crucially linked to growth in intermodal co-ordination. Since Piaget assumes that the modalities are initially unco-ordinated, facial imitation must be impossible in early infancy. Piaget argues:

[Before eight to twelve months old] the intellectual mechanism of the child will not allow him to imitate movements he sees made by others when the corresponding movements of his own body are known to him only tactually or kinesthetically, and not visually (as, for instance, putting out his tongue). To be able to make the connection between his own body and those of others, the child would require mobile indices which are not yet at his disposal. Thus, since the child cannot see his own face, there will be no imitation of movements of the face at this stage, provided that training, and therefore pseudo-imitation, is avoided. (Piaget, 1962, p.19).

Table 4.1. Piaget's stages of imitation in infancy

Levels of imitative development	Stages of imitative development	Approximate age (months)	Selected developments in imitation
Level 1	1	0–1	Imitation of crying
	2	1–4	Imitation of hand gestures (hand opening/closing)
	3	4–8	Imitation of actions-on-objects (hitting or banging an object)
Level 2	4	8–12	Facial imitation (mouth opening, tongue protrusion)
	5	12–18	Imitation of certain new behaviours never before performed by the infant
Level 3	6	18–24	Deferred imitation

Level 3 consists of the imitation of gestures that have disappeared from the perceptual field, 'deferred imitation'. Deferred imitation is classified in the most difficult level of imitative development because no direct perceptual comparison, whether intra- or intermodal, can be used to guide the infant's behaviour. Performing facial imitation in a deferred form would be doubly difficult, because the infant would have to imitate a gesture that was no longer visible with a part of his body he could not see.

Piaget assumes there is no capacity for mental representation at birth (Piaget, 1952, 1954, 1962; Piaget and Inhelder, 1971, 1973). One central problem for his theory is to explain how and when this capacity develops. Herein lies the critical importance of imitation for

Piaget's theory, for he claims that imitative development underlies the development of representation. His argument, as I understand it, is the following. Piaget sees imitation as a reconstruction of events in overt motor action, and representation as the reconstruction of events in covert mental activity. If there is no mental representation at birth, why not suppose that mental reconstruction (representation) develops from motor reconstruction (imitation)? This is the position Piaget adopts. He postulates that sensory-motor imitation is eventually 'internalized' to become internal imitation—that is, mental representation. Only after the infant develops through all the stages of sensory-motor imitation is his imitative ability flexible enough to 'internally imitate' (mentally represent) absent objects and events. This is what Piaget means when he states: When the accommodation of sensory-motor schema takes the form of visible gestures, it constitutes imitation proper, but when, sufficiently developed to need no external experiment, it remains virtual and interior, would it not lead to interiorized imitation, which would be the image? (Piaget, 1962, p.70). Or again: Then, sooner or later, comes the mental image, no trace of which is observed on the sensory-motor level (otherwise discovery of the permanent object would be greatly facilitated). It appears as an internalized imitation. (Piaget and Inhelder, 1969, p.54). In short, infants have no capacity for mental representation at birth; this capacity develops as an outgrowth of sensory-motor imitation.

Further clarifications of Piaget's theory.
The developmental links Piaget forges between imitation and representation are commonly confused in two ways: one by advocates of his theory, the other by critics.

The first confusion arises from theorists who agree with Piaget's claim that representation is late to develop but use object permanence to index the growth of this capacity (Schaffer, 1971). They claim that infants do not search for hidden objects before approximately one year old because, as Piaget says, they have no ability to represent absent objects before that age. The successful recovery of hidden objects is then taken as a landmark development that indexes the birth of mental representation. More specifically, one-year-olds are said to begin searching for hidden objects because they can, for the first time, use some representation of the absent object to guide their search. Although advanced to support Piaget's theory, this claim that representation underlies the one-year-old's search behaviour is incompatible with it in a truly fundamental way. Piaget cannot allow that the one-year-old's search is guided by a representation of the hidden object because he postulates that representation is an outgrowth of level 3 imitation, and the latter develops at approximately eighteen to twenty-four months old. The logic of Piaget's theory compels him to explain successful recovery of hidden objects without reference to any representational capacities. According to Piaget, search before eighteen months is not guided by any representation, but rather by a series of visible indices that lead the infant step by step to recover the hidden toy:

Searching for an object under a screen when the subject has seen it disappear there (stages IV and V) does not necessarily presuppose that the subject 'imagines' the object under the screen, but simply that he has understood the relation of the two objects at the moment he perceived it (at the moment the object was covered) and that he therefore, interprets the screen as sign of the actual presence of the object. (Piaget, 1954, p.85).

In Piagetian theory, then, development in object permanence in the first year do not index development in representational capacities for two reasons: 1) imitation, not object permanence, is the precursor to representation, and 2) representation itself does not appear in the first year. Only after all the stages of imitation have been passed (approximately eighteen to twenty-four months) can imitation be internalized and allow for mental representation.

All this does not mean that a new theory of the development of object permanence cannot be constructed to address the representational capacities of young infants (see Moore and Meltzoff, 1978). It suggests, however, that the standard, Piagetian search tasks are not appropriate for such assessments, since Piaget himself explains successful search on these tasks without resorting to any sort of representational ability.

The second confusion concerning Piaget's position about representation and imitation arises from Piaget's critics. Since even young infants demonstrate visual recognition memory (Fantz, 1964; Fantz, Fagan and Miranda, 1975; Fagan, 1970; Cohen and Gelber, 1975), some argue that Piaget is incorrect in claiming that mental representation first develops at the end of the second year. Piaget's arguments linking sensory-motor imitation and representation are seen as excess baggage. This criticism, however, overlooks Piaget's discussion of early recognition memory (Piaget, 1952, 1954; Piaget and Inhelder, 1973). He emphasizes the difference between 'recognition' and 'recall' memory and argues that recognition does not require any mental representation of the world, at least as he defines it. According to Piaget, the young infant does not necessarily recognize an object on the basis of a stored representation of the distal stimulus. Rather, he recognizes his own actions when he repeats them in perceiving the object the second time:

> But in the elementary examples now under consideration, recognition does not necessitate any evocation of a mental image. For recognition to begin, it is enough that the attitude previously adopted with regard to the thing be again set in motion and that nothing in the new perception thwart that process. The impression of satisfaction and familiarity peculiar to recognition could thus stem only from this essential fact of the continuity of a schema; the subject recognizes his own reaction before he recognizes the object as such. (Piaget, 1954, p.5).

As in the object permanence case, new tests could be designed explicitly to evaluate Piaget's position. Suffice it to say that Piagetians have been able to incorporate existing reports of early recognition memory using paired-comparison and habituation procedures without abandoning their claims concerning the late development of mental representation.

Conclusions
Piaget makes two important assumptions about the newborn infant's psychological status: 1) newborns begin with independent sensory systems; intermodal co-ordination comes with later development, and 2) newborns lack the capacity for storing representations of absent objects and events; this ability is the culmination of infant development. Imitation is conceived as playing a critical role because it reflects progress in intermodal co-ordination and, in turn, is the developmental precursor to mental representation.

Piaget offers a tidy (and widely accepted) theory linking imitation, intermodal co-ordination and representation in infancy. Recently, we conducted a series of interlocking experiments designed to test some of Piaget's hypotheses about these issues. Contrary to Piaget, we found that infants under one month old can imitate facial gestures and succeed on certain intermodal matching tasks. These findings lead us to propose a radical departure from Piaget's theory. We will argue that imitation, intermodal co-ordination and representation are indeed linked, but that *the neonate is already capable of storing abstract representations of perceptually absent objects and events, and this underlies their unexpected performance on imitation and intermodal matching tasks.*

Facial Imitation in Neonates
Our study of facial imitation addressed three major questions (Meltzoff and Moore, 1977):

1. Methodology: what would constitute evidence for facial imitation in neonates?
2. Existence: do neonates have the competence to perform such
   imitation?
3. Mechanism: what mechanism(s) underlies such imitation, if it
   exists?

Methodology.   Consider the first of these questions, that of an
adequate methodology. The chief issues to be solved are:
(1) distinguishing true imitation from an arousal response,
(2) avoiding possible shaping of the imitative response, (3) developing an objective scoring system, and (4) devising test conditions that
are sensitive to the special needs of neonates. These methodological
issues are examined in turn below.

What are the proper controls for distinguishing true imitation
from an arousal response? It is clearly insufficient to compare the
infant's response to a tongue protrusion demonstration to his 'baseline reaction' when a stationary face (or no face at all) is displayed. If
infants respond with more tongue protrusions to the former than the
latter, true imitation need not be implicated. A more parsimonious
explanation is that infants are aroused by a moving face, and
increased oral activity, including tonguing, is part of the infant's
arousal response. In our research, therefore, we distinguished true
imitation from arousal by comparing each infant's response to one
gesture with his response to other gestures that were performed by
the same adult, at the same distance from the infant, and at the same
rate of movement. For instance, we tested whether infants responded
with more tongue protrusions after an adult demonstrated tongue
protrusion than after he demonstrated mouth opening and *vice
versa*. Even if the presentation of a moving face arouses infants, a
global arousal of oral movements could not account for such differential responding.

The second methodological issue consists of controlling interactions between adults and infants that might shape the imitative
response. It is common practice to inform parents about an experiment before they come into the laboratory. Unfortunately, imitation
tests are easy to simulate, and we found that if parents were
informed, they tended to practice with their infants 'so they would do
well on the test.' Neonates can be conditioned to perform certain

head movements in response to a tone or buzzer (Lipsitt, 1969), so they could presumably be conditioned to perform tongue movements in response to an adult's tongue protrusion. Piaget has referred to such reactions as 'pseudo-imitation.' It is clear that both the theoretical puzzle of facial imitation and Piaget's prediction that it is impossible before one-year-old are addressed only if such training, and therefore pseudo-imitation, is avoided.

The experimenter's interaction with the infant must also be controlled for similar reasons. In reviewing films of preliminary work, we noticed that untrained experimenters often smiled when infants copied their behaviour. Such interactions raise questions about whether infants are being shaped during the experimental session.

Our experiments were designed to control for these difficulties. Participating parents were kept uninformed about the true nature of the tests before visiting the laboratory. They were told that we were interested in assessing infants' visual discrimination and responses to moving objects. In addition, the experimental design prevented the experimenter from shaping the infant's behaviour during the response period.

The third methodological issue concerns the scoring of infant's responses. Unobtrusive machine measurement of infant facial movements is beyond the limits of existing technology. There is also no standardized method for quantifying infant facial movements comparable, say, to the corneal reflection technique (Fantz, Fagan and Miranda, 1975) or forced-choice preferential looking procedure (Teller, 1979) developed for assessing infants' visual fixations. Evaluating neonatal facial imitation required the development of new scoring systems that quantified infants' facial movements—not an easy task (Barker, 1963; Birdwhistell, 1973; Eckman, Friesen and Ellsworth, 1972; Oster and Eckman, 1978). Additionally, infant facial movements are not generally produced in a discreet and unambiguous fashion, thus, scoring biases are possible if infants are scored 'live' by the experimenter himself. It is crucial, therefore, that we videotaped the infants and had the recordings scored by observers who were blind to the gesture shown to the infant they were scoring.

Our identification of these three methodological points (arousal, shaping, and scoring) and our solutions are significant, since other studies of infant imitation have not adequately dealt with them. The early work by Zazzo (1957) is anecdotal in nature with no attempt to address these issues in any way. The Gardner and Gardner (1970) report (which is a study of a single infant) and Maratos (1973) experiment can be criticized because the experimenter herself scored the infants' reactions live without the aid of videotaped recordings, thus raising the possibility of scoring bias. Finally, no previous study of infant imitation at any age included adequate safeguards against shaping before or during experimental sessions.

Beyond these three methodological points, we also considered a fourth category of issues related to the special purpose of our study. 'By 'special purpose' I mean that our goal was to assess the neonate's imitative competence, and this question about underlying *competence* requires a different approach than does a more *normative* question. Our question, 'Can any infant perform these tasks under any circumstance?' is a different question from the more common one, 'Do average infants normally perform these tasks in everyday circumstances?' (Abravanel, Levan-Goldschmidt and Stevenson, 1976; Bruner, 1969, 1975; McCall, Parke and Kavanaugh, 1977; Uzgiris and Hunt, 1975). It is important to emphasize the safeguards we instituted to ensure that we tested neonates at their best and to prevent possible obscuring of imitation effects. There are at least nine major steps we took to ensure that we would not spuriously obscure the imitation effect. Those listed below as Group I are precautions followed in many studies of neonatal behaviour; those in Group II are more specialized procedural points; Group III consists of an interesting issue, perhaps unique to imitation testing.

Group I:
(1) Birthweight and gestational age are known to influence infant behaviour (Als, Tronick, Adamson and Brazelton, 1976; Fantz, Fagan and Miranda, 1975; Sigman and Parmelee, 1974). Therefore, we tested only infants within a narrow band of birthweight (2500-4300 g) and gestational age at birth (38–40 weeks). (2) Method of delivery may influence infant behaviour (Als, Brazelton, Lester and Landers, 1980; Zaslow, 1980). Thus, no infants delivered by Caesarean section were admitted into our study. (3) Maternal medication administered during labour and delivery is thought to affect a wide range of neonatal behaviour (Aleksandrowics and Aleksandrowics, 1974; Brazelton, 1961; Conway and Brackbill, 1970; Stechler, 1964). Therefore, only infants whose mothers received no medication, or who received solely local or regional anesthetics, were admitted into the study (represented as 'drug group 1' by Aleksandrowics and Aleksandrowics, 1974). (4) Neonates are not maximally receptive to external stimuli while lying in a supine position (Caesaer, O'Brien and Prechtl, 1973; Bower, 1972). Thus, all infants were tested while seated in a semi-upright posture in a well-padded infant seat. (5) The room lights were dimmed so that infants remained wide-eyed and alert, and the experimental room was kept

free from auditory distractions (for example, the videotape recorders were housed in sound-dampening boxes).

Group II:
(6) There are major technical difficulties in obtaining detailed high-resolution video recordings of fine motor activity such as neonatal lip and tongue movements. For example, we found it impossible to count accurately the infant's oral movements if we used only one camera that 'zoomed out' far enough to photograph both the infant's face and hands. In such a set-up, the image of the infant's oral region is simply too small to allow the scorer to make valid decisions about the infant's oral movements. Therefore, in our research, one camera was devoted solely to obtaining a closeup recording of the infant's face alone. This close-up picture allowed a careful microanalysis of the oral movements. Further, since the lighting on the infant's face was dim, we used a special camera with low-light capabilities (Sony model AVC–3260 with an AV–3650 recorder). Photographs taken from our closeup, high-resolution video record are displayed in Fig. 1 in Meltzoff and Moore (1977) and Figs. 2 and 3 in this chapter. (7) The experimenter's face was illuminated by a spotlight and presented against a homogeneous backdrop that surrounded the infant. This ensured that the face was the brightest object in the infant's visual field, and there was virtually nothing but this face to look at (the cameras were behind the backdrop, with the lenses poking through small holes). (8) All testing was done in the laboratory rather than at home. One reason for this is that the lighting and background conditions described above are difficult to achieve outside the laboratory. Additionally, the portable video systems normally carried to home settings do not provide as high-quality videotape records as the special system we used (Sony, 1971 a, 1971 b; 1972, 1979).

Group III:
(9) In preliminary work, we found that infants performed poorly on imitation tests if they had already seen the experimenter smiling, laughing and talking to the parents, thereby demonstrating a wide array of mouth gestures before the imitation test began. This is understandable since, from the infant's point of view, the pre-test period is not separated from the experiment itself. In tests of facial imitation, the experimenter's face *is* the test stimulus, and pre-test exposure to the experienter's face must be controlled. To ignore this would be somewhat analogous to suspending a mobile containing checkerboards or bulls-eyes in front of infants before formal testing using these patterns. Therefore, in our tests a research assistant greeted participating families and gave them preliminary instruc-

tions so that the infant never saw the experimenter's face until the experiment began.

Existence.   We conducted two studies of imitation in infants ranging from twelve to twenty-one days old. In the first experiment, we obtained evidence that infants could imitate four different adult gestures: lip protrusion, mouth opening, tongue protrusion and sequential finger movement. A second study was then designed to assess whether infants could accurately imitate two of these gestures, mouth opening and tongue protrusion, even if their motor response was delayed until after the adult's demonstration had ended. In this experiment, the gestures were demonstrated to the infants while they were sucking on a pacifier (see Fig. 4.1). The experimenter then stopped gesturing, assumed a passive face pose, and *only then* removed the pacifier. It is noteworthy that infants' sucking responses seemed to take precedence over any imitative reactions while the pacifier was in their mouths. Infants did not tend to push the pacifier out with their tongue during the tongue protrusion demonstration; nor did they show a tendency to open their mouths and let the pacifier drop out during mouth opening demonstrations. Thus, the pacifier technique seemed effective in delaying imitative responding until after the experienter stopped demonstrating the target gesture.

Even using these procedures, infants were able to imitate the two facial gestures shown to them. Infants responded with more tongue protrusions after the tongue protrusion demonstration than they did during the baseline period (p<.005) or after the mouth opening gesture (p<.005). Similarly, they produced more mouth openings in response to the mouth opening demonstration than during baseline (p<.05) or after the tongue protrusion gesture (p<.05).

Infants imitated the adult gestures with surprising accuracy (see Fig. 4.2 for illustrations). Indeed, the accuracy of the responding is manifest in the findings themselves, since we adopted very stringent criteria for imitation. We demanded that infants thrust their tongues clearly beyond their lips to score a tongue protrusion, and that they fully open their mouths to score a mouth opening. Smaller baseline oral movements did not count as imitative responding. Thus, the findings reported reflect a pattern of accurate imitation (large, forceful behaviours accurately matched to the model) and were not derived from tiny tongue flicks or partial lip separations.

The temporal organization and morphology of the imitative reaction are especially intriguing. Accurate imitation does not burst forth immediately after the pacifier is removed. Rather, infants respond in fits and starts. They often pause before beginning their response and

Condition	Baseline Exposure	Baseline Period 150-sec	Experimental Exposure 1	Response Period 1 150-sec	Experimental Exposure 2	Response Period 2 150-sec
Experimenter	Passive Face	Passive Face	Gesture 1	Passive Face	Gesture 2	Passive Face
Infant	Pacifier	No Pacifier	Pacifier	No Pacifier	Pacifier	No Pacifier

Fig. 4.1. Schematic illustration of the pacifier technique used for assessing infant imitations. Half the infants were exposed to the gestures in the order tongue protrusion, mouth opening; and half were exposed to the gestures in the reverse order.

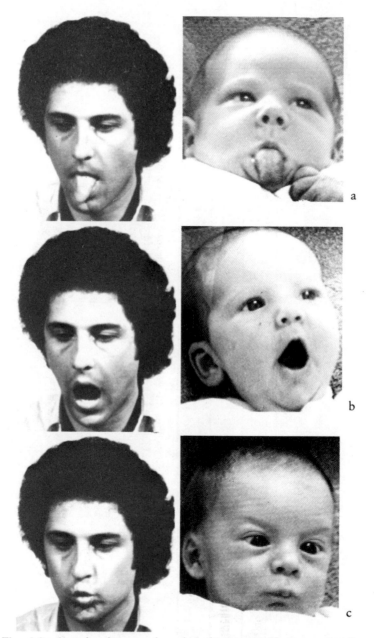

Fig. 4.2 Sample photographs taken from our videotape recordings of neonates imitating: (a) tongue protrusion; (b) mouth opening; and (c) lip protrusion.

produce approximate matches before producing large, forceful behaviour accurately matched to the model. Infants thus converge from
approximate to accurate imitative matches, seeming to correct their
behaviour over time (Meltzoff, 1977a, 1977b, Meltzoff & Moore, in
prep.). We refer to this phenomenon as 'convergence' and think it has
important implications for theories about early imitation, as discussed below. Fig. 4.3 shows examples of different levels of accuracy
in imitating a tongue protrusion demonstration. The temporal organization of the imitative response is captured in the following description of one infant's response to a tongue protrusion demonstration:

Obs. 12: The infant makes two small tongue movements that push his
bottom lip forward but remain well within his mouth. Next he knits his
eyebrows and very slowly slips his tongue forward with the tip held between
the lips. The tongue is then retracted. The infant now pauses, looks away and
closes his eyes. He makes one small tongue movement, then stares intently at
the experienter and finally protrudes his tongue between his lips. Suddenly,
he thrusts his tongue far beyond his lips, then quickly repeats this a second
time, farther still, with noticeable brightening round the eyes.

Mechanism.   What mechanism(s) might underlie these early imitative reactions? Three major possibilites immediately suggest themselves: (1) reinforcement, (2) innate-releasing mechanisms, and (3)
active, intermodal matching. The available data seem to me to
support the third, although future experiments are surely necessary
to explore the details of this account. These three major accounts are
considered in turn below.

First, it could be that the imitative reactions were somehow
shaped. Infants old enough to be spoon fed will be reinforced for
imitating mouth opening. Mothers typically open their mouths and
wait for the infant to do the same before popping in a spoonful of
food. It would not be surprising, then, if certain infants imitated
mouth opening at six months or so. However, the infants we tested
were only twelve to twenty-one days old, and a history of reinforcement for imitating facial gestures is unlikely at this age. Observations
in naturalistic, home settings of infants this young show that parents
rarely (Whiten, 1975) demonstrate 'anti-social' gestures such as
tongue protrusions while reinforcing their infants for sticking out
their own tongues. In our experiment, shaping during the experiment
was avoided by requiring that the experimenter adopt a passive face
pose throughout the response period. The experimenter's face was
videotaped, and analyses revealed that he adhered to this design.
Thus, shaping by parents at home or the experimenter during the
testing session seems an improbable basis for the effects obtained in
these young infants.

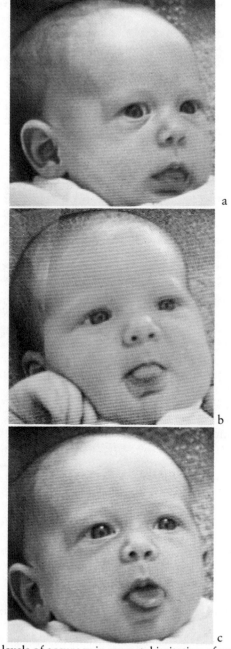

a

b

c

Fig. 4.3.   Three levels of accuracy in neonatal imitation of an adult tongue
protrusion gesture.

The second possibility is that this early imitation is based on releasing mechanisms such as those postulated by Lorenz and Tinbergen to explain complex animal behaviours (Lorenz and Tinbergen, 1938; Tinbergen, 1951). For example, the mandible patch of an adult herring gull acts as a sign stimulus that releases mouth opening (food begging) in gull chicks. Similarly, man may have evolved so that adult mouth opening acts as a sign stimulus, releasing mouth opening in the human infant.

There are two arguments against considering these imitative reactions as released responses. First, our study showed imitation not of one, but several different gestures. Moreover, recent studies not only replicated our effects but now have extended our findings by reporting early imitation of additional non-oral behaviours (Dunkeld, 1978; Burd and Milewski, 1981). Clearly, one cannot postulate a Lorenzian releasing mechanism for 'imitation in general', and it would be *ad hoc* in the extreme simply to declare that every new behaviour that is shown to be imitated represents another, released response. Second, the morphology of the imitative reaction is different from what one would expect if it were released in the classic sense. The hallmark of released reactions—fixed action patterns (FAPs), as they are called—is that they are stereotypic, rigidly organized reactions that 'run off' independent of feedback mechanisms (Lorenz and Tinbergen, 1938). For example, once released, the egg-retrieving behaviour of the grey lag goose continues in a sterotypic manner even if the egg slips away, or if the experimenter substitutes a giant egg that cannot possibly be retrieved. This rigidity is further demonstrated by the 'simple head throw', a courtship behaviour of the goldeneye drake, that has an average duration of 1.29 seconds and *never* varies more than a *few hundredths* of a second from this (Dane and Van der Kloot, 1964). As described above, early imitation bears little resemblance to such reactions. On the contrary, infants continue to suck on a pacifier while the model is displayed, often pause before responding, and seem to correct their initial behaviour so that it more and more accurately matches the model over time. There is also substantial variability in the organization of the response across infants. In sum, early imitation seems to be far from a sterotypic, fixed-action pattern that is automatically tripped by a certain adult display.

If we reject the reinforcement and releaser accounts, what other mechanism could underlie this early imitation? The hypothesis we favour is that this early imitation is accomplished through a more active matching process than admitted by these other two accounts. The heart of this view is that imitation is based on the infant's capacity to utilize equivalences between the body movements he sees, and the body movements he feels himself perform. It is precisely this point that is denied by the other two accounts. Both explain early imitation without postulating that infants utilize such equivalences. After all, neither a 'cue' nor a 'sign stimulus' need match the response it elicits. Any two gestures could presumably be paired through reinforcement, and the released behaviours of most animals are not morphologically similar to the sign stimuli that trigger them (for example, herring-gull chicks open their mouths in response to seeing a mandible patch, not to mouth opening by the adult gull).

In contrast, we postulate that imitation, even this early imitation, involves active intermodal matching in which infants recognize an equivalence between the act seen and their own act which is done at a later time. That is our major claim about early imitation. If true, one might further ask what mediates such intermodal matching. Our corollary hypothesis is that this imitation is mediated by a representational system that unifies different modalities. Such a representational system does not register sense-specific elements, but rather utilizes what can be called 'supramodal' or 'transmodal' information. According to this view, information picked up by the proprioceptive and visual systems can be represented in a form common to both. This allows infants to compare information from their own unseen movements to a supramodal representation of the visually perceived model and to produce the motor match required.

Jacobson (1979) recently published a paper in which she supported our findings about the *existence* of early facial imitation. However, she disagreed with the *mechanism* we favoured (active intermodal matching) and opted instead for one of the other accounts we discussed, namely the releaser account. Her work may broaden our understanding of early imitation, but, in my view, it does not actually bear on the mechanism question. Consider the study. First and foremost, she found, in agreement with our research, that young infants do indeed respond to adult tongue protrusion by producing tongue protrusions of their own. Jacobson further reported tonguing in response to the in-out movements of a pen, while 'a ball was somewhat less effective, suggesting that the shape of the object moving toward the mouth may also be important and that tongue protrusion is probably not an epiphenomenon to arousal generated by directing objects to the face' (p.329).

Possible methodological criticisms of the study need not concern us here. My principal point concerns the logic underlying this research. The exploration of what features of the stimulus are effective in eliciting tongue protrusion is an interesting line of research. However, even if one isolated these features, as say, 'long narrow objects moving in and out,' this would not constitute evidence that the imitative reaction is a released response. All three of the possible mechanisms discussed above could incorporate such data: (1) the reinforcement account would explain these findings as an example of stimulus generalization; (2) the releaser account would call the effective stimuli the class of sign-stimuli; and (3) our active matching account would say that infants can detect similarities between their own tongue movements and other tongue-like shapes making similar movements.

In fact, Piaget (1962) himself discussed data similar to Jacobson's in an effort to disprove the releaser and reinforcement accounts and to support the idea that active matching underlies imitation in one-year-old infants. For example, Piaget observed that one-year-olds sometimes open their mouths not only to mouth opening, but also to adult eye opening and closing. He also reported finger protrusion in response to tongue protrusion. Werner and Kaplan (1963) report similar 'imitative' reactions to both animate and inanimate objects. Both these theorists cite such cases to show that imitation involves active assimilatory processes in which 'intelligent confusions' are possible (Piaget, 1962, p.44). Surely if one finds tongue protrusion in response to tongue protrusion, finger protrusion, and/or pen protrusion (but not to other appropriate controls), she cannot claim that this is evidence for the 'releaser' hypothesis and reject the hypothesis of active matching with 'intelligent confusion' simply because the infants are younger than Piaget's.

In my view, more relevant data about underlying mechanism is obtained, not by examining the effective stimulus, but by evaluating the organization of the response. I noted earlier that infants 'converge' toward a more accurate match to the modelled gesture without any shaping by the experimenter. If infants can actually correct their response by utilizing proprioceptive information from their unseen movements, this argues against the hypothesis of released, fixed-action patterns and for our hypothesis of active, intermodal matching.

One way of enriching the viewpoint I have been advancing so far is to conduct converging experiments. For example, one might test whether neonates show any ability to utilize intermodal equivalences in a situation other than early imitation. The work discussed next was designed toward this end.

Intermodal Matching by Neonates[2]
In this study, we returned to Molyneux's original problem concern-

ing the recognition of shapes across modalities (Meltzoff and Borton, 1979). Recent experiments show that infants ranging between six and twelve months old can succeed on certain tactual-visual matching tasks, that is, after touching an object they can subsequently recognize that same object by vision alone (Bryant, Jones, Claxton and Perkins, 1972; Gottfried, Rose and Bridger, 1977; Ruff and Kohler, 1978).

However, this research does not address the original question raised by Molyneux, nor our own hypothesis about intermodal functioning in human neonates. Infants of the age tested in the above studies commonly reach out and handle objects they see (Bower, 1974; Bruner and Koslowski, 1972; White, Castle and Held, 1964; Piaget, 1962). This bimodal exploration of shapes presumably offers ample opportunity for infants to associate the visual and tactual impressions of them. Thus, Locke and Piaget would hardly be surprised by these recent findings of intermodal matching in six to twelve-month-old infants. Indeed, Piaget uses facial imitation by one-year-olds to illustrate that certain intermodal correspondences can be established by that age, and so he would have little reason to deny that similar correspondences could also be established for inanimate shapes. As Piaget points out: 'Between three and six months of age the child begins to grasp what he sees, to bring before his eyes the objects he touches, in short, to coordinate his visual universe with his tactile universe' (Piaget, 1954, p.13).

Given our interpretation of neonatal imitation, however, we predicted a result that was unexpected by Piaget and Locke and went beyond the existing findings on intermodal functioning. We predicted that infants too young to have watched themselves handling different objects could, nevertheless, recognize equivalences in shapes across modalities (see also Bower, 1974, 1979; E. Gibson, 1969; J. Gibson, 1966).

To test this idea, we modified the paired-comparison techniques typically used for assessing recognition memory in older infants (Fagan, 1970; Fantz, Fagan and Miranda, 1975). Such tests begin with a brief familiarization period during which the infant is allowed to look at a stimulus. Next, the infant is shown a pair of stimuli, one matching the original stimulus, the other novel. If infants show differential visual fixation to the familiar versus novel stimulus, this is taken as evidence for visual discrimination and recognition memory. Our experiment followed the same logic and general experimental procedure, except the infants were not allowed to look at the initial stimulus. Instead, they were given the object to explore tactually during the familiarization period. The tactual object was then removed and the infants given the paired-comparison visual test.

In preliminary work, we attempted putting objects in infants' hands during the tactual familiarization period. However, we abandoned this procedure, because neonates tended to grasp the objects rigidly rather than to explore them actively, and for obvious reasons we needed to ensure that they had, at least, explored the tactual objects before presenting the visual test. Next we tried putting the objects in their mouths and found that neonates actively explored them with their lips and tongue. We therefore took advantage of this by modifying pacifiers so that small, hard-rubber shapes could be mounted on them (Fig.4.4). The objects used in the paired-comparison visual test were 6.4 cm in diameter and painted a bright orange.

Three experimenters were used to ensure objectivity of the results. One experimenter administered the tactual stimulus. He was not informed about the left-right positioning of the visual shapes. A second experimenter observed the infant's visual fixations through a peephole in the rear wall of the testing chamber. He was unaware of both the tactual shape and the left-right positioning of the visual shapes. Corneal reflections of the test objects were visible to this scorer, but the shapes of the objects were not resolvable. He scored the infant as fixating the left object when the left reflection was visible

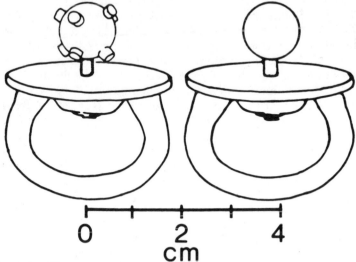

Fig. 4.4. The tactual objects used in assessing intermodal matching by neonates.

in either of the infant's pupils, and as fixating the right object when the right reflection was visible (Fantz, Fagan and Miranda, 1975). A third experimenter randomly selected the tactual shape and the left-right positioning of the visual shapes. This experimenter was not involved with testing the infant.

Two experiments were conducted involving thirty-two infants each (mean age = 29.4 days). Both experiments started with a ninety-second tactual familiarization period during which the infants orally explored either the sphere or the sphere-with-nubs. The tactual object was then carefully removed without the infant seeing it, and the infant presented with the visual choice. In both experiments, the tactual object, the positioning of the visual shapes and the sex of the infants were completely counter-balanced.

The results clearly show that twenty-nine-day-old infants are capable of intermodal matching. Of the thirty-two infants tested in the first experiment, twenty-four fixated the shape matching the tactual object longer than the non-matching shape ($p < .01$, binomial test). The mean per cent of total fixation time directed to the matching shape was 71.8 per cent, as compared with the chance level of 50 per cent ($t = 3.07$; $p < .01$). The second experiment, conducted by a different team of experimenters, fully replicated these effects. Of the thirty-two infants tested, twenty-two fixated the matching shape longer than the non-matching one ($p = .05$); the mean per cent of fixation to the matching shape was 67.1 per cent ($t = 2.14$; $p < .05$).

These results with twenty-nine day-old infants show that neonates can: (1) tactually and visually discriminate between the shapes presented; (2) store some representation of the tactually perceived shape; and (3) relate a subsequent visual perception to the stored representation of the tactually perceived shape. The results do not isolate the exact nature of this stored representation. Infants could be storing information about specific features such as edges or information about whole forms. However, even without specifying the nature of the intermodal invariants, the results show that neonates are not limited to processing sense-specific elements such as retinal images or tactual sensations. If they were limited to registering such sensory bits, they could not succeed on these intermodal tasks.

It is noteworthy that our study shows preferences for the shape matching the tactual object, while Fantz's and Fagan's classic studies of intramodal recognition memory report preferences for novel stimuli. It will be important for future studies to investigate why infants prefer familiarity under certain conditions and novelty under others (Greenberg, Uzgiris and Hunt, 1970; McCall and McGhee, 1977; Weizmann, Cohen and Pratt, 1971; Wetherford and Cohen,

1973). However, there are four important differences between Fantz's and Fagan's research and our own that already offer helpful clues for understanding what determines whether infants prefer the familiar or the novel test objects. Specifically, our experiments, unlike this previous work: (1) assess intermodal rather than intra-modal recognition; (2) test infants younger than typical with the paired-comparison technique; (3) use three-dimensional forms rather than two-dimensional patterns; and (4) use a ninety-second tactual familiarization period. There are theoretical reasons for thinking that all these interact to influence the direction of infant visual preference. For example, our findings that neonates preferred the matching shape probably indicate that they had not yet habitu-ated to the familiarization stimulus (Cohen and Gelber, 1975). On the assumption that older infants habituate more quickly than younger ones, we would expect them to prefer the novel object given the same ninety-second tactual familiarization period and the same intermodal task as the neonates. In short, I do not think there is a simple 'natural tendency' to prefer a physically new stimulus, as others have suggested (Fantz, Fagan and Miranda, 1975). Instead, I believe a variety of factors influence the direction of infant fixation including: age (developmental level), familiarization time, percep-tual modalities used in familiarization and test periods, and com-plexity of stimuli. The infant's direction of visual preferences prob-ably reflects the degree of encoding of the familiarization stimulus. These ideas can be tested, and we are currently doing so (Meltzoff, 1981).

To summarize, Molyneux's original question concerning the rela-tion between touch and vision has inspired a plethora of studies aimed at testing blind patients who recovered their vision (Gregory and Wallace, 1963; Valvo, 1968; von Senden, 1960). These studies have not provided a clear answer to Molyneux's question, primarily because of one major stumbling block. That is, it is difficult to draw firm conclusions about the initial, unlearned relation between touch and vision (the subject of Molyneux's question) from adult patients who have suffered a lifetime of visual deprivation (blindness) and may therefore have experienced abnormal development and/or de-generation of various sorts. Our study with human neonates pro-vides a cleaner test of Molyneux's question, and the results show that we must reverse his answer. Human beings are able to recognize equivalences in information picked up by different modalities with-out the need for learned correlations. Apparently, this is an innate ability.[3] One can only wonder about possible differences in the history of philosophy and psychology had Molyneux framed his provocative philosophical question in terms of newborn infants instead of blind adults who recovered their vision.

Conclusions

Our tests were designed so that success on them would imply some representational capacities. In our test of imitation, we used the pacifier technique so that infants could not imitate while the target gesture was in the perceptual field. The gesture was demonstrated while the infant sucked on a pacifier. The adult then stopped gesturing, assumed a passive face pose, and only then removed the pacifier. Moreover, imitative responses did not immediately burst forth once the pacifier was removed, as if they had been barely held back. Infants at first produced approximate matches that seemed to be corrected over the course of the response period. Given the experimental design, these findings imply that infants are storing some representation of the original model against which they are comparing their own unseen motor movements. Similarly, the inter-modal task was designed to avoid simultaneous matching between objects that were in the perceptual field. The tactual object was removed before the infant was presented with the paired-comparison visual test. Success on this type of successive intermodal task neces-sarily implies some representational capacities.

The imitation task is perhaps the more demanding of the two, because in that case the infant does not merely fixate longer on the matching stimulus ('recognition memory'), but generates the match-ing behaviour himself after the target has disappeared (suggesting 'recall' or 'reconstructive memory'). Both experiments, however, show neonates are capable of storing some representation of a perceptually absent stimulus.

If we are to invoke representation in the neonatal period, what kind of representation is it? The results suggest that neonates are capable of storing surprisingly abstract representations or descrip-tions of the world (Bower, 1979). Consider our intermodal matching experiment. Infants must be storing information abstract enough, at least, to allow recognition at a different point in time, across changes in size, orientation and modality of perception.

This brings me to the crux of the argument. I think Piaget was correct in seeing theoretical links between intermodal coordination, imitation and representation. However, the data and interpretations advanced here stand his argument on its head. They reverse two major assumptions in his developmental theory. (1) Instead of seeing intermodal coordination as a product of many months of postnatal development, I think it characterizes the newborn's initial state.

Development in infancy apparently does not consist of a stitching together of initially independent sense-modalities. On the contrary, it may well be characterized by a gradual differentiation of an initial intermodal unity. The implications for our research programs are important. A classic developmental question was framed as follows: When (and by what mechanism) do infants first detect equivalences in information perceived through different modalities? Our results suggest a new question: When (and by what mechanism) do infants differentiate the modalities enough to represent tactually and visually perceived information in a form that is different from one another? This question is difficult to address experimentally, but would seem to be well worth the effort. (2) Instead of seeing mental representation as an outgrowth of sensory-motor imitation, I think representation underlies imitation. In my view, neonatal imitation and intermodal matching are both mediated by the representational capacities available at birth.

In conclusion, I am proposing the following thesis. Sensory-motor behaviour is not 'internalized' to give birth to the infant's representation capacities at eighteen to twenty-four months of age. Quite the contrary. The ability to act on the basis of abstract representations or descriptions of perceptually absent events needs to be considered as the starting point of infant development, not its culmination.

Notes

1. For Piaget's account to work, he must assume that infants can categorize the sight of the adult's hand and the sight of his own hand as the same or similar to one another. (Indeed, Piaget argues that the infant actually 'confuses' these two.) This is by no means trivial, since the adult's and infant's hands are of such different size, texture, and so forth. However, Piaget seems willing to attribute this level of sophistication to the young infant (Piaget, 1952, 1962), and recent experiments can be cited in support of Piaget's assumption that this is not beyond the capacities of young infants (Cohen, 1979; Cohen and Strauss, 1979). Piaget does not appear to have overestimated the infant's categorization abilities, although he may well have underestimated them.

2. I follow the common use of the term 'intermodal matching' to describe experiments where subjects relate information picked up through two different modalities. In using this standard label, I do not mean to specify anything about the psychological processes used by the infant. For example, if, as suggested in the text, neonates utilize a supramodal or transmodal representational system, then the tactually and visibly perceived information may be represented in the same (supramodal)

form. Other possible labels such as 'intermodal perception' or 'cross-modal transfer' could also be criticized if they were to be taken as descriptions of underlying processes used by the infants, and not as mere labels.

3. We tested twenty-nine-day-old infants, and one would need to test newborns to disprove all possible learning arguments. Nevertheless, the existing data strongly suggest an innate capacity, since it is unlikely that a normally-reared infant could learn these tactual-visual correspond-ences in the first twenty-nine days. The classic learning arguments rely on *simultaneous* tactual and visual exploration of shapes. Thus an infant is said to run his finger over an edge while he visibly inspects the edge. It is this simultaneous bimodal experience (the temporal and spatial contiguity) that leads to associating the two impressions. However, twenty-nine-day-old infants do not reach out and tactually explore objects, so the learning arguments, as classically outlined, do not apply. They must be revised to apply to neonates.

    Could sucking on objects lead neonates to learn certain intermodal correlations? Extending a learning argument to neonatal oral experi-ence has serious pitfalls, because this oral experience differs critically from manual exploration in older infants. Neonates can never see what is in their mouth while they are sucking on it; simultaneous oral and visual exploration is therefore impossible. Indeed, everyday circum-stances would probably lead neonates to make erroneous intermodal linkages if they were actually relying on learned associations between sensory impressions. Consider the neonate's world. Since he cannot see inside his mouth, he will usually see a different shape from the one he is simultaneously perceiving tactually. For example, he would see the mother's face or breast while tactually perceiving a nipple shape. If simple association were operating, the infant should come to link the tactual impression of a nipple-shape with the visual impression of a breast-shape or face!

    Perhaps, one could revise the learning argument to claim that neo-nates learn to associate visual and tactual stimuli even when they are perceived in succession and not simultaneously. There are, however, two reasons for thinking this revision still will not account for the present findings. First, infants under one-month-old usually do not visually inspect an object before it is inserted into their mouths. For example, before and during nursing, neonates are more likely to ex-amine the mothers face than to inspect visually the mother's nipple itself (Spitz, 1965). Second, even if neonates periodically inspected the mother's nipple before sucking it, such experience would not be condu-cive for learning, because the relevant visual perception precedes the tactual experience on a highly irregular basis (there are many violations of the contingency), and even when this occurs there is a temporal delay between the visual and tactual experience (Millar, 1972; Ramey and Ourth, 1971; Watson, 1967). At best, then, a detailed learning argu-ment designed to account for our results would probably have to assume what it is attempting to prove—namely, that prior to any learning experiences, neonates have a 'natural tendency' to link certain visual and tactual perceptions.

Acknowledgements
This work was supported in part by grants from the Spencer Foundation and the National Institute of Child Health and Human Development (HD–13024). I thank Keith Moore, Jerome Bruner, Richard Borton and Craig Harris for help in conceptualizing the issues discussed in the chapter as well as for assistance in conducting the research. I also thank Craig Harris, Charles Marks, Richard Borton, Barbara Mackoff, Alison Gopnik and Calle Fisher for useful comments on preliminary versions of this chapter. Figs. 4.1 and 4.2 are reproduced with the permission of *Science*, and Fig. 4.4 with the permission of *Nature*.

References

Abravanel, E., Levan-Goldschmidt, E. and Stevenson, M. (1976) 'Action imitation: The early phase of infancy', *Child Development*, 47, 1032–44.

Als, H., Brazelton, T., Lester, B. and Landers, B. (1980) 'Caesarean section: Differential impact on newborn behavior', paper presented at the International Conference on Infant Studies, New Haven, April, 1980.

Als, H., Tronick, E., Adamson, L. and Brazelton, T. B. (1976) 'The behavior of the full-term yet underweight newborn infant', *Developmental Medicine and Child Neurology*, 18, 590–602.

Aleksandrowics M. and Aleksandrowics, D. (1974) 'Obstetrical pain-relieving drugs as predictors of infant behavior variability', *Child Development*, 45, 935–45.

Barker, R. (1963) *The Stream of behavior*, Appleton-Century-Crofts, New York.

Berkeley, G. (1709) An essay toward a new theory of vision. Dublin: Pepyat.

Birdwhistell, R. (1973) *Kinesics and Context: Essays on Body Motion.*, Penguin, Harmondworth.

Bower, T. (1972) 'Object perception in infants', *Perception*, 1, 15–30.

Bower, T. (1974) *Development in Infancy*, W. H. Freeman, San Francisco.

Bower, T. (1979) *Human Development*, W. H. Freeman, San Francisco.

Brazelton, T. (1961) 'Effects of maternal medication on the neonate and his behavior', *Journal of Pediatrics*, 58, 513–8.

Bruner, J. S. (1969) Origins of problem solving strategies in skill acquisition. Paper presented at the XIX International Congress of Psychology. London.

Bruner, J. S. (1975) The beginnings of intellectual skill: 1. *New Behaviour*, October, 20–4.

Bruner, J. S., & Koslowski, B. (1972) Visually preadapted constituents of manipulatory action. *Perception*, 1, 3–14.

Bryant, P., Jones, P., Claxton, V. and Perkins, G. (1972) 'Recognition of shapes across modalities by infants', *Nature*, 240, 303–304.

Burd, A. P., and Milewski, A. E. (1981) 'Matching of facial gestures by young infants: Imitation or releasers? Paper presented at the meeting of the Society for Research in Child Development, Boston, MA.

Caesaer, P., O'Brien, M., and Prechtl, H. (1973) 'Postural behaviour in human newborns.' *Aggresologie*, 14, 49–57.

Cohen, L. B. (1979) Our developing knowledge of infant perception and cognition. *American Psychologist*, 34, 894–9.

Cohen, L. B., and Gelber, E. R. (1975) 'Infant visual memory'. In L. Cohen & P. Salapatek (Eds.), *Infant perception: From sensation to cognition* (Vol. 1). CA: San Francisco, Academic Press.

Cohen, L. B., and Strauss, M. S. (1979) Concept acquisition in the human infant. *Child Development*, 50, 419–24.

Conway, E., and Brackbill, Y. (1970) Delivery medication and infant outcome: An empirical study. *Monographs of the Society for Research in Child Development*, 35 (4, Serial No. 137), 24–34.

Dane, B., and Van der Kloot, W. G. (1964) 'An analysis of the display of the goldeneye duck (*Bucephala clangula L.*).' *Behavior*, 22, 283–328.

Dunkeld, J. (1978) 'The function of imitation in infancy', Unpublished doctoral dissertation, University of Edinburgh.

Eckman, P., Friesen, W., and Ellsworth, P. (1972) *Emotion in the human face*. New York: Pergamon Press.

Fagan, J. F., III. (1970) Memory in the infant. *Journal of Experimental Child Psychology*, 9, 217–26.

Fantz, R. (1964) 'Visual experience in infants: Decreased attention to familiar patterns relative to novel ones', *Science*, 146, 688–76.

Fantz, R. L. Fagan, J. F. and Miranda, S. B. (1975) 'Early visual selectivity as a function of pattern variables, previous exposure, age from birth and conception, and expected cognitive deficit', in Cohen, L. and Salapatek, P. (eds) *Infant Perception: From Sensation to Cognition, Vol. 1*, Academic Press, San Francisco.

Gardner, J. and Gardner, H. (1970) 'A note on selective imitation by a six-week-old infant', *Child Development*, 41, 1209–13.

Gibson, E. J. (1969) *Principles of Perceptual Learning and Perceptual Development*, Appleton-Century-Crofts, New York.

Gibson, J. J. (1968) *The Senses Considered as Perceptual Systems*, Houghton Mifflin, Boston.

Gottfried, A., Rose, S. and Bridger, W. (1977) 'Cross-modal transfer in human infants', *Child Development*, 48, 118–23.

Greenberg, D. J., Uzgiris, I. C. and Hunt, J. McV. (1970) 'Attentional preference and experience: III. Visual familiarity and looking time', *Journal of Genetic Psychology*, 117, 123–5.

Gregory, R. and Wallace, J. (1963) 'Recovery from early blindness: A case study' *Experimental Psychology Society Monograph* No. 2.

Jacobson, S. (1979) 'Matching behavior in the young infant', *Child Development,* 50, 425–430.

Locke, J. (1690) *An essay concerning human understanding*, London, Bassett.

Lorenz, K. and Tinbergen, N. (1938) *Zeitschrift Tierpsychologie*, 2, 1.
Lipsitt, L. (1969) 'Learning capacities of the human infant', in Robinson, R. (ed) *Brain and Early Behaviour*, Academic Press, New York.
Maratos, O. (1973) 'The origin and development of imitation in the first six months of life', unpublished doctoral dissertation, University of Geneva.
McCall, R. B., and McGhee, P. E. 1977 The discrepancy hypothesis of attention and affect in infants. In I. C. Uzgiris and F. Weizman (Eds), *The structure of experience*. Plenum Press, New York.
McCall, R. B., Parke, R. D. and Kavanaugh, R. D. (1977) 'Imitation of live and televised models by children one to three years of age'. *Monographs of the Society for Research in Child Development*, 42 (5, Serial No. 173).
Meltzoff, A. N. (1977a) 'Imitation in neonates'. Paper presented at the meeting of the American Psychological Association, San Francisco, CA.
Meltzoff, A. N. (1977b) 'Imitation in early infancy: Some implications for Piaget's theory of representation'. Paper presented at the meeting of the Seventh Annual Symposium of the Jean Piaget Society, Philadelphia, PA.
Meltzoff, A. N. (1981) 'Intermodal matching in early infancy'. Paper presented at the meeting of the Society for Research in Child Development, Boston, MA.
Meltzoff, A. N. and Borton, R. W. (1979) 'Intermodal matching by human neonates'. *Nature*, 282, 403–4.
Meltzoff, A. N. and Moore, M. K. (1977) Imitation of facial and manual gestures by human neonates. *Science*, 198, 75–8.
Meltzoff, A. N. and Moore, M. K. (in prep.) 'Neonatal imitation' in Lipsitt, L. P. (ed.), *Advances in Infancy Research*, Ablex, New York.
Millar, W. S. (1972) A study of operant conditioning under delayed reinforcement in early infancy. *Monographs of the Society for Research in Child Development*, 37 (2).
Moore, M. K. and Meltzoff, A. N. 'Object permanence imitation and language development in infancy: Toward a neo-Piagetian perspective on communicative and cognitive development', in Minifie, F. and Lloyd, L. (eds.), *Communicative and Cognitive Abilities – Early Behavioral Assessments*, University Park Press, Baltimore, 1978.
Oster, H. and Ekman, P. (1978) 'Facial behavior in child development', in Collins, A. (ed.) *Minnesota Symposia on Child Psychology, Vol. 11*, Laurence Erlbaum, Hillsdale NJ.
Piaget, J. (1952) *The Origins of Intelligence in Children*, Norton, New York.
Piaget, J. (1954) *The Construction of Reality in the Child*, Basic Books, New York.
Piaget, J. (1962) *Play, Dreams and Imitation in Childhood*, Norton, New York.
Piaget, J. and Inhelder, B. (1969) *The Psychology of the Child*, Basic Books, New York.
Piaget, J. and Inhelder, B. (1971) *Mental Imagery in the Child*, Basic Books, New York.

Piaget, J. and Inhelder, B. (1973) *Memory and Intelligence*, Basic Books, New York. 1973.

Ramey, C. T. and Ourth, L. L. (1971) Delayed reinforcement and vocalization rates of infants. *Child Development*, 42, 291–7.

Ruff, H. A. and Kohler, C. J. (1978) *Infant Behavior and Development*, 1, 259–64.

Schaffer, H. (1971) *The Growth of Sociability*, Penguin, Harmondsworth.

Senden, M. von (1960) *Space and Sight*, Free Press, Glenese.

Sigman, M. and Parmelëe, A. H. (1974) 'Visual preference of four-month-old premature and full-term infants', *Child Development*, 45, 959–65.

Sony Corporation (1971a) *Sony Service Manual AV-3650*, Sony, Japan.

Sony Corporation (1971b) *Sony Service Manual AVC-3400*, Sony, Japan.

Sony Corporation (1972) *Sony Service Manual AV-3400*, Sony, Japan.

Sony Corporation (1979) *Sony Service Manual AVC-3260*, Sony, Japan.

Spitz, R. (1965) *The first year of life*, International Universities Press, New York.

Stechler, G. (1964) 'Newborn attention as affected by medication during labor', *Science*, 114, 1–2.

Teller, D. (1979) 'A forced-choice preferential looking procedure: A psychological technique for use with human infants', *Infancy, Behavior and Development*, 2, 135–53.

Tinbergen, N. (1951) *The Study of Instinct*, Oxford University Press, London.

Uzgiris, I. C. and Hunt, J. McV. (1975) *Assessment in Infancy*, University of Illinois Press, Chicago.

Valvo, A. (1968) 'Behavior patterns and visual rehabilitation after early and long lasting blindness', *American Journal of Ophthalmology*, 65, 19–23.

Watson, J. S. (1967) 'Memory and "Contingency Analysis" in infant learning'. *Merill-Palmer Quarterly*, 13, 55–76.

Werner, H. and Kaplan, B. (1963) *Symbol Formation*, John Wiley. New York.

Weizmann, F., Cohen, L. B. and Pratt, J. (1971) 'Novelty, familiarity, and the development of infant attention', *Developmental Psychology*, 4, 149–54.

Wetherford, M. J. and Cohen, L. B. (1973) 'Developmental changes in infant visual preferences for novelty and familiarity', *Child Development*, 44, 416–24.

White, B. L. Castle, P. and Held, R. (1964) 'Observations on the development of visually-directed reaching', *Child Development*, 35, 349–64.

Whiten, A. (1975) 'Neonatal separation and mother-infant interaction', paper presented at the Meeting of the International Society for the Study of Behavioral Development, Guildford, July, 1975.

Zaslow, M. (Chairperson) (1980) 'The psychological impact of Caesarean childbirth', Symposium presented at the International Conference on Infant Studies, New Haven, April, 1980.

Zazzo, R. (1957) 'Le Problème de l'imitation chez le nouveau-né', *Enfance*, 10, 135–42.

5 Action and Perception of Displacements in Infancy

WILLIAM A. BALL AND ELIANE VURPILLOT

Introduction

Some of the most commonplace events are striking in the contrast between the apparent directness of the visual perception they produce and the complexity of the psychological and philosophical problems suggested by what is seen. Suppose, for instance, that an observer were to catch a thrown ball or to run after it. This statement of the events is partly a description of perceptual experience: the observer sees an object coming closer, or sees himself moving toward the object. In short, the observer perceives movement of an object or of himself in a three-dimensional space. The broad issues contained within the perception of these ordinary events include the problems of depth and motion perception as well as the powerful tendency to see a stationary world within which objects and the self can move. Despite changes in a two-dimensional retinal image, adult visual perception involves experience of movement in a three-dimensional space, as well as a correct distinction between states of the world and of the self. These skills have long been objects of epistemological discussion. They are also themes familiar from Piaget's (1937) work, and one of his most important contributions has been to argue that the study of human development cannot be divorced from reflection on the nature of knowledge of the self and the external world.

In the present chapter, we propose to examine aspects of Piaget's theory of spatial understanding in infancy. Piaget has chosen motor activity as the cornerstone of a complicated account of spatial development in infancy. Why he does so will be shown to be inseparable from the philosophical debate he sought to resolve. This broader debate will serve as a context for discussing Piaget's treatment of problems implied by the perceptual examples described earlier. A guiding question can be quickly stated: What is the origin of human visual knowledge of movement in a three-dimensional space?

Motoric Descriptions of Space

At the centre of centuries of debate surrounding this question is the role of motor activity in creating the visual perception of space. Intuitively, it is reasonable that common activities such as reaching, walking and head movements would play a key theoretical role because the distance and location of a surface relative to an observer can be represented in terms of the displacements (movements) needed to contact a point on the target. Indeed, one of the physicists' descriptions of space involves a set of three-dimensional vectors that can be conceived as representing the directed displacements needed to move from one point to another. Given a point of reference, all the locations within the three-dimensional space can be specified by giving appropriate values to the horizontal, vertical, and depth components of the vector. Each component can be thought of as a directed movement having a given magnitude. Thus, humans' workaday space can be described in terms of the left–right, up–down, and in–out movements needed to go from place to place. From the standpoint of elementary physics, the displacements could, in principle, involve any moving object, human or otherwise, and the rigid movements of an observer are isomorphic to displacements of an inanimate object.

The Action Hypothesis.

A description of space having psychological relevance almost inevitably involves some element of displacement, whether produced by muscular action or another source. Humans have to locomote and reach in order to adapt to the world, and space must in some sense be perceived in terms of the possibilities of movement if vision is to be useful in detecting the spatial layout and displacements within it (see Gibson, 1958). Theorists as diverse as Berkeley (1709), Piaget (1937) and Gibson (1958, 1966) have not really differed over the issue of whether the visual perception of space can usefully be described in terms of a specification of the motor activity or other displacements needed to reach a point. Rather, the theories concerning the relation of action and vision have differed in the role assigned to motor activity in *creating* the visual perception of a stable, three-dimensional world. On this issue, opinions have fallen into roughly two categories: one stressing that action gives three-dimensional spatial significance to visual perception (the action hypothesis) and one de-emphasizing the role of action in creating the visual skills. Piaget, at least in his early writing (1937), clearly falls into the former category, but a fair amount of the non-Genevan work in infant spatial perception has been done with the intent of discrediting the action hypothesis. The organization of the rest of the chapter will sketch the lines of this debate in three major sections. In a first section, some of the philosophical problem Piaget tried to solve will be made explicit, and hence, there will be an attempt to clarify what motivated his adopting the views he expressed. Next, this theory will be examined in light of selected, empirical work done within a framework critical of Piaget's views. Finally, these criticisms will be re-examined from a perspective more sympathetic to Piaget's undertaking.

Piaget's Theory and Certain Knowledge of Space

Piaget's treatment of the role of action in spatial development is imposing in the subtlety with which he tries to seize a middle ground between views presented as polar opposites. No polar set of doctrines is more fundamental to Piaget's work than nativism and empiricism. His discussion (1937) of the development of the infant's spatial understanding can be construed as an elaborate argument that this knowledge results neither from *a priori* structures nor from inductive experience. The classic debates of nativism and empiricism (Kant and Hume) constitute a backdrop indispensable to understanding why Piaget's theory of infancy takes the form it does. What is original in Piaget is not so much that he argues that the two philosophical extremes must be reconciled. Rather, what is striking is the way in which he tries to overcome the traditional dichotomy. The problem, although not always clearly articulated in his 1937 work *Construction du réel* is the origin of sure or deductive knowledge that space can be represented in terms of displacements and motor activity having the property of a mathematical group.

Piaget (1937) echoes Kantian and skeptic empiricist-philosophers in holding that knowledge of space derived from repeated exposure can never be perfectly certain or perfectly general. Induction in this view only allows an observer to make a best guess that the same conditions will be followed by similar events in the future. There is no logical certitude that (no way to deduce the possibility that) the subsequent events must have the properties observed earlier. A slightly contrived Piagetian example, one presented in the introduction, will clarify the relevance of this epistemological position to theories of spatial understanding. Suppose that a naive baby monitored a series of events that, from *an adult's point of view*, consisted of an object moving closer, stopping and moving away to the original position. A baby wearing an empiricist bonnet would have no logical guarantee that the initial displacement toward his or her must be reversible, that the object can return to its initial position. However many times the sceptical infant viewed the successive movements, he or she could never claim to deduce that one kind of change can always be followed by the other. The infants could, of course, predict the likelihood that movement toward can be followed by movement away, but the discovering of an empirical regularity does not allow infants to deduce that the displacements will continue to be as orderly as in the past. For Piaget (*Ibid*. p.85), however, spatial knowledge in infancy comes to have a deductive quality that detection of empirical regularities does not suffice to explain.

Groups of Displacements and Deductive Knowledge.
In Piaget's view, the baby's understanding eventually becomes a 'theory' that displacement of self and objects conform to the properties of a mathematical group. The group of displacements in three-dimensional space can be considered a set of elements (movements) that can be combined such that any movement is reversible and successive movements are associative. Associability in this context simply means that there are multiple routes available to reach the same location. If infants were to have a theory that movements in general have group properties, they would have a powerful basis for *deducing* that any specific movement has the same properties of being reversible or being potentially executed in more than one way. Suppose, to continue the earlier example, that an object approached an infant and stopped. The infant with a knowledge of groups could deduce that the object could, in principle, return to the original point. The infant's chain of 'reasoning' might consist of something analogous to the following: I see a displacement, displacements have group properties including reversibility, therefore, this displacement has a potential inverse. It should also be noted that a disappearance of an object behind a barrier is only a special case of a displacement (whether of a cover or an object moving under one). Thus, a disappearance can also be known to be reversible once the infant's knowledge of groups is acquired. The belief in the reversibility of the movement of an object resulting in disappearance is, of course, one manifestation of object permanence. Piaget (*Ibid*. p.85) argues that the infant's knowledge of objects is 'rational' or deductive precisely because it hinges on an understanding of space, an understanding of the group properties of displacements.

Piaget further holds that the baby's knowledge of groups is not derived from merely viewing regularly co-occurring events. He does not, however, accept the Kantian or neo-Kantian perspective (Poincaré, 1925) that this understanding of groups is innate. Rather, he has maintained that during the first few weeks of life

. . . nothing is given of space except the perception of light and the accommodation appropriate to this perception (pupillary reflex to ambient lighting and blinking reflex in dazzling light). All else, that is the perception of form, size, distance, position, etc., are elaborated little by little . . . . (Piaget, 1937, p.87).

Piaget's view seems to be that veridical spatial perception depends on an understanding of groups. Infants do not see depth or constant form directly. They begin to see constant form of a rotated object only when they can actively reverse the rotation; such constancy of form becomes deductive when the rotation is known to conform to the properties of a group. A movement can undo the rotation and restore the initial orientation. Visual distance between objects or depth relative to the observer becomes objective only to the extent that the infant knows that the spatial layout can be represented in terms of the reversible and associative movements needed to go from point to point. This knowledge is held to be based neither on innate structures nor on inductive experience. Piaget thus rejects both nativist views that an understanding of groups is innate and empiricist views that mere visual observation of successive movements can result in knowledge of groups.

Sensorimotor Alernative to Induction and Nativism
What is the 'middle' alternative to nativism and induction? The middle ground between radical nativism and empiricism is rooted in Piaget's description of the development of sensorimotor intelligence. Piaget argues (*Ibid.* p.306) that the categories of object and space are outcomes of intellectual development that is marked by the progressive co-ordination of actions into means–ends relations. But sensorimotor intelligence reaches mature form only through active experience of the individual. Therefore, because the categories of knowledge (space, object, causality) are held to be the outcomes of the development of sensorimotor intelligence, these categories, in turn, depend on active experience for their emergence. What is crucial to note is that the active experience does not lead merely to an accumulation of memories for specific events. Rather, active experience results in a global change in the organization of the schemes of action into which particular events can be assimilated.

The ties between sensorimotor intelligence, spatial understanding, and the theoretical construct of the group can now be made clearer. It is crucial to note that the group is a mathematical structure that describes both the motor actions of the infant and the displacement of external objects. Both motor activity and movements of things are associative and reversible. Piaget's theory that the re-organization of internal sensorimotor schemes underlies the development of spatial understanding thus can lean heavily on the group construct to make the link between intelligence and spatial knowledge adherent. An example is in order. A stage-four baby can retrieve a ball he or she threw by pulling the cover it landed on or crawling to it directly. The goal of grabbing the ball can be achieved in two active ways, pulling or crawling, and this means–end relation of activities is the hallmark of true intelligence. Furthermore, the behaviour of throwing the ball is reversed by retrieval, and the retrieval is associative because it can be accomplished in more than one way. But, as previously described, the in–out movements of the ball itself—its displacements—are also reversible and associative: the object can be returned to its original position via more than one path.

The essential point of Piaget's theory hinges on this isomorphism of the group of displacements of external objects and the group characterizing the infant's behaviour. If infants were to become aware of the properties of their own behaviour, they would have just the sort of knowledge required to deduce the properties of displacements of objects in space. In the context of sensorimotor intelligence, becoming aware of the properties of action is synonymous with knowing before acting that there are multiple ways to achieve a goal such as retrieving an object. But this awareness is precisely what characterizes an intelligent baby between stages four and six. Intelligent behaviour requires active experience for development, not in the sense that the baby accumulates memories for discreet movements, but in the sense that experience leads to a reorganization of internal action schemes. What emerges in development is a group structure into which the perception of moving objects can be assimilated. Infants can know about the group properties of objects only to the extent that they are aware of these same properties in their own behaviour. In highly schematic form, the argument seems to be as follows: In acting on objects, babies become aware of the group properties of their own action. They are then able to attribute the properties of their own activity to objects (that is, assimilate perceived events to schemes of action). Experience is needed for the reoganization of action schemes into a group structure, and this structure, in turn, can serve as a basis for deducing the properties of any actual event in space. If displacements are believed to be like actions, and if actions are believed to have group properties, the infant can deduce essential properties of any given displacement of an object.

Some Empirical Implications
The central role of action and displacements in Piaget's theory suggests that one important area of research would involve young infants' perception of displacements. If babies too young to show means–ends behaviour were nonetheless able to perceive displacements as real movements in space, the implication would be that the development of sensorimotor intelligence plays little role in creating the visual perception. The following discussion will lean heavily on a particular example of perceived displacement, the perception of movement of an object or an observer along the line of sight. This case will receive particular attention because there is some evidence that infants can use optical information specifying movement of objects toward them and movement away from them. It is obvious that these displacements are the inverse of each other, and thus babies potentially could begin at an early age to discover reversible, group properties of motion without 'waiting' for manual intelligence to give meaning to their visual experience. Conceivably, mere observation of many examples of motion and its inverse could allow infants to induce empirical clues such as 'any movement can be undone'. This kind of empiricist alternative to Piaget's account would gain plausibility if infants too young to reach, crawl or show intelligent activity were able to see displacements veridically. These ideas will be elaborated in the ensuing sections of the chapter.

Studies of Perceived Displacement in Depth
One skill fundamental to the perception of displacement is mainly ignored in Piaget's treatment of the sensorimotor period (1936, 1937). Piaget assumed, but rarely attempted to observe directly, the ability to discriminate stimulus variables that are an infant's source of information about events in space. For instance, there is little discussion of what properties of the visual stimulus stage four babies use in seeing that the toy they are pulling is getting closer. How infants are able to see such events as 'approach' is a problem subordinated in his 1937 theory to the creation of visual meaning through action. Even if infants must develop an understanding of the properties of displacements, they still must discriminate displacements from other kinds of events such as the dissolving of a sugar cube or from changes of form for example of a hand opening. Apart from occasional allusions to motion parallax or convergence, however, the description of the effective stimuli is severely limited. The position in Piaget (1937) seems to be that whatever visual discriminations are involved, the perception of displacements is incomplete without the intelligent, means–ends co-ordinations of

schemes of action. Piaget, later (1967), qualified this view in acknow-
ledging that the visual perception of depth is possibly innate, but
recent secondary accounts (for example, Vurpillot, 1972) continue
to reflect chiefly his earlier statement. The 1937 view will continue to
be dubbed Piaget's theory in the rest of the paper.

Several investigators have within the past decade examined depth
perception of infants from a perspective quite different from Piaget's.
The investigators have leaned heavily on work with adult subjects
(for example Gibson, 1966) for a description of the stimuli that
infants could potentially use in perceiving depth. The Gibsonian
view that changes in a stimulus (that is transformations) carry
information about displacements in general and movement in depth
in particular has provided a focal point for arguing that active
experience is not necessary for the creation of visual perception of
three-dimensional space. Because optical stimuli are informative, it
seemed to many investigators that a baby need only attend to the
correct stimulus variables in order to have valid knowledge of an
external world. Anglo-American researchers thus have implicitly and
explicitly stressed continuities in visual functioning from infancy to
later life, and this theoretical orientation is at variance with classic
Piagetian views. In the more recent work, the description of the
effective visual stimulus has been a central concern rather than an
adjunct, as in Piaget's treatment of spatial perception.

Perception of Movement of an Object in Depth.
Results of a number of investigations strongly suggest that infants
under two months old can detect movement of an object in the third
dimension. Bower, Broughton and Moore (1970) found that infants
aged six to twenty-one days rotated their heads upward and pulled
away from an object approaching their faces. Ball and Tronick
(1971) replicated these findings in infants as young as fourteen days
and also showed that the head movements were affected markedly by
the path of approach of the object. Infants withdrew from the object
when its movement was along the line of sight, but not when the
object moved to the side as it approached. A horizontal turning of the
head was the modal response in the latter 'miss' trials. When the
object moved away, no avoidance was observed. Babies thus seem to
avoid approaching objects at an age substantially prior to the
hierarchical organization of action schemes that are the hallmark of
Piaget's sensorimotor intelligence. Also, active retrieval of objects
does not seem to be crucial in creating the response because most
observers do not report this skill before three or four months of age
(White, 1969).

Although the data do not seem compatible with a purely Piagetian view, they do not, however, rule out entirely some role of tactile contact in the origin of the avoidance response. Infants are exposed from birth to contact with moving objects such as bottles, breasts, wash cloths, bonnets and so on. It is possible that contact might rapidly be associated with optical variables specifying potential collision. The learning interpretation presupposes a very precocious discrimination of stimuli accompanying movements in depth. Indeed, one of the present authors has observed the head back avoidance with his son who was under eighteen hours old at the time! There is no systematic evidence concerning the frequency of manifestly painful stimuli such as collision with a hard or rough object moving quickly. It seems doubtful, however, that infants are universally exposed to such obviously harmful situations, and other forms of contact would have to be examined for their 'unpleasant' properties to make a learning position plausible. Unless very young babies are actually exposed to aversive contact together with visual stimuli specifying approach, withdrawal from moving objects becomes difficult to explain within a learning framework.

Whatever the ultimate origin of the avoidance, there is good evidence that visual variables by themselves can produce withdrawal in young infants. Current work with adult subjects (summarized in Braunstein, 1976) indicates optical expansion or contraction of a closed pattern centered on the line of sight is a powerful source of information about movement of an object toward or away from an observer respectively. Bower, Broughton and Moore (1970) and Ball and Tronick (1971) found that the optical equivalent of an approaching object—an expanding shadow—produced avoidance in babies as young as ten days. The optical equivalent of movement away—contraction of a shadow—resulted in few instances of head withdrawal. As with real objects, the head avoidance was specific to the apparent path of 'approach' of the shadow. When the centre of expansion shifted away from the line of sight, the shadow appeared to move to one side, and infants displayed mainly tracking, not avoidance (Ball and Tronick, 1971).

Head withdrawal: avoidance or tracking? Yonas, Bechtold, Frankel, Gordon, McRoberts, Norcia and Sternfels (1977) raised a possible objection to the view that young babies perceive the expanding shadow as an approaching object. These authors argued that head rotation upward during expansion of a pattern could have represented tracking of a contour as it moved up the projection screen. Apparent avoidance would have been an artifact of tracking.

In their study, they replicated the findings of Ball and Tronick (1971) in showing that when the centre of expansion is near the line of sight, babies one to two months old showed more upward head rotation and less horizontal tracking than when shadows expanded and also moved to the side. They further showed, however, that if the top edge of an expanding shadow remained at eye level, upward head rotation (avoidance) rarely occurred. With no upward-moving contour to track, the infants exhibited no pseudo-avoidance.

The upward tracking hypothesis is flawed on at least two counts, however. First, it fails to account for why the downward-moving contour of a symmetrically expanding shadow failed to produce a significant amount of downward tracking. There is no obvious reason why babies should exhibit a bias to track upward given an equal opportunity to track in either direction. Second, Bower (1977a, 1977b) has shown that a shadow mimicking the downward rotation of the edge of a plank resulted in avoidance. Although there was no upward-moving contour to track, babies nonetheless pushed away from the projection screen when the apparently rotating 'object' was about to hit them on the nose!

Why then did infants in the Yonas, Bechtold, Frankel, Gordon, McRoberts, Norcia and Stemfels (1977) study fail to show avoidance when the top of an expanding shadow remained at eye level? A study by Ball[1] (1978) indicated that the eye-level condition here was probably perceived as an object moving below the face. As Gibson noted (1958, 1966), the position of the centre of an optical expansion pattern specifies the path of approach. Deviation of the centre of expansion from the line of sight corresponds to movement of a surface on a miss path with respect to the face. In support of this view, Ball found that if the end point of the centre of shadow expansion was at face level, avoidance was frequently observed in infants thirty to sixty days old. If the end point was below the face, avoidance declined. In both conditions, the top edge of the shadows remained at a constant height, above the head or at eye level, respectively. Therefore, tracking of a contour moving upward could not have been responsible for the avoidance, and the results underscored the sensitivity of young infants to the path of apparent displacement. Yonas and his co-workers' results can be best seen as replicating the data of the Ball and Tronicks (1971) study with shadows, and the controversy over tracking has led to a demonstration that infants are sensitive to the path of approach in the vertical dimension as well as the horizontal one.

Thus, for infants under two months old, expansion of a closed visual pattern can specify both that objects are approaching and the direction of movement. Optical transformations such as expansion or contraction have ecologically valid (invariant) relations to real events (Gibson, 1966), and babies too young to retrieve objects or to crawl use the available transformations in ways appropriate to the distal situation. The view that young infants use invariant transformations is further supported by a recent study performed by Ball[2] (1978). Babies viewed a film that alternated two kinds of trials: in one, an object continuously changed form (for example, from a solid square to a Y form), but in the other, the same form changes were included in continuous expansion of the changing figure. Infants aged thirty to sixty-four days showed the typical avoidance response mainly during expansion trials, even though the top edge of the stimuli did not change height. The babies apprently processed the optical invariant of expansion despite a variable figure embedded in the apparent movement in depth. The results suggest, although not conclusively, that perception of an event, continuous movement in depth, cannot be confounded with a perception of a constant object. Perceiving continuous movement does not necessarily require the presence of a constant form, a fact perhaps suggesting at least some independence of the mechanisms underlying event and form perception.

The hands as external objects. The data reviewed are consistent with the view that, prior to systematic reaching, babies are able to perceive events that could have combined to form a group. It seems plausible that movement toward the infant is seen as different from movement away. The claim is not necessarily that babies under four months see groups; rather, at a minimum, they have the ability to use optical information that specifies two distinct events, each of which is the inverse of the other. The baby, wearing its empiricist bonnet, might well have the perceptual pre-requisites to learn that one movement exactly undoes the effects of the others. For example, the expansion of a stimulus can be followed by a contraction leading to a state of affairs corresponding to the initial conditions. One outcome in development may well be a rule that one event can usually be done by another.

It is important to stress that such skills appear in babies as young as one to three weeks, ages at which systematic reaching is rarely observed. Action does not create the ability to use optical transformations, but it certainly is possible to consider hands and other extremities as providing examples of movements of the sort already described. The latter possibility is important from the stand point of determining how infants guide their own hands visually. A hand can open, close and spread while being displaced, and babies could use the resulting complex optical transformations to monitor their own hand movements. As the Ball (1979) study indicates, changing depth and location of the hands could be seen by even young infants despite the form changes inherent in fluid movement of animate objects (Gibson, 1958). To paraphrase Walk and Gibson (1961), whenever infants are ready for systematic prehension and retrieval of objects, their visual system is ready to facilitate guidance of the behaviour.

Detailed observation of reaching in four-month-old infants nicely illustrates the kind of visual control that is possible. McDonnel (1975) found that babies wearing wedge prisms frequently showed two components in their reaching for an object. A first component was often a relatively smooth ballistic motion covering a good portion of the distance to the object. A second consisted of corrective movements *prior to* arrival at the target, movements that brought the hand back into a trajectory producing contact. Guidance of the hand may thus depend on multiple sources of optical information and the kind of information used may vary according to whether the baby is performing to the initial triggered component or the later corrective movements.

As McDonnell noted (1975), the ballistic movement may be programmed on the basis of depth information given, for example, in motion parallax. But corrective movements occuring prior to the arrival of the object pre-supposes that a discrepancy has been detected between the position of the object and the current or predicted trajectory of the hand. Lasky's finding (1977) that sight of the hand produced more accurate reaching in four-month-old babies further suggests that corrective movements involve visual monitoring of the trajectory of the moving hand.

Detecting the discrepancy between the target and trajectory perhaps represents a special case of perceived movement of an object in depth along a particular path. A hand moving away produces an optical contraction pattern and the centre of change specifies the direction of movement. Young infants have been shown to use this very type of information in perceiving movement of external objects. To predict the end point of a hand moving away from the self, an infant could use information given by the centre of contraction of the optical pattern. Opening, closing or rotating the hand should have no effect on the infant's perception of the trajectory. If the predicted path were discrepant with the location of the target, a corrective movement could be initiated. The visual reafference of the new movement would be, among other things, a new contraction pattern that would confirm that the action was of the right sort (for example, movement away and to the right). Of course, an optical expansion pattern would be produced once the object is grasped and retrieved. The effects of motor commands—movements of the hands closer or farther away—can be given by optical transformations of a kind used by infants from an early age. The visual skills needed for guidance of action need not originate in active experience itself.

The hands have thus far been treated as if they were external objects. But they are external objects with an important perceptual property: their state of movement can potentially be monitored both visually and internally by proprioceptive and efferent motor information. Even if the group properties of action are ignored for the moment, guidance of the hands would still require a theoretical explanation of the co-ordination of action and vision. How infants know that a seen hand will be responsive to 'voluntary' changes in direction remains an open question. For example, how did McDonnell's (1975) babies know that the hand viewed as going off target was their *own* hand and, hence, a thing subject to motor commands? Piaget (1936) anticipated this issue in arguing that young infants do not necessarily know that a thing perceived visually is the same one being felt. The problem in the present context is one of explaining how infants can see their hands as their own rather than as independent external objects.

It is difficult to fathom how purely optical information would resolve this problem of discriminating between internally and externally generated movement. Expansion patterns, motion parallax, or binocular parallax can specify what is happening but it is less obvious that visual information suffices to inform the baby that the hand moving belongs to him or her. What the invariant visual information specifying one's own hand would be is not self-evident. Optical expansions, contraction and form changes produced by movement of a limb could just as well have arisen if the limb were an external object.

The argument is that optical information specifying movement of a limb is consistent with at least two states of affairs:

1   movement of an object external to the self; and
2   movement of a part of the self.

Babies seem to behave as if the latter were the case because they appropriately correct their own hand movements. It is possible to speculate that babies monitor their efferent motor commands. [For a discussion of skill see Bruner 1973]. They would have a potential basis for correlating efforts to move and visual reafference in the form of optical changes already discussed. In the present view, action does not create visual skills such as perceived movement in depth. Rather, one of its roles is to disambiguate optical information that could correspond to movement of the self or movement of part of the world. Action may help specify the cause; that is, the source of the optical transformations discriminated. It should be noted that the efferent monitoring involved need not require the emergence of intelligent behaviour for its development. The mechanism for integrating information across modalities may be part of of the young infant's perceptual hardware (see Meltzoff, 1981, this volume Ch4), and an understanding of groups is not obviously crucial to perceiving the distal cause of the different stimulus changes.

The Visual Perception of Locomotion
As Piaget (1937) brilliantly pointed out, the awareness of group properties of displacements of objects may have its counterpart in the awareness of group properties of locomotion. Furthermore, movements of the self must be distinguished from movements of the world if a stable three-dimensional world is to be perceived. For Piaget, the co-ordination of action schemes into means–ends, group-like behaviour is at the root of the distinction. Only after such co-ordination is achieved can the infant clearly distinguish movement of the world from changes produced by the infant's own action. For instance, when infants crawl, walk, or are carried, their visual field undergoes a dramatic change: there is an expansion of all the elements in the field and the inter-element spaces get bigger. Adults universally see such changes as results of their own motion, not dramatic products of expansion of their surroundings. Piaget's classic views seem to imply that this perceived stability of the world is a developmental consequence of sensorimotor intelligence. Only when infants know that their own movements can be reversed would it become 'obvious' that their own movements do not alter the state of things independent of their actions. Movements must be known to be reversible in order for a baby to deduce the stability of the environment. As with an external object, the issue is whether action creates the visual skills required to see motion veridically.

Studies of perceived locomotion. Studies to date have shown a clear reliance on vision in monitoring the observer's own movement. The visual perception of locomotion along the line of sight is a special case of perceived movement in depth. Adult observers usually can see both that they, not the world, are in motion and that the distance to surfaces ahead of them is being reduced (Gibson, 1958, 1966). Indeed, if an observer rides in a vehicle at a constant velocity, vision is the only source of information specifying continued movement. Lishman and Lee (1973) provided a dramatic demonstration that adults generally use vision in monitoring their own displacements. Despite being objectively at rest, observers reported they were moving forward or backward when a surrounding enclosure moved towards or away from them, respectively.

This line of work begun with adult subjects has been extended to infants by Lee and Aronson (1974), who observed twelve-month-old babies standing in a four-sided enclosure. Movement of the walls of the enclosure toward the babies led to their falling backward; movement of the wall away from the infants led to their stumbling forward. Babies 'compensated' for their apparent movement by losing their balance in the opposite direction. Butterworth and Hicks (1977) obtained qualitatively similar behaviour with seated nine-month-olds, too young to stand.

When babies *begin* to monitor their locomotion visually and the role of action in creating the skill are unclear. Walters and Walk (1974) lowered infants toward the surface of a visual cliff, but the babies did not place the palms down and extend their arms in anticipation of contact until eight or nine months of age. Bower (1977a, 1977b) has argued that findings such as those of Walters and Walk suggested that visual perception of locomotion is not fully in evidence until the last third of the first year. But placing responses perhaps depend for their development on extensive experience in reaching and crawling. Manual indices would tend, therefore, to inflate the estimate of when visually perceived locomotion can be observed in babies.

In considering another method of assessing perceived locomotion, it is important to reiterate that the perception involves babies detecting both that movement in depth occurs and that they are the 'things' moving. There is no reason to assume that the two perceptual abilities have the same developmental history. One skill might emerge earlier in life than the other, and an account of when perceived locomotion begins must include this possibility. For instance, young babies could see a depth change without necessarily perceiving that they, not the world, were in motion. In fact, as was already shown in earlier sections of this report, babies between two and eight weeks saw movement in depth of an object toward them. Head rotation up and away from the target was the typical reaction. Babies apparently see movement in depth of an external object, and they avoid potentionally dangerous collisions ny withdrawing their heads.

In the case of the infant's own displacement, Ball and Dibble (1981) argued that head movements might provide a more sensitive index of perceived depth changes than the manual placing responses used by Walters and Walk (1974). Head withdrawal could be used to assess depth perception during displacement of babies too young to crawl. Ball and Dibble lowered babies in a prone position toward a patterned surface. Infants ranging in age from thirty to 104 days rotated their heads up and away at about five cm from the surface, just prior to facial contact. The response appeared to be the same observed when an object approached the babies in the work discussed earlier. Rapid deceleration and stopping the baby's descent at ten to twenty cm from the surface did not produce withdrawal. Interestingly, movement of the baby horizontally near the surface (five to eight cm) did not yield avoidance, which thus appears direction-specific. Movement toward a surface, not parallel displacement, seems to underlay the response. Even young infants may rely on vision to detect depth changes while they themselves are in motion.

Locomotion and the active resolution of spatial ambiguity. A theoretically important ambiguity remains, however. Pooling the results of several studies suggests that young babies' avoidance of a surface can be observed in two different situations: during movement of an object toward the infant and during movement of the infant toward a surface. Babies under three months old seem to detect a reduction in the distance between themselves and a surface but avoidance of a surface is an appropriate response whether approach is produced by locomotion or movement of the world. Present knowledge does not rule out the possibility that they do not see locomotion and movement of the world as different distal events. This possibility is reinforced by findings obtained with purely optical displays. Ball and Vurpillot (1976) noted that optical magnification of a large display containing discreet textural elements resulted in head withdrawal in babies as young as twenty-one days. This condition provided an optical analogue to the visual transformation produced by locomotion towards a large, flat surface (Gibson, 1958, 1966). Thus, avoidance has been obtained during movement of babies, movement of a single object, and optical magnification of displays that mimic the two types of distal events. Furthermore, these visual skills exist well prior to a period in which intelligent behaviour is evident. Action does not create the visual skills.

The questions raised by current work in perceived-movement-in-depth highlight the developmental issue raised earlier. As in the perception of movement of the limbs, it is possible that perception of locomotion in depth and perception of the locus of movement have distinct developmental histories. How babies distinguish between locomotion and deplacement of the world is unclear. Gibson (1966) maintained that simultaneous transformation of the entire visual field specified locomotion, but the same transformation could, in principle, be the outcome of movement of the world. Suppose that an observer were placed on roller skates, and the whole Earth slid by under him or her. The optical changes produced would have the same properties as visual transformations produced by movement of the observer. Although the example is somewhat far-fetched, the description of the ambiguity seems correct. What is especially important, however, is that adult observers almost universally report that they are in motion during the transformation of the whole visual field. That such ambiguous optical information gives rise to specific visual perceptions suggests that processing contraints of the visual system are revealed (Johansson, 1964). Observers go beyond information inherent in the stimulus.

Speculative mechanisms of resolving optical ambiguity. At present, no definitive answer can be given to the question of how infants come to perceive large-scale optical changes as movement of the self in depth. Some possibilities can be raised, however. First, a transformation of the whole visual field filled with discrete elements may be seen innately as locomotion. The babies' visual system may arbitrarily 'interpret' the stimulus events as being produced by self motion. The innateness hypothesis is plausible given the high ecological validity of the stimulus. In most real-world situations, optical expansion of the whole field, for example, is produced whenever an observer walks over a textured surface. An evolutionary 'bet' that the expansion pattern of the entire visual field corresponded to locomotion would generally be sound because of the very great likelihood of the correlation. Also, movement of an external, single object in depth is usually accompanied by the expansion of only a single item in the visual field. Betting that expansion of a single closed pattern meant that an external object was approaching might also be a sound innate 'wager'. Thus, it is possible that the nervous system of infants inherently decodes whole-field transformations and transformations of an isolated pattern as locomotion and movement of an object, respectively. There are other possibilities, however.

Seeing reduction in the distance between the observer and the observed does not logically entail that an observer perceives what is in motion, himself or an external surface. A potential source of information to infants about their state of motion is self-produced activity itself. Active movement need not be seen in this view as developmentally prior to perceived movement in depth. Instead, activity may serve to specify what optical changes correspond to locomotion, and displacement of the head is one early form of locomotion of the eyes that might allow correlation of efforts to move and visual inputs. Head movements such as arching toward or away from a real crib surface produce optical transformations, expansion or contractions, over the entire visual field. Head 'locomotion' occurs long before actual crawling and, hence, it may provide an early occasion for the baby's correlating optical transformations with efferent motor commands, vestibular inputs, and proprioceptive information. The visual reafference of active head movements toward or away from a surface is the very transformation of the whole visual field that seems to produce visually perceived locomotion in adults and older infants. Young babies could differentiate local transformations of the visual field not usually produced by head movements from simultaneous transformations of all elements in the visual field regularly produced by activity of the head. In both cases, movement in depth would be seen but only one optical transformation would eventually correspond to locomotion. That vestibular information can modify visually perceived locomotion in adults has been suggested by Wong and Frost (1978), and such non-visual input may have an important developmental role in meaning that large-scale optical transformations rapidly come to be seen as being produced by the self.

Implications for Piaget's theory

Piaget's action hypothesis is inadequate in one important respect. Displacements are detected and responded to appropriately by infants lacking the co-ordinated schemes of action that Piaget has called 'intelligent'. Infants under four months old perceive the direction of movement of objects in the third dimension as well as discriminate their own locomotion parallel to a surface from movement toward it. Although the visual perception of these events possibly requires information from the motor system to become entirely unambiguous, this point remains highly speculative. What does seem clear is that intelligent behaviour does not create the ability to use optical transformations specifying distal events like movement in a three-dimensional space. Rather, vision may serve as a means of guiding immediate behaviour at any age at which babies are ready to reach, move their heads, or locomote.

Infants, therefore, possess the minimum requirement for seeing that one movement 'undoes' the effects of another, and this skill would be a *sine qua non* for infants' inducing knowledge of the reversible and associative properties of movements. In watching an object approach, then recede or move back to an initial position via an indirect route, babies could learn that the effects of a variety of movements can be achieved in more than one way. Infants could discover, for example, that a thrown toy can be retrieved readily by an inverse movement produced by a left hand or a right one, and performed in roundabout way or a direct movement. In principle, all such movements could be observed and no deductive set of action schemes need be invoked to explain the acquired knowledge. Babies could see that many movements of an object can be undone— including disappearance—and part of what is meant by the object concept could be derived from observing events without directly acting on them. Babies use optical invariants such as expansion and contraction in seeing movements and their paths, and this information in principle could reveal the group properties forming the core concepts of Piaget's theory.

Are the Objections Fundamental?
The issue of whether early visual sophistication is contradictory to Piaget's theory is perhaps the major question to arise from a decade of research in infant perception. The answer clearly depends on what is considered to be central to Piaget's account of infancy. In the case of spatial development, extreme Piagetian claims of the sort noted at the beginning of this chapter are certainly wrong, and Piaget (1967), in fact, recognized that such complex skills as depth perception could be innate. That perceived movement in depth might also be innate need not be considered by Genevans to be a particularly damaging blow to Piaget's theory.

Why is this? The Piagetian defence perhaps lies in what Vurpillot (1972) has called structured wholes. Piaget's theory has never reduced the older infant's knowledge of objects to mere empirically derived facts. As was stressed in the introduction, Piaget asserts that an infant's knowledge of space comes to have a deductive quality rooted in the assimilation of any particular event (for example, displacement) to an *organized* set of action schemes having the properties of a mathematical group. Piaget has never argued that infants do not use vision to detect empirical regularities. Rather, he has emphasized that visual perception takes place in the context of motoric action of the infant. That babies can see displacements as movement in space at an early age does not necessarily mean that mature sensorimotor knowledge of space results from repeated visual exposure to movements. Action may be required as a 'glue' for incorporating isolated, visually perceived displacements into a structured role. Piaget's view is that the structural whole only emerges with the intelligent co-ordination of actions.

Let us be more specific. Piaget (1936) early argued that infants are inherently active. The complexity of infant behaviour increases strikingly over the first eighteen months, and the necessity of guiding more and more complex behaviour may require babies to become aware of the properties of their own activities. Suppose a stage three infant were confronted with the problem of retrieving a ball he had thrown. If the infant was prevented from reaching the ball directly, he would eventually be able to pull the cover on which the ball fell and, hence, retrieve the object 'indirectly'. The goal in this case is to perform some behaviour—throwing, retrieval, etc. With direct action impossible, the infant in Bruner's (1973) phrase is forced to 'turn around' on his own behaviour. He becomes aware that actions can be combined to achieve a goal: the retrieval of a displaced object. The essential point is that the development of complicated action obliges the infant to go beyond the moment-to-moment guidance of behaviour. Failure of an activity to be performed readily is the occasion upon which the infant must co-ordinate action in new ways. This 'disequilibrium' is the engine driving Piaget's version of sensorimotor development.

The potential relation of action and vision in Piaget's theory can now be stated. Infants perhaps have a precocious ability to see individual movement of objects or their own locomotion correctly. They see movement in three-dimensional space. But the visually perceived movements are not necessarily related to each other in a coherent representation of space. In prompting an infant to reorganize his or her behaviour, 'unsuccessful' action also prompts infants to reorganize their visual perception of displacements such as movement of hand and ball. Indeed, what infants frequently see, their own activity directed to objects, is precisely that which is being structured. Babies may well have to act on objects by reaching or locomoting before a seen displacement is known to be a member of a group structure including all possible movements. Knowledge of groups requires that, for example, a seen movement toward can be *combined* with movement away. Action reveals that optical events such as expansion and contraction can be related to each other in a set of movements characterized by associativity and reversibility.

Some conclusions

The speculative nature of this chapter would be evident. It is prompted by a belief that all the information relevant to evaluating Piaget's theory is not yet in hand. Part of the difficulty is that Piaget's theory itself is frequently unclear. Hopefully, the present chapter has done more than add to the obscurity. Beyond restating Piaget's views, however, the intent of the authors has been to suggest that Piaget's use of the group structure is so fundamental to his views that any evaluation of his theory must deal with this concept. Piaget's theory probably can accommodate the findings discussed in this chapter. Action does not create skills such as perceived motion in depth, but it may well be an essential condition for relating visually perceived displacements to each other in a structure allowing deduction of the properties of any observed movement.

Reference

Ball, W. (1978) 'Infant's responses to optical expansion; avoidance not tracking', paper presented at 1978 Meeting of the Southern SRCD in Atlanta.

Ball, W. (1979) Unpublished data.

Ball, W. and Tronick, E. (1971) 'Infant responses to impending collision: optical and real', *Science*, 171, 818–20.

Ball, W. and Dibble, A. (1981) 'Perceived movement in the visual crib', *Journal of Genetic Psychology* (in press).

Ball, W. and Vurpillot, E. (1976) 'La perception du mouvement en profoundeur chez le nourrisson', *Année psychologique*, 76, 383–400.

Berkeley, G. (1709) *An Essay Towards a New Theory of Vision*, various editions.

Bower, T. G. R. (1977a) *A Primer of Infant Development*, W. H. Freeman, San Francisco.

Bower, T. G. R. (1977b) 'Comment on Yonas and Col. Development and sensitivity to information for impending collision', *Perception and Psychophysics*, 21, 281–2.

Bower, T. G. R., Broughton, J. M. and Moore, M. (1970) 'Infant responses to approaching objects: An indictor of response to distal variables', *Perception and Psychophysics*, 9, 193–96.

Braunstein, M. L. (1976) *Depth Perception through Motion*, Academic Press, New York.

Bruner, J. S. (1973) 'Organization of early skilled action', *Child Development*, 44, 1–11.

Butterworth, G. and Hicks, L. (1977) 'Visual proprioception and postural stability in infancy', *Perception*, 6, 255–262.

Gibson, J. J. (1958) 'Visually controlled locomotion and visual orientation in animals', *British Journal of Psychology*, 49, 182–94.

Gibson, J. J. (1966) *The Senses Considered as Perceptual Systems*, Houghton Mifflin, Boston.

Johansson, G. (1964) 'Perception of motion and changing form. A study of visual perception from continuous transformations of a solid angle of light at the eye', *Scandinavian Journal of Psychology*, 5, 181–208.

Lasky, R. E. (1977) 'The effect of visual feedback of the hands on the reaching and retrieval behavior of young infants', *Child Development*, 48, 112–7.

Lee, D. and Aronson, E. (1974) 'Visual proprioceptive control of standing in human infants', *Perception and Psychophysics*, 15, 529–532.

Lishman, J. and Lee, D. N. (1973) 'The autonomy of visual kinesthesis', *Perception*, 2, 287–94.

McDonnell, P. M. (1975) 'The development of visually guided reaching', *Perception and Psychophysics*, 18, 181–5.

Meltzoff, A. N. (1981) 'Imitation, intermodal co-ordination and representation', in Butterworth G. (ed.) *Infancy and Epistemology*, Harvester Press, Brighton, this volume pp.85–114.

Piaget, J. (1936) *La naissance de l'intelligence chez l'enfant*, Delachaux & Niestlé, Paris.

Piaget, J. (1937) *La construction du réel chez l'enfant*, Delachaux & Niestlé, Paris.

Piaget, J. (1967) *Biologie et connaissance*, Gallimard, Paris.

Poincaré, H. (1925) *La valeur de la science*, Bibliothèque de Philosophie Scientifique, Paris.

Vurpillot, E. (1974) 'Les débuts de la construction de l'espace chez l'enfant', in *De l'espace corporel á l'espace écologique: Symposium de l'Association de Psychologie Scientifique de langue francaise, Bruxelles, 1972*, Presses Universitaires de France, Paris, pp. 81–132.

Walk, R. D. and Gibson, E. J. (1961) 'A comparative and analytic study of visual depth perception', *Psychological Monographs*, 75, Whole No. 519, 1–44.

Walters, C. P. and Walk, R. D. (1974) Visual Placing by Human Infants, *Journal of Experimental child psychology*, 18, 34–40.

Wong, S. C. P. and Frost, B. J. (1978) 'Subjective motion and acceleration induced by movement of the observer's entire visual field', *Perception and Psychophysics*, 24 (2), 115–20.

White, B. L. (1969) 'The initial co-ordination of sensorimotor schemes in human infants. Piaget's ideas and the role of experience', in Elkind, D. and Flavell, J. (eds) *Studies in Cognitive Development*, Oxford University Press, London.

Yonas, A. Bechlold, G., Frankel, D., Gordon, F., McRoberts, G., Norcia, A. and Sternfels, S. (1977) 'Development of sensitivity to information for impending collision', *Perception and Psychophysics*, 21, 97–104.

6 Object Permanence and Identity in Piaget's Theory of Infant Cognition

GEORGE BUTTERWORTH

Space and also time and all its determinations *a priori* can be cognised by us because, no less than time, it inheres in our sensibility as a pure form before all perception or experience and makes all intuition of the same and therefore all its phenomena possible.
Immanuel Kant, *Prologomena to any Future Metaphysics*)

Introduction
An assumption basic to Piaget's theory of cognitive development is that sensory perception cannot provide objective information about reality. Throughout the sensorimotor period, perception becomes slowly structured by patterns of instrumental activity that serve to introduce the infant to the invariant properties of objects. The 'object concept' is a belief that eventually allows the infant to perceive objects as:

Permanent, substantial, external to the self and firm in existence even though they do not directly affect perception and to conceive of them as retaining their identity whatever the changes in position (Piaget, 1954, pp.5 and 7).

Piaget's account of the developmental dependencies between perceiving, acting and knowing is based on the premise that the initial relation between infant and environment is one of profound adualism. The infant cannot tell the difference between sensory events that are independent of his own activity and sensory feedback that is contingent on activity. According to Piaget, there is no information in the structure of stimulation itself that will allow response contingent feedback to be distinguished from independent sensory data. Consequently, the infant cannot discriminate a *change of place* from a *change of state* of an object because the baby cannot tell whether transformations in the sensory array arise from its own movements or from independent movements of an object in the environment. The essential difference is that a *change of place* can be reversed by the observer taking up a new position, whereas a *change of state* is not reversible by a movement of the observer. Hence, the discrimination requires a distinction between observer and observed and monitoring of object (or self) movement relative to an external, stable, spatial framework.

The assumption that development begins from a state of profound adualism is fundamental to Piaget's constructionist theory of object permanence. When a visible object disappears the event is equivalent to a change of state and, from the infant's point of view, the object is annihilated at the moment it vanishes. As far as babies up to the age of eight months or so can tell, vanished objects simply cease to exist. Infants not only lack the co-ordinated motor structures that would allow them to reverse the observed sensory transformation in order to restore the object to immediate experience but also they lack the capacity to represent the absent object and thereby 'bridge the gap' in experience. Even after the baby is able to search, an object that moves from place to place is not perceived as a single thing that has changed its position because the infant cannot tell whether this change may have arisen from a change in its own position. Perception of permanence and spatio–temporal identity is not veridical until the object concept is acquired. The concept acts as the 'first invariant', the 'lynch pin', of the cognitive system and it is considered a necessary condition for objective perception.

For Piaget, as for Kant, the object concept is a 'category without content', an abstract constraint on experience that makes objectivity possible. Whereas Kant maintained that the basic categories (space, time, causes and objects) are *a priori*, Piaget insists that they are derived from experience. For Piaget the concept of the permanent object is abstracted from the infant's interactions with physical and social objects. Thus whereas Kant might have argued that abstract, *a priori* categories give structure to empirical experience, Piaget argues that empirical experience *gives rise* to abstract concepts.

Piaget's departure from Kantian theory begins in his attempt to deal with the problem of unambiguously defining when a concept is available. Piaget is (correctly) reluctant to attribute innate ideas to the infant and so he marks the acquisition of the object concept as the moment when the infant becomes able to deal with the world not simply as perceived but as imagined. When the infant consistently and correctly infers the path of movement of an invisibly displaced object and demonstrates the ability to recall information from memory, this marks the transition from sensorimotor activity to pre-operational thought. In so far as such a criterion is at least consistent with the definition of a concept as a basic unit of *thought* this formulation may lend precision to discussions of the development of knowledge from its pre-conceptual origins.

Nevertheless, despite Piaget's attempt to establish precise behavioural criteria for possession of conceptual knowledge, his theory of the relation between perception and objective experience suffers major drawbacks. Piaget is among those authors who stress the 'hypothetical' nature of perception, an assumption that has its origin in Bishop Berkeley's (1709) constructionist theory of spatial vision. It is assumed that perception of the third dimension depends on correlation of vision with touch and supplementation of the two dimensional retinal image by motor kinaesthesis. This makes it impossible to consider perception in the infant independently of constructive processes derived from action because visual perception of space and substance ultimately depends on motor supplementation. Kant however distinguished *percepts* from *concepts*. He stressed that space and time are *a priori percepts* and contemporary theories of perception such as Gibson's (1966), 1979) also make a similar distinction.

Gibson holds perception to be a direct, unmediated process of attending to reality. He argues that information for spatial extension is contained in the structure of light reflected from differently textured surfaces in the environment. Gradients of texture and the interposition of differentially textured surfaces specify space directly. Percepts and concepts are different levels of cognitive processing because perception of invariance *necessarily* depends on sensory information whereas a concept, which may incorporate the invariant properties of an object or a class of objects, can be independent of sensory support. The important point made by this type of theory is that 'direct' perception does not depend on prior construction of conceptual categories. All the necessary information is available in the structure of stimulation itself. For a further discussion see Costall (1981, this volume, Ch2).

The thesis expounded in this chapter is that Piaget draws attention to the infant's conceptual deficiencies when it may be more useful for our understanding of infant adaptation and for genetic epistomology to consider the infant a proficient sensory and perceptual organism. Reformulating the contribution of infant perception to the process of cognitive growth may lead to a more satisfactory account of the relation between perceiving and knowing than characterizes Piaget's theory. This contrast between perceptual proficiency and conceptual deficiency is not synonymous with the familiar distinction in cognitive development between competence and performance. Percepts and concepts imply different, although ontogenetically related kinds of awareness and they are different levels in a hierarchy of control systems over action. Contemporary research shows that there may exist a pre-reflective level of sensory and perceptual awareness that precedes the acquisition of self-conscious concepts or beliefs and that forms a secure foundation for the process of cognitive growth by ensuring coherence and continuity of early experience.

The aim of this chapter is to review evidence pertinent to the question whether infants can distinguish 'a change of place from a change of state' at the level of sensory perception. The question at issue is whether development is better understood from the perspective of 'adualism' as Piaget maintains, or from a perspective of 'dualism', at least in so far as the relation between infant and environment incorporates an implicit polarity.

In the following pages, Piaget's constructionist theory of object concept development will first be briefly outlined to set the stage for subsequent sections of the chapter. Then, three aspects of infant perception will be considered to establish whether babies may be able to distinguish between reversible and irreversible changes in the sensory array. The first and most basic example concerns the distinction between 'self' and 'environment' implicit in the perception of self movement. The second example concerns the perception of object permanence and this will be considered in the context of alternative theories put forward by Michotte (1950) and Gibson (1966, 1979). The final example concerns the spatial determinants of error in infant manual search for an object hidden at successive locations. This example was selected because Piaget considers these perseverative errors to be definitive evidence for the subordination of perception to action in development.

Each of the examples illustrates the general thesis that the infant can distinguish between 'a change of place and a change of state' and the concluding section draws the arguments together. It will attempt to reconcile the evidence that a distinction between 'self' and 'environment' is implicit in infant perception, with Piaget's insight that objective knowledge of self and world are correlative and only slowly acquired during infancy.

Development of the Object Concept: Piaget's theory

Piaget's 'object concept' includes the development of processes such as intersensory co-ordination and the perceptual constancies which will be omitted here. Only a brief account of his stages in the development of permanence and identity will be given to make clear his constructionist theory.

Evidence on perceptual constancy, substantiality and intersensory co-ordination in infancy has been reviewed elsewhere (Butterworth

1978, 1981) and is touched upon in other chapters of this volume. For an outline of Piaget's complete sensorimotor theory the reader is referred to Russell (1981), this volume, Chapter 1), Beilin (1971) or Wolff (1960).

According to Piaget, all knowledge is derived from reflexive actions with which the neonate is biologically endowed. The logic behind this assumption is well expressed by Baldwin (1894): 'In the absence of alternative considerations, reflections, the child acts and act it must, on the first sensation which has any meaning in terms of its sensations of movement' (p.5).

The fundamental question addressed is how can the unreflective infant acquire knowledge except in so far as knowledge originates in particular responses to particular stimuli? The question leaves open the possibility of complex inbuilt relations between distal sensory input and motor output, such as visual–manual co-ordinations of the kind reported by Bower (1974) in precocious reaching for objects, responses to 'looming' objects (Ball and Vurpillot, 1981, this volume Ch5) imitative responses of neonates reported by Meltzoff (1981, this volume Ch4) or the temporal synchronies in interpersonal behaviour thought to be precursors of language by Trevarthen (1979).

But Piaget did not consider it possible for aspects of *distal* perception to be built in; instead the repertoire of the neonate is restricted to reflexive responses to *proximal* stimuli as in sucking and rooting. There is no pre-adaptation to perceive events to occur in a space external to the infant's body and consequently, cognitive growth begins with the infant locked into a world of proximal experience. The theoretical problem is how the infant is to *construct* an external world of space, time, causes and objects.

Piaget introduces order into experience by adopting Baldwin's mechanism of the 'circular reaction'; the infant repeats an action in order to reproduce the sensory stimulation previously contingent on it. To the extent that the infant succeeds, invariant spatio-temporal parameters are *imposed* on sensory feedback. Through accommodation and assimilation, elementary repetitive activities become co-ordinated and hierarchically organized until, by the end of the sensorimotor period, the infant deliberately varies actions in experiments that allow him to deduce objects to be the permanent and enduring 'building blocks' of reality (this is called a 'constructive deduction').

At any point in development, the circular reactions are considered equivalent to partially formed, overt concepts linked to sensory input. Construction of tertiary circular reactions eventually allows the 'constructive deduction' of an abstract 'object concept' that is not tied to any particular sensory experience.

Mechanisms mediating permanence in Piaget's theory.

The problem of object permanence concerns how we know objects to endure even though our experience of them is discontinuous. In Piaget's description of the sensorimotor substages three successive mechanisms for continuity of experience can be discerned: the earliest is the simple repetition of an activity, the second is permanence of a vanished object by association with a perceived sign of its location and the most advanced is permanence through representation of the vanished object. Representation, 'making an absent object present to the senses' or the ability to recall information from memory, ensures spatio-temporal continuity by 'bridging the gap' between successive experiences. These mechanisms serve to impose spatio-temporal continuity on sensory events and each marks a further degree of objectivity in the child's comprehension of reality. For convenience, the mechanisms will be considered in two groups, those that occur in the stages preceding manual search and those that follow it.

Sensorimotor stages one, two and three

Reflexes, Primary and Secondary Circular Reactions. In the earliest stages, continuity of experience is assured only by the prolongation of an action. For example, Piaget (1954, p.11) maintains that the very young infant simply stares at the place where an object vanishes and makes no attempt to search: 'The vanished object is not yet for him a permanent object that has been moved, it is a mere image that returns to the void as soon as it vanishes.'

Like any primitive organism, the infant only prolongs the action that initially gave rise to the experience. Etiènne (1973) has compared this mechanism to the behaviour displayed by the dragonfly larva (*Aeschra Cyaneam*) to vanished objects. It will remain oriented to the location of its vanished prey for a duration related to the initial intensity of behavioural activation but makes no attempt to search because it lacks any awareness of the independent existence of the food object.

With differentiation of primary into secondary circular reactions there is progress in the development of objectivity because the infant now comes into possession of motor strategies to 'make interesting events last'. Also information from different sensory modalities is related to the self-same object by the co-ordination of the activities of looking, seeing and touching. However, the permanence of the object remains an extension of the infant's activity. For example, Piaget's son Laurent at seven months loses a cigarette box that he has been swinging to and fro: 'Far from considering the loss as irremediable he begins again to swing his hand although it is empty, after this he looks at it once more . . . it is impossible not to interpret such behaviour as an attempt to make the object come back' (1954, p.22). To the end of the third stage, objects exist for the infant only in so far as search continues an on-going activity, such as tracking along a particular trajectory or completing a prehensile movement that was initiated before the object disappeared. When an object is hidden *before* the infant has initiated a response, the baby makes no attempt to retrieve it and behaves as if the object had ceased to exist, even though the necessary motor skills for retrieval are available.

Stages four, five and six: Co-ordinated secondary circular reactions, tertiary circular reactions and representation
Acquisition of a new mechanism for permanence is marked by the onset of manual search for a hidden object at about eight or nine months. The infant discovers that objects continue to exist adventitiously through a secondary circular reaction such as striking an obstacle, which is then co-ordinated with the act of grasping the revealed object. However, the object concept retains a subjective element because infants perseverate in searching at an initial location (A), even after *the same object* has been seen to disappear at a new location (B). Despite being sufficiently skilled the infant thereby betrays the fact that objects are not yet known as independent entitites that can move from place to place. Etiènne (1973) has described this mechanism as 'permanence by association'. The child's response to the hidden object is under the control of cues associated with it before it disappeared; there is no understanding of spatio-temporal identity beyond a primitive topological concept of space that depends on presence of a perceived 'sign' for the object's continued existence.

A necessary temporal corollary of Piaget's spatial explanation for error is that the infant cannot remember the sequence of positions: 'Faced with the disappearance of the object, the child immediately ceases to reflect. He does not try to remember the sequence and thus merely returns to the place where he was successful first time' (1954, p.61). Lacking the object concept, the infant has no organizing principle at his disposal to allow him to remember the sequence of places. Errors are not simply a matter of forgetfulness but of failure *to store* locative information. In summary, the object is conceived to occupy a special place linked to the initially successful action. The baby fails to distinguish 'a change of place from a change of state' and the object is experienced 'as if it had a limited number of distinct forms, intermediate between unity and plurality'. (*Ibid*. p.63).

From the fifth stage, beginning at about twelve months, the infant gradually takes into account the spatial relations between perceived images and will find an object hidden at successive locations, so long as all the movements remain visible. This marks a further advance because the infant will search only at the most recent location at which the object was seen to disappear. However, this mechanism is still purely strategic and permanence is known only in relation to a visible cue. For example, when an object is hidden in a cup and the cup is transported under several screens before being emptied, the baby searches in the (empty) cup but not under the screens. The infant is not aware that the object must share the cup's spatial trajectory and therefore will be found somewhere on the path of movement of the cup. Permanence is still only assured by association of the object with the container and not by a representation of the spatial relation between object and container.

Representation is an aspect of figurative knowledge. It develops with the acquisition of tertiary circular reactions (the operative or transformational aspect of the cognitive system). Through experiments, the infant becomes aware of the spatial relations between objects (for example, in stacking and nesting them) and through his own mobility, of distant space and of the self. By the end of the sensorimotor period the infant has constructed sufficient regularity in activity to deduce that objects are permanent and retain their identity through space and time. The baby will now search systematically for a hidden object until it is retrieved, inferring from lack of success at one location that it must be elsewhere. The object is freed from action and perception alike because representation provides an interiorized spatio-temporal framework to bridge gaps in experience. At the same time as the object concept is acquired, the infant acquires a concept of self as an object and henceforth banishes the ontological egocentrism of the sensorimotor period.

Direct perception as an alternative to constructivism

Piaget's genetic evidence, on the development of manual search, convinced him that perception must be subordinate to action in the acquisition of knowledge. Michotte (1950) and more recently, Gibson (1966, 1970) have presented alternative accounts, in which all the properties of substance assumed by Piaget to be constructed are directly specified in sensory stimulation. Perception of object permanence is said to be an 'amodal' property that does not depend on the continuous availability of sensation from an object but on relations within the sensory array when an object disappears. In a symposium attended by Piaget, Michotte discussed their basic disagreement:

When I speak of a prefiguring of ideas of causality, permanence and so on [in perception] I have never tried to pretend that these ideas are preformed in the sense of classical, innate ideas. What I have in mind is the existence of 'intrinsic signs' of certain [mental] structures . . . . One can perceive something slide behind another object without having to have the *concept* of a permanent object. Prior to any individual experience, the transformation itself is full of meaning (Michotte, 1955, p.57).

In these remarks, Michotte wished to establish a clear distinction between *perception* of a disappearing object that continues to exist after it vanishes and the *concept* that objects are permanent. He argued that patterning of the sensory array in the course of an object's disappearance is inherently structured in such a way as to specify the event taking place. Elsewhere, Michotte (1950) drew an analogy with the distinction between figure and ground in visual perception to make the same point. Even though the figure occludes the background, the ground is nevertheless perceived to exist beneath the figure. He implied that these aspects of perception are innate and described them as 'amodal', in the sense that perception of continued existence occurs in the absence of sensory stimulation from the object itself, (see also Michotte, Thinès and Crabbé 1964). From the perspective of theories of direct perception it is not necessary for an object's permanence that local stimulation from the object itself should be continuously available nor does permanence require a representation or memory image of the vanished object.

Before considering these questions in detail it will be useful to address the more fundamental question; whether there is information in the sensory array sufficient to allow a distinction between self and environment. If such information is available, and infants can be shown to make use of it, then Piaget's assumptions of complete adualism and failure to distinguish a change of place from a change of state may be mistaken. This evidence will provide a framework for interpreting subsequent sections on perception of object permanence and identity.

Optic flow patterns and the distinction between self and world
Gibson (1966) coined the term 'visual proprioception' to draw attention to the role of vision in providing information for self-

motion over and above the traditional mechanical–vestibular cues of the kinaesthetic system. Vision specifies movement of self by perspective transformations of the retinal image that arise when an observer moves through a stable space. According to Gibson, total motion of a structured visual array, outward from a stationary central point, specifies movement of the observer in a particular direction given by the focus of optical expansion. Under ecologically valid conditions such a flow pattern would only arise when the observer moves relative to a stable space and it is thought sufficient directly to specify the distinction between 'self' and the world. Gibson argued that such flow patterns contain 'invariants' that need not be constructed during development. However, this remains largely an assumption and it is quite possible that optic flow patterns only acquire their significance as a consequence of the infants' developing mobility. In that case, Gibson's theory, based on the structure of sensory events, would be the reciprocal of Piaget's description of the schemes of action that give rise to structured sensory events. A number of studies have been carried out recently that allow the theories to be separated and these will now be reviewed.

The first demonstration that infants use visual information to monitor their posture was carried out by Lee and Aronson (1974). Infants who had recently learned to stand unsupported were tested on a stable floor inside a moveable room comprising three walls and a ceiling. The infants stood facing the interior end wall of the room and the whole structure, except the floor, was moved so that the end wall slowly approached or receded. Babies compensated for a non-existent loss of balance and they consequently swayed, staggered or fell in a direction appropriate to the plane of instability specified by the misleading visual flow pattern. For example, if the end wall moved away thus providing discrepant visual feedback consistent with backward loss of stability, the babies compensated and fell forwards.

Vision does not acquire its proprioceptive function as a result of learning to stand because Butterworth and Hicks (1977) found that younger babies compensated at least as intensely for visually specified instability when *sitting* as older infants. Postural compensation occurred both to forward and backward motion of the room and to lateral movements across the visual field, always in a direction particular to the plane of instability specified by the misleading visual feedback. In a further study, Butterworth and Cicchetti (1978) investigated the effect of postural experience on responses to discrepant visual feedback in sitting and standing infants. There was a consistent *decline* in the intensity of response to misleading visual proprioception with experience of the respective postures (see Fig. 6.1).

During the first three months after learning to walk, the babies would invariably fall over but by the time they had had twelve months experience standing they would sway slightly and often laughed while they turned to see 'what was making the room move', as if it was an incongruous event relatively independent of their postural stability. We can be sure that these effects of misleading visual feedback were not learned through locomotor activity because

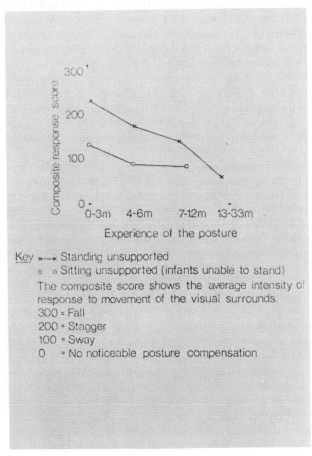

Fig. 6.1. Effect of misleading visual feedback on postural stability in infants of varying postural experience.

the youngest sitting infants were not yet able to crawl. Furthermore, the consistent decline in the intensity of response with experience of the postures suggests that far from motor activity slowly giving structure to the visual flow patterns, infants make use of the invariant information contained in the flow pattern to gain control over posture. The data suggests that skilled, voluntary control may be gained by calibrating the unskilled, postural regulation system against information from the stable surround.[1]

It is essential to consider the implications of such experiments for adaptation in the normal environment, where the background can be considered stable. Under ecologically valid conditions the relationship between organism and environment can be considered a feedback control loop in which self-motion is specified in the optic flow pattern which contains an implicit distinction between self and surround. Even under conditions of passive movement, the distinction between observer and environment would be imposed by the natural ecology. On the other hand, it is clear that the infant has no *objective knowledge* of self because postural compensation occurs even though the infant is objectively stable. Voluntary control over the body is obtained slowly and sequentially as each postural sub-system is calibrated against the stable surround.

In summary, the distinction between self and environment is *implicit* in the sensorimotor relation between the infant and the stable visual surround. The implicit relation becomes explicit (to the degree that the infant can eventually over-rule misleading visual information in favour of what is objectively the case) as part of the process of gaining voluntary control over action and this process may involve motor activity. However, activity may build on a pre-structured intersensory relation, rather than giving rise to the structure *de novo*.

It is instructive to compare the infant's response to movements of the whole surround, as in the moving room situation, with the evidence on infant's responses to 'looming' (Ball and Vurpillot, 1981, this volume). This is another way of determining whether babies can tell the difference between motion of self relative to the environment and motion of objects in the environment relative to the self, a further occasion for the distinction between a change of place and a change of state. 'Looming' is progressive expansion of a portion of the visual field to which defensive responses occur when the expansion pattern reaches a maximum relative to the stationary background. In the 'moving-room' situation, responses occur immediately the surround is displaced. Another difference is that defensive responses to looming are specific to the pattern of optical expansion (Ball and Tronick, 1971) whereas postural compensations in the moving room occur to forward, backward and lateral movements of the surround (Butterworth and Hicks, 1977). Thus, the evidence suggests that infants discriminate between an optic flow pattern specifying an approaching object and optic flow patterns that are, in the normal ecology, contingent on self-motion. This again implies that the basic distinction between object-movement and self-movement must be available, if implicitly, in the structure of sensory stimulation.

Some recent research with adults has clarified the visual processes that may be involved in making these discriminations. Johannson (1977) showed that a visual flow pattern over a very small area of the extreme retinal periphery was sufficient to induce an illusion of self-movement in adults, despite the simultaneous availability of information for a stationary environment over the rest of the retina. Motion of an object on the other hand depends on detection of a circumscribed optic flow pattern *relative to* information for a stationary background in the periphery (Harris, Cassel and Bamborough, 1974).

This formulation of the problem of distinguishing self from environment may be compatible with recent descriptions of the visual system in primates and man as comprising 'ambient' and 'focal' processes (Trevarthen, 1968). The ambient system is specialized for spatial orientation to the wider visual field and is connected with a phylogentically ancient mid-brain visual system that governs locomotion in vertebrates. The phylogentically more recent 'focal' system governs precise attention to events in central, behavioural space and is concerned with fine motor control. In the acquisition of voluntary control over posture, for example, there may be a developmental 'embedding' of regulatory processes between sub-cortical and cortical systems that (at least in the sighted), depends on pre-structured visual feedback inherent in the relation between the infant and a stable visual surround.

If it could be shown that postural compensation to movement of the whole surround is innate (as the evidence suggests for looming) it would imply that the infant is pre-adapted to respond not only to proximal but also to distal events. A great deal of evidence has accumulated to demonstrate that infants perceive distal properties of objects such as shape and size constancy (Butterworth, 1978, 1981) long before the opportunity could have arisen to construct these invariants by correlating vision with touch. So it is reasonable to speculate that information for the basic distinction between infant and environment may be available and effective. However, it must be re-emphasized that although the distinction between self and sur-round may be *specified*, it is not objectively known. The infant lacks objective knowledge of self and repeatedly compensates for a non-existent loss of balance. The distinction is as yet *implicit* in the relation between organism and environment. Only after prolonged experience does the infant acquire voluntary control over posture so that what is perceptually specified can, at least in part, be over-ruled in favour of what is objectively the case. It is tempting to hypothesize that objective knowledge of postural stability (one aspect of a concept of self), has its roots in pre-structured sensorimotor relations that 'pre-figure' conceptual processes, just as Michotte originally maintained.

Direct perception of object permanence
In the previous section it was argued that the distinction between infant and environment may be *implicit* in the structure of the sensory array. We can now consider the problem of object perma-nence; the interpretation of transformations of the visual field that occur when an object disappears. The question is whether such events are necessarily perceived from an *adualist* perspective, in which case there can be no permanence of the vanished object or from a '*dualist*' perspective that at least allows the baby to discrimin-ate events that are dependent upon its own activity from independent events in the world.

As Bower (1975) has pointed out, perception of object perma-nence and perception of depth are complementary problems because both require the organism to respond to information that is not in any obvious way present in the two-dimensional retinal array. According to traditional theories of perception, there is no stimulus-specifying distance on the surface of the retina, while objects that are out of sight cannot possibly provide any stimulation to inform the perceiver of their continued existence. However, in the previous section it was suggested that optic flow patterns can unambiguously specify the occlusion of one surface by another, as in looming, to yield an impression of movement in depth. The question is whether such an analysis can be extended to the problem of object permanence.

Michotte's (1950) demonstration of the 'screen effect' is one of the earliest studies of the psychophysics of object permanence. In this demonstration, one of two coloured squares of light projected onto a ground glass screen is slowly moved into contact with the second, stationary square. The moving square is then progressively narrowed until it vanishes. Adults describe this sequence of events as 'one square sliding behind the other', without mentioning any change in the shape or size of the moving square. The effect has been extensively investigated by Gibson, Kaplan, Reynolds and Wheeler (1969) who used a cinematic projection of a randomly moving textured surface containing no visible boundaries. When part of the surface was made to move in such a way that it progressively deleted texture in the remainder of the array, observers described the deleted surface to be behind the moving surface. The authors argued that texture deletion is sufficient *to establish* a boundary in depth in the random pattern. Another way of thinking about the effect is that the deleting pattern immediately becomes 'figure' relative to the 'ground' of the deleted pattern, which continues to exist although occluded. These studies suggest that perception of occlusion and by implication, permanence, may depend on structured visual information within a moving array but they are not sufficient to establish whether such transformations are directly perceived, or whether they depend on acquisition of the object concept (as Piaget argues).

Bower (1967) has carried out a series of studies that suggest there is a perceptual form of object permanence available in early infancy. He calls it 'existence constancy', to differentiate it from a later conceptual form, likening it to other perceptual constancies such as size and shape in that it requires the ability to perceive an attribute (existence) as invariant under transformations of appearance and disappearance. Infants aged seven weeks were conditioned to suck on a sealed nipple at a constant rate in the presence of a 'bullseye' patterned stimulus. The conditioned stimulus was then made to disappear either by drawing a screen in front of it slowly or by making it vanish instantaneously using an arrangement of mirrors. To an adult, these transformations respectively specify continued existence or annihilation of the object. After the disappearance of the conditioned stimulus, infants continued to suck at the operant rate following the object's occlusion by a screen but they stopped sucking when the visual event specified annihilation. Depending on what was specified perceptually, babies behaved as if the conditioned stimulus was 'present' but invisible, or 'absent'.

Bower described a new pattern of responses that emerged at about twelve months old, which he attributed to 'conceptual constancy', a rule that objects continue to exist no matter what the perceptual transformation specifies. He distinguished it from the earlier, perceptual form because twelve-month-old infants searched particularly enthusiastically for an object made to disappear by 'annihilation' (an instantaneous disappearance brought about with mirrors). Although perception specifies that the object has ceased to exist, the baby knows, 'it must be somewhere'. Perception is over-ruled by disbelief, in a manner analogous to an adult watching a magician. Bower's studies offer some support for Michotte's distinction between perceptually and conceptually specified forms of permanence and, important from the theoretical point of view, the perceptual form is primary in ontogenesis.

If it is the case that infants make use of textured information specifying a stable background from an early age it seems reasonable to argue that background texture deletion is the critical variable leading to perception of the screen effect. It is possible to offer the following taxonomy of stimulus relations, each unique to a particular movement of object or observer which makes it unnecessary to postulate a profound adualism as a necessary condition of early perception:

(i)   In the case of the 'screen effect', the moving screen will progressively delete texture in the background at its leading edge (and accrete texture at its trailing edge) thus specifying its own motion relative to the background. Once the screen starts to occlude the object, its leading edge will delete texture internal to the object, which itself partially occludes the textured ground. When the object finally disappears, it is located 'behind' the screen but 'on' the background, by virtue of the multiple relations of occlusion.

(ii) The 'screen effect' is quite different from the visual transformation which occurs when one object occludes another through movement of the observer. Although there is deletion of the internal texture of the further object by the nearer, there is also an optic flow pattern *in* the background which corresponds to the direction of motion of the observer.

(iii) Combinations of object and observer movement also occur but disappearances brought about by movement of the observer will always result in different optic flow patterns in the background than those brought about by movement of the object (so long as the background is stationary as under normal ecological conditions).

(iv) The sequence of optical transformations in 'annihilation' or impermanence, can be thought of as replacement of the internal texture of an object by the textured ground. Annihilation is perceived, for example, when an object vanishes into a mist, when a puddle evaporates or when an object disappears instantaneously as in Bower's (1967) study. It occurs at the moment when the visual field becomes 'all ground' and 'no figure'. Phenomenologically this is the opposite of 'looming' where an expanding optic flow on a 'hit' course, specifies a collision at the moment when the visual field becomes 'all figure' and 'no ground'.

Thus, it is logically possible that there exist relationships within a structured optic array that are sufficient to allow the infant to discriminate between temporary object disappearance and annihilation and which may underlie Bower's (1967) psychophysical studies. Even though the baby may not be self-consciously aware of the meaning of these events, the capacity to make the discriminations carries implicit and differential significance for interpreting events at a distance. In summary, reversible and irreversible sensory events that take place with respect to a stable background may be structurally discriminable from each other and from transformations of the sensory array that arise as a consequence of the infant's own movements. There is no need to assume an absolute adualism if sensation is inherently structured.

Direct perception of another's point of view
Quite apart from the problem of interpreting sensory transformations, there is another aspect to the problem of permanence that merely entails the *possibility* of sensation. Some recent studies of how infants follow an adult's line of regard may serve as a convenient vehicle to discuss this issue. The technique is simple; adult and infant are engaged in face to face interaction until, at a pre-arranged moment, the adult turns to inspect an object located somewhere in the room. Infants as young as two months of age will turn head and eyes in the appropriate direction as if to discover the object at the focus of the adult's attention. (Scaife and Bruner, 1975). The most straightforward interpretation would be that the infant responds to the adult's signal of 'something there', a *possible sensation* that is potentially available to the infant.

Although this interpretation is obvious, it is difficult to reconcile with Piaget's theory since it entails that the infant perceives the adult to refer to something that is '*already there*'. On a Piagetian account, the response would have to be explained as a circular reaction that is merely *terminated* by a visual consequence, rather than *arising* from joint reference to a common external, spatial objective.

Butterworth and Cochran (1980) carried out a series of experiments to try and establish the mechanism underlying the capacity for joint visual attention. Subjects were babies aged between six and eighteen months and their mothers who were seated opposite each other in the centre of a laboratory with pairs of targets presented at various positions arranged to left and right (see Fig. 6.2).

The mother was instructed to interact naturally with her baby and when she felt sure the infant's attention was on her she was to turn and inspect one of the targets which had been designated by a

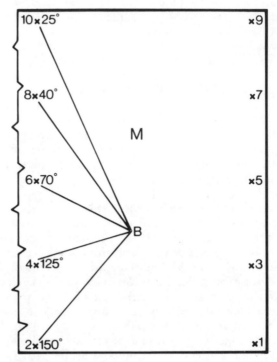

Key:

M – Mother

B – Baby

1 to 10 – Target Locations
(A subset of targets was presented on any one trial)

Approximate visual angles of targets with respect to baby are shown.

Fig. 6.2.   Joint visual attention: target locations and laboratory layout (Butterworth and Cochran, 1980).

pre-arranged signal. The targets were presented two at a time (for example, 1 and 2, 5 and 6 etc.) until the mother had looked at all ten locations. The most striking result was that infants *hardly ever* succeeded in locating a target behind them (locations 1, 2, 3, and 4, see Fig. 6.2). When the mother fixated a target in that region, infants would turn in the appropriate direction but they would scan the space *in front of them* up to a visual angle of about 40° (where locations 7, 8, 9 and 10 would have been). On the other hand, for targets within the infants' visual field, they were perfectly capable of localizing positions as extreme as 70° (locations 5 and 6). Thus, when the nearest target was at 125° behind the baby, the infant would terminate the scan at 40°, even though perfectly capable of localizing targets displaced up to 70° from the mid-line. In other experiments[2] Butterworth and Jarrett (1980a) have shown that twelve and eighteen month-old infants can accurately localize the target the mother is looking at even when it is second along the scan path (from the infant's mid-line) so long as it is in the infant's visual field. This shows that the baby is not simply turning until a target is encountered. Rather, the infant seems to have the ability to compensate geometrically for the difference between its own and the adult's lines of gaze in broad zones of its own visual space. The major constraint on joint visual reference in infancy is that it is limited to targets within the infant's visual field.

Quite a different explanation is required to account for these phenomena than is available in Piaget's solipsistic account of infant perception. William James offered a clue when he said:

Practically then our minds meet in a world of objects which they share in common, . . . if my reader will only allow that the same dollar goes into his pocket as came out of mine . . . that the same now both ends his past and begins his future . . . he will also in consistency have to allow that the same object may conceivably play a part in, as being related to the rest of any number of otherwise unrelated minds (James, 1912, p.79).

On James account, joint visual attention is made possible by objects *held in common* (that is, those which have an objective existence) in a common external space. In scanning the infant's visual space, the adult is also scanning her own visual space and *vice versa*. The *consensibility* of sensory perception may provide the key to early social reciprocity and perhaps to the wider problems of scientific knowledge that are Piaget's ultimate concern (Ziman, 1979).

The fact that the adult's action is interpreted in immediate perception sets spatial limits on the domain within which the adult and the infant can share common objects. To engage in joint visual attention beyond the boundaries of immediate perception may indeed require the infant to acquire a concept of an extended space. However, to behave with respect to another *as if* the world contains permanent objects does not itself depend on co-ordination of motor schemes, nor on possession of a concept of object permanence or a concept of space.

In summary, it has been argued here that perception of object permanence may be possible before the object concept is acquired. A taxonomy of sensory relations has been suggested that specifies unambiguously the distinction between observer and observed. A temporary disappearance of an object presents a different set of optic flow patterns relative to a stable background than does the annihilation of an object. Similarly, movement of an observer within a stable space presents different stimulus relations in the optic flow pattern than movements of objects relative to the observer. Thus, under the ordinary circumstances of everyday life, the distinction between 'self' and 'object' may be implicit in the inter-relations among motion patterns in the optic array.

Quite apart from what is specified in the transformations of the optic array when an object vanishes, permanence also implies the 'possibility' or 'potential availability' of sensation. Joint visual attention between infant and adult is a behaviour that seems to presuppose objects held in common. Gibson's theory of space perception offers an explanation for the phenomenon and its limits that Piaget's theory has difficulty in encompassing. Thus it seems likely that perception of permanence is not the fundamental problem in the infant's cognitive development.

Perception of Object Identity

Some of Piaget's major evidence for 'adualism' in infant perception comes from perseverative errors in manual search tasks. Even though the baby of eight to eleven months will search for a hidden object, the distinction between self and object is as yet incompletely constructed and the baby is said not to perceive that an object retains its identity over a change in position. Perception remains subordinate to the previously successful action, a further example of 'adualism'. But in the previous sections it was suggested that the infant may be able directly to perceive self-motion and the referential actions of another. If perception of self and perception of reference do not depend on Piaget's 'object concept' it should also follow that infants may be able directly to perceive the identity of an object *before* the object concept is acquired. In this section some recent, critical experiments on the determinants of perseverative error will be discussed. Butterworth (1978), Bremner (1980) and Harris (1975), have reviewed the general background to this problem so the reader is referred to these authors for a more extensive overview.

According to Piaget (1954) infants between the ages of eight and eleven months search for an object hidden at an initial location (A) but they continue to search at A even after they have seen the same object moved to a new location (B). The AB or stage four error is his definitive evidence that the object is perceived as an extension of the infant's activity and not as a thing with independent properties of movement. Piaget's explanation for the phenomenon is complex and his interpretations take slightly different forms depending on whether the error is taken as evidence for the child's concept of an object, of space, time or causality. What all his explanations have in common is that the infant is said not to distinguish movements of the object from apparent changes in the object's position brought about by changes in the infant's own position. It is precisely because the infant still cannot distinguish 'a change of place from a change of state' that he cannot tell whether a single object has moved from A to B. The object retains its identity only within the boundaries of a topological space linked to the first position where it was found, a limited 'group' of spatial displacements defined by the relation between the infant and the object's initial position. When the object is hidden at B, the infant cannot perceive that a single object has moved so 'the act of finding the displaced image is confused in the infant's consciousness with the act of recreating it' (*Ibid.* 1954, p.103). The secondary circular reaction of repeating the successful response is said to *confer* identity on the object.

A great deal of research has now been carried out on the stage four error and it seems reasonable to argue that the phenomenon may indeed reflect the infant's difficulty in identifying an object over a change in its position. The major findings have been that response-produced cues are not necessary for error because observation of the object at A results in perseveration after the object is moved (Landers, 1971; Butterworth, 1974, Bremner 1978a, 1978b). Thus, it is difficult to sustain the argument that the object is literally known as an extension of the successful response, although changes in egocentric radial position may still be responsible. A second consistent result has been that errors do not occur unless there is a delay between hiding the object at the new location B (about three secs) and allowing retrieval (Gratch, Appel, Evans, Le Compte and Wright, 1974). This may indicate that the infant has some limited capacity to represent the hidden object (that is, to hold it in mind while it is hidden rather than recognize it when it reappears) or delay may simply disrupt a postural set to the correct location. A third result has been that errors occur even when the object is visible at A and B and the infant merely has to search where the object can be seen (Harris, 1974; Butterworth, 1977; Willats, 1979). This is interesting because even when a pragmatic solution to the problem of retrieving the object would work (that is, the infant can simply search where the object is visible) some other criterion over-rides sight of the object in favour of search at A. [This also suggests that there may be no need to invoke memory or representation]. Another consistent finding has been that search on B trials is rarely exclusive to the original location. In many cross-sectional studies, infants are equally likely to search at the initial location A or at the final location B after the object is moved (Butterworth, 1974, 1975, 1977). In longitudinal studies, the same infant may be correct or consistently incorrect on successive occasions of testing (Bower and Wishart, 1972). In these studies, the object is usually placed *on* a table surface and hidden at successive locations. As we shall see, it is possible to generate persistent errors to the initial location (A), as Piaget describes, but this pattern of errors occurs only under spatial conditions where the object's movements cannot be monitored in relation to a continous background.

Testing the spatial aspects of Piaget's explanation presents complex problems because even a simple, two-position discrimination task may involve a multiplicity of spatial coding processes in interaction. However, the critical question is whether there exist spatial conditions under which an infant can search correctly for an object that is visibly displaced between successive locations, since this would require infants to distinguish a change of place from a change of state.

Butterworth, Jarrett and Hicks (1981) carried out a series of experiments to establish the spatial conditions leading infants to make perseverative errors in the stage four task. All possible combinations of simultaneous change in three position codes were made between trials and at A and at B. After the experiment, all infants were retested on a 'standard' stage four task to establish that performance had indeed been a function of the earlier spatial conditions.

Fig. 6.3 summarizes the results. It shows in descending order of accuracy, data for all seven combinations of change in spatial code relative to a control condition where no spatial changes occurred. Infants searched accurately in three conditions and in two of them, (2 and 4) the display on B trials corresponded to a simple spatial transformation that would have occurred if the infant had been

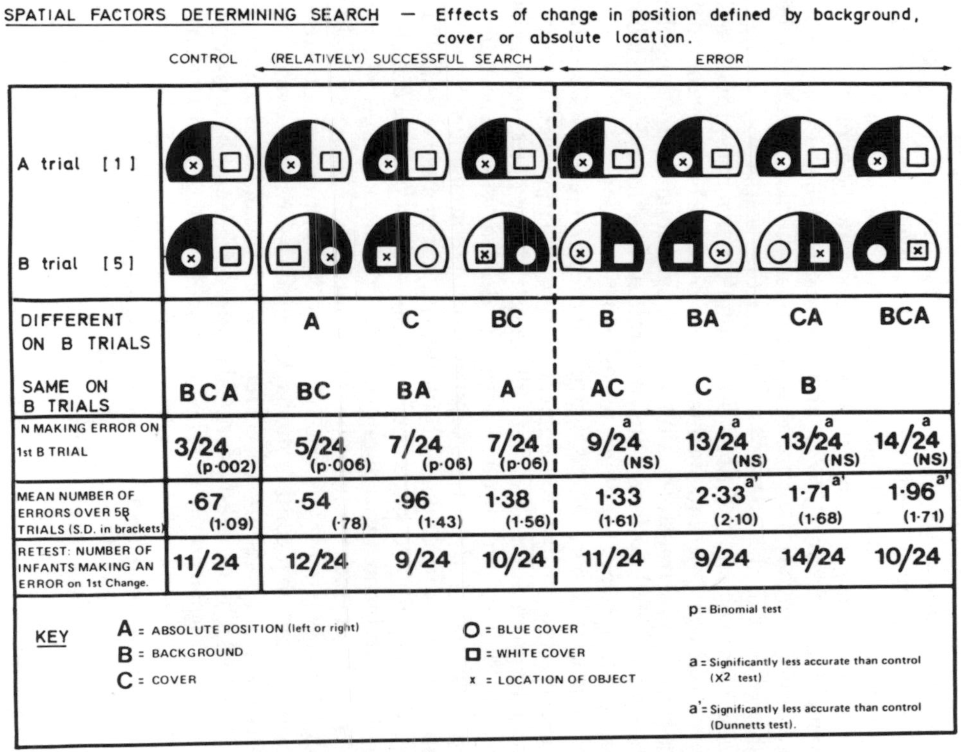

SPATIAL FACTORS DETERMINING SEARCH — Effects of change in position defined by background, cover or absolute location.

	CONTROL	(RELATIVELY) SUCCESSFUL SEARCH			ERROR			
A trial [1]								
B trial [5]								
DIFFERENT ON B TRIALS	BCA	A	C	BC	B	BA	CA	BCA
SAME ON B TRIALS		BC	BA	A	AC	C	B	B
N MAKING ERROR ON 1st B TRIAL	3/24 (p·002)	5/24 (p·006)	7/24 (p·06)	7/24 (p·06)	9/24 [a] (NS)	13/24 [a] (NS)	13/24 [a] (NS)	14/24 [a] (NS)
MEAN NUMBER OF ERRORS OVER 5 B TRIALS (S.D. in brackets)	·67 (1·09)	·54 (·78)	·96 (1·43)	1·38 (1·56)	1·33 (1·61)	2·33 [a] (2·10)	1·71 [a] (1·68)	1·96 [a] (1·71)
RETEST. NUMBER OF INFANTS MAKING AN ERROR on 1st Change.	11/24	12/24	9/24	10/24	11/24	9/24	14/24	10/24

KEY

A = ABSOLUTE POSITION (left or right)
B = BACKGROUND
C = COVER

O = BLUE COVER
□ = WHITE COVER
x = LOCATION OF OBJECT

p = Binomial test
a = Significantly less accurate than control (X² test)
a' = Significantly less accurate than control (Dunnetts test).

Fig. 6.3. Spatial factors determining search.

rotated 180° around the A display. That is, the spatial transformation was a simple invariant function of the A display, compatible with those engendered by a mobile organism. In the conditions where search was incorrect, the B display cannot be derived from the A display by a simple rotation. On the retest, where spatial cues were minimal (identical covers, continuous background) every group showed the typical equiprobable pattern, where half the infants searched persistently at A and half searched persistently at B.

It is interesting to compare these results with those obtained by Bremner and Bryant (1977) and Bremner (1978a, 1978b) who actually moved the infant around a stationary display, or rotated the table relative to the infant. They found that search was accurate under some spatial conditions (for example, when background and cover were constant) and the infant was moved but errors occurred if the same spatial transformation was brought about by rotating the table relative to the infant. Thus, the table surface may act as a stable external framework for object (or infant) movement.

It has usually been found that infants search correctly when the object enters a constant topological relation with its immediate cover and background. Piaget might still argue that the object retains its identity only at an absolute location defined with respect to a particular context. But, a 'perceptual' explanation emerges from two further studies carried out by Butterworth, Jarrett and Hicks (1981) and Butterworth and Jarrett (1980b).[3]. In the first of these evidence for successful search was obtained under spatial conditions where a simple 'topological' explanation would not apply. The spatial conditions are shown in Fig. 6.4 and comprised two distinctively different covers resting on a continuous background. Now thirty-five out of forty-eight infants searched correctly when the object was moved from A to B. On the retest (identical covers on the same background) the babies displayed the usual equiprobable pattern of search to A or B.

The significant majority of infants consistently searched correctly at the B location, thus demonstrating that they distinguished a change of place from a change of state and identified the object. How can this pattern of results be explained?

We begin our analysis with the retest data which always showed that search was equiprobably divided between A and B (it is important to note that the object was always *on* the surface when hidden). In the retests, identical covers were placed on a continuous surface connecting A and B. There is nothing *intrinsic* to such a spatial array to differentiate A from B and the infant may be forced to rely on an egocentric code to do so. By contrast, where the background was

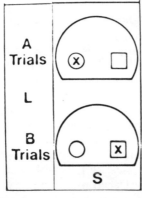

Key

X - Location of object on A and B trials
L - Side of first cover on A trials
S - Subjects midline

◯ - Blue Cover ⬜ - White Cover

Fig. 6.4.   One group of spatial conditions allowing successful search in the stage four infant.

continuous and the covers distinctively different (Fig. 6.4), initial and final locations can be differentiated without reference to an egocentric code. The visual space defined by the table surface and the different covers is sufficient to allow the object to be localized without reference to the observer's position relative to the space. In Piaget's terms, the 'group' of visible displacements of the object is independent of the observer and this competence is inherent in *perception* of the object in relation to the surround.

Whether perceptual specification also serves the infant in the natural environment, where people and things generally come and go in a stable context structured with landmarks, is an open question but Acredelo (1979) has found that babies tested on the stage four task in their own homes are less likely to err. A perceptual mechanism for object identification, may assure the infant of continuity of experience, even though the object concept is lacking.

In a second series of experiments Butterworth and Jarrett (1980b) set out to investigate spatial factors which lead infants consistently to search at the initial location (A) after an object has been moved. In this series, the A and B locations (with identical covers) were arranged in the vertical plane (see Fig. 6.5). There were three conditions: background behind both locations, background behind the lower location and background behind the upper location only.

When the background extended behind upper and lower locations, search was equally likely at A or B whatever the direction of movement. When the background extended immediately behind the lower location only (Fig. 6.5) there was an asymmetry in the error pattern. The significant majority of infants searched at 'up' after the object was moved from 'up' to 'down' but the equiprobable pattern occurred when the object was moved from the lower to upper location. Finally, when the background extended behind the upper container but not the lower (Fig. 6.5) the asymmetry was reversed. Now all the infants searched at A when the movement was from 'down' to 'up' and the equiprobable pattern occurred with the opposite movement. These studies show that persistent search at the initial location by the majority of infants in a sample occurred when A *lacked an immediate background*.

It is interesting to observe that many of Piaget's observations may effectively have been made under similar spatial conditions. Objects were often hidden under large carpets, coverlets or cushions (for example, Piaget, 1954 Observation 40) and consistent perseveration may have occurred because the object disappeared in such a way that a background was not continuously visible. Similarly, in many experimental versions of the stage four task, the object is hidden in 'wells' in the table surface and infants consistently perseverate to A (Bremner, 1978a, 1978b). Under these circumstances, the infant may perceive the object to pass *through* the background, into an indeterminate space beneath the table so that it effectively undergoes an invisible displacement. Since the stage four task is supposed to measure comprehension of *visible* displacements certain aspects of procedure may deprive the baby of the essential perceptual support necessary for judgements of object identity to be made.

In summary, patterns of search in the stage four task vary with the visual spatial information available. Babies are not restricted by a prior successful response but they are restricted by the perceived context in relation to which objects move. The infant can distinguish a change of place from a change of state, when the environment affords sufficient afferent support. The baby does not have a concept that the object *will* retain its identity despite any movement it might make; infants at stage IV *perceive* invariance but do not conceive of it. Difficulties arise when the spatial frames of reference that define 'place' come into conflict but even so, the rule that an object can only be in one place at one time is implicit in perception.

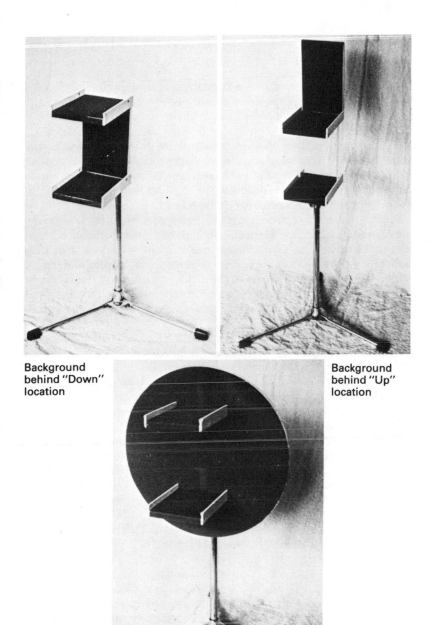

Background
behind "Down"
location

Background
behind "Up"
location

Background Complete

Fig. 6.5.   Presence or absence of background and perseverative error in the
stage four infant.

Conclusion

This chapter has considered a fundamental assumption of Piaget's theory, namely the proposition that the relation between infant and environment is one of profound 'adualism'. Evidence was reviewed and in each case, it was concluded that the distinction between self and environment is implicit in the structure of the sensory stimulation to which the baby responds. Piaget's developmental model, based on a theory of solipsistic perception, seems inadequate to account for the data. It is necessary to consider how the theory might be reformulated from a 'realist' perspective.

The fact that perception in the infant appears to function 'directly' has developmental implications, perhaps the most immediate is that the roots of objective knowledge may be discovered in structures inherent in the processes of sensory perception. If infants perceive objects and events in relation to the *distal* environment, then it might be argued that spatial and temporal processes inherent in distal perception form the constraints and guiding processes for subsequent, qualititative changes.

If the hypothesis that distal information can control the infant's responses is accepted, then other implications follow. Baldwin (1894) had the insight that for knowledge to develop, action systems must from the outset be linked to the environment. Objective knowledge may have its origins in direct sensorimotor links that function as pre-structured feedback loops within a system composed of infant and environment.

Evidence for such-pre-adaptive sensorimotor links is accumulating rapidly and some has been reviewed in this volume (for example, visually elicited reaching in neonates (Bower, 1974; Van Hofsten 1979) precociious imitation of facial movements (Meltzoff, 1981, this volume) responses to 'looming' (Ball and Vurpillot, 1981, this volume,) visual-motor integration, (Bullinger, 1981, this volume) and aspects of intersensory co-ordination Meltzoff, 1981, this volume) or the innate link between seeing and hearing (Butterworth, 1981). What these behaviours have in common is an intimate interconnection between complex response systems and afferent information from the distal environment. In each case, the distinction between self and environment is *implicit* in the relations between perception and action. The infant is an unreflective *participant* in the environment, but it is not lost in the sensory effects of its own activity. Development begins with a pre-established harmony, not an adualistic confusion, between infant and world.

The major problem is to define the qualitative transformations of the sensory system that give rise to new cognitive capacities such as recall, conceptual knowledge and autonomous control over action. One way to tackle this problem is to consider the structured sensory stimulation to which the infant is innately attuned to constitute the 'programming' language for the internal, neural processes that constitute the 'machine' language (see Mounoud and Vinter, 1981, this volume), where both programme and machine language have been mutually pre-adapted by evolution. It is precisely because *adaptation* requires an initial, intimate link between infant and environment (as Baldwin recognized) that it makes sense to speak of perception as 'direct' in the neonate. This need not entail any pre-suppositions about *what* will be perceived. It is merely to state that whatever *can be* perceived will not require mediation through action, although there must exist direct links with complex response systems.

In order to make the transition from a perceptual to a conceptual mode of intellectual functioning, the infant must acquire self-conscious awareness and awareness of the permanence and the individual identity of physical and social objects. Interiorization of the invariant information specifying self and objects, constantly available in the sensory array, should serve to categorize memory and to lay down a body image. Development also requires some means of gaining access to that information, which seems to require a 'reversal of perspective' that will allow reflection upon interiorized information. If objective knowledge has roots in pre-structured feedback, with an implicit subject—object distinction, this may ensure that as representations develop they are automatically assigned to their appropriate referents (aspect of self or aspect of the environment). By 'interiorizing' aspects of the physical and social environment, the baby simultaneously 'externalizes' the self to produce the reversal of perspective necessary for self reflection. This need not involve a 'reflection on action', even though action may drive the whole process along, but perception of the perceptual process itself.

In conclusion, perception necessarily involves a point of view but this need not involve solipsism. The tasks for the future are to describe how qualitative transformations in cognitive growth come about through interaction with the world, to relate them to their neurological substrate (see Gibson, 1981, this volume) and to clarify the functional utility of 'direct' sensory perception in the social and cognitive economy of the infant.

Notes

1 	What are the implications of these findings for the problem of distinguishing between a change of place and a change of state? It will be recalled that a change of place is defined as any pattern of sensory data that can be reversed by a movement of the observer, whereas a change of state cannot be 'undone' in this way. The infant's involuntary postural compensation to the misleading optic flow pattern might be considered an attempt to reverse a change of *place* of the infant's own body, in order to maintain postural stability. Of course, the true state of affairs is a change of *state* of the surround (from stationary to moving). Thus, it might be argued that the infant fails to make the crucial distinction but this would be to ignore the constraints of the normal ecology. (Furthermore, early in the acquisition of postural control, infants *invariably* interpret the visual information as signifying a change of place, that is there is no question of confusion.)

2 	Research funded by a grant from the Social Science Research Council of Great Britain.

3 	Research funded by a grant from the Medical Research Council of Great Britain.

References

Acredolo, L. P. (1979) 'Laboratory versus home: the effect of environment on the nine month old infant's choice of spatial reference system', *Developmental Psychology*, 15 (6) 666–7.

Baldwin, J. M. (1894) *Mental Development in the Child and the Race*, Macmillan, London.

Ball, W. A. and Tronick, E. (1971) Infant responses to impending collision optical and real, *Science*, 171, 818–20.

Ball, W. A. and Vurpillot, E. (1981) 'Action and the perception of displacements in infancy', in Butterworth, G. (ed.) *Infancy and Epistemology*, Harvester Press, Brighton, this volume pp.115–36.

Beilin, H. (1971) 'The development of physical concepts', in Mischel, T. (ed.) *Cognitive Development and Epistemology*, Academic Press, London, pp.85–119.

Berkeley, G. (1709) *A New Theory of Vision*, Dent/Everyman, London.

Bower, T. G. R. (1967) 'The development of object permanence, some studies of existence constancy', *Perception and Psychophysics*, 2 (9), 411–8.

Bower, T. G. R. (1974) *Development in Infancy*, W. H. Freeman, San Francisco.

Bower, T. G. R. (1975) 'Infant perception of the third dimension and object concept development', in Cohen, L. and Salapatek, P. (eds) *Infant Perception from Sensation to Cognition, Vol II*, Academic Press, London, pp. 29–49.

Bower, T. G. R. and Wishart, J. G. (1972) 'The effects of motor skill on object permanence', *Cognition*, 1 165–72.

Bremner, J. G. (1978a) 'Egocentric versus allocentric spatial coding in nine-month-old infants: Factors influencing the choice of code', *Developmental Psychology*, 14, No.4, 346–55.

Bremner, J. G. (1978b) 'Spatial errors made by infants: inadequate spatial cues or evidence of egocentrism?' *British Journal of Psychology*, 69, 77–84.

Bremner, J. G. (1980) 'The infant's understanding of space', in Cox, M. V. (ed.) *Is the young child egocentric?* Concord Books, London.

Bremner, J. G. and Bryant, P. E. (1977) 'Place versus response as the basis of spatial errors made by young infants', *Journal of Experimental Child Psychology*, 23, 162–77.

Bullinger, A. (1981) 'Cognitive elaboration of sensorimotor behaviour', in Butterworth, G. (ed.) *Infancy and Epistemology*, Harvester Press, Brighton, this volume pp.173–99.

Butterworth, G. E. (1973) 'The development of the object concept in human infants', unpublished DPhil thesis, University of Oxford.

Butterworth, G. E. (1975) 'Object identity in infancy: the interaction of spatial location codes in determining search errors', *Child Development*, 46, 866–70.

Butterworth, G. E. (1977) 'Object disappearance and error in Piaget's stage IV task', *Journal of Experimental Child Psychology*, 23, 391–401.

Butterworth, G. E. (1978) 'Thought and things: Piaget's theory' in Burton, A. and Radford, J. (eds) *Perspectives on thinking*, Methuen, London, pp. 65–89.

Butterworth, G. E. (1981) 'The origins of auditory–visual perception and visual proprioception in human development', in Walk. R. and Pick. H. (eds) *Perception and Perceptual Development Vol. II*, Plenum Press, New York.

Butterworth, G. E. and Cicchetti, D. (1978) 'Visual calibration of posture in normal and motor retarded Down's Syndrome infants', *Perception*, 7, 513–25.

Butterworth, G. E. and Cochran, E. (1980) 'Towards a mechanism of joint visual attention in human infancy', *International Journal of Behavioural Development*, 3, 253–72.

Butterworth, G. E. and Hicks, L. (1977) 'Visual proprioception and postural stability in infancy: a developmental study', *Perception*, 6, 255–62

Butterworth, G. E. and Jarrett, N. (1980a) 'The geometry of pre-verbal communication', paper presented to the Developmental Psychology Section of the British Psychological Society, Edinburgh.

Butterworth, G. E. and Jarrett, N. (1980b) 'Asymmetrical search errors in infancy: background to the problem', Unpublished manuscript University of Southampton.

Butterworth, G. E., Jarrett, N. and Hicks, L. (1981) 'Spatio-temporal identity in infancy: perceptual competence or conceptual deficit?', *Developmental Psychology* (in press).

Costall, A. (1981) 'On how so much information controls so much behaviour', in Butterworth, G. (ed.) *Infancy and Epistemology*, Harvester Press, Brighton, this volume pp.31–51.

Étienne, A. S. (1973) 'Developmental stages and cognitive structures as determinants of what is learned', in Hinde, R. A. and Hinde, J. S. (eds) *Constraints on Learning*, Academic Press, London, pp. 371–95.

Evans, W. F. and Gratch, G. (1972) 'The stage IV error in Piaget's theory of object concept development—difficulties in object conceptualisation or spatial localization?' *Child Development*, 43, 682–8.

Gibson, J. J. (1966) *The Senses Considered as Perceptual Systems*, Houghton Mifflin, Boston.

Gibson, J. J. (1979) *The Ecological Approach to Visual Perception*, Houghton Mifflin, Boston.

Gibson, J. J., Kaplan, G. A. Reynolds, H. W. J. R. and Wheeler, K. (1969) 'The change from visible to invisible: a study of optical transitions', *Perception and Psychophysics*, 5, 113–6.

Gibson, K. R. (1981) 'Comparative nuero-ontology: its implications for the development of human intelligence', in Butterworth, G. (ed.) *Infancy and Epistemology*, Harvester Press, Brighton, this volume 52–84.

Gratch, G., Appel, K. J., Evans, W. F. Le Compte, G. K. and Wright, N. A. (1974) 'Piaget's stage IV object concept error: evidence of forgetting or object conception?' *Child Development*, 45 (1), 71–7

Harris, P. L. (1974) 'Perseverative search at a visibly empty place by young infants', *Journal of Experimental Child Psychology*, 18, 535–42.

Harris, P. L. (1975) 'Development of search and object permanence during infancy', *Psychological Bulletin*, 82 (3), 332–44.

Harris, P. L., Cassel, T. L. and Bamborough, P. (1974) 'Tracking by young infants', *British Journal of Psychology*, 65, 345–9.

James, W. (1912) *Essays in Radical Empiricism, A Pluralistic Universe*, Longman, London, new edition 1947.

Johansson, G. (1977) 'Studies on visual perception of locomotion', *Perception*, 66, 365–76.

Landers, W. F. (1971) 'Effects of differential experience on infants' performance in a Piagetian stage IV object concept task', *Developmental Psychology*, 5 (1), 48–54.

Lee, D. N. and Aronson, E. (1974) Visual proprioceptive control of standing in human infants. *Perception and Psychophysics*, 15, 529–532.

Michotte, A. (1950) 'A propos de la permanence phenomenale, faits et theories', *Acta Psychologica*, 7, 298–322.

Michotte, A. (1955) 'Discussion entre les trois rapporteurs', in *La Perception: Deuxieme Symposium De L'association de Psychologie Scientifique de Langue Francaise, Louvain, 1953*. Presses Universitaires de France, Paris, pp. 53–61.

Michotte, A., Thinès, G. and Crabbé, G. (1964) *Les complements amodaux des structures perceptives*, Studia Psychologia, Louvain.

Mounoud, P. and Vinter, A. (1981) 'Representation and sensorimotor development', in Butterworth, G. (ed.) *Infancy and Epistemology*,

Harvester Press, Brighton, this volume pp.200–35.

Piaget, J. (1954) *The Construction of Reality in the Child*, Basic Books, New York.

Russell, J. (1981) 'Piaget's theory of sensorimotor development: outlines assumptions and problems', in Butterworth, G. (ed.) *Infancy and Epistemology*, Harvester Press, Brighton, this volume, pp.3–31.

Scaife, M and Bruner, J. S. (1975) 'The capacity for joint visual attention in the infant', *Nature*, 253, 265.

Trevarthen, C. (1968) 'Two visual systems in primates', *Psychologische Forschung*, 31, 299–377.

Trevarthen, C. (1979) 'Instincts for human understanding and for cultural cooperation: their development in infancy', in von Cranach, M., Foppa, K., Lepenies, W. and Ploog, D. (eds) *Human Ethology*, Cambridge University Press, pp. 530–71.

Von Hofsten, C. (1979) 'Development of visually directed reaching. The approach phase', *Journal of Human Movement Studies*, 5, 160–78.

Willats, P. (1979) 'Adjustment of reaching to change in object position by young infants', *Child Development*, 50, 911–3.

Wolff, P. H. (1960) 'The developmental psychologies of Jean Piaget and psychoanalysis', *Psychological Issues*, 2, 1–181.

Ziman, J. (1979) *Reliable Knowledge: An Exploration of the Grounds for Belief in Science*, Cambridge University Press.

PART III
THE DEVELOPMENT OF REPRESENTATION

7 Cognitive Elaboration of Sensorimotor Behaviour

ANDRÉ BULLINGER, (translated by John Churcher and Karen Clarke)

Introduction

This paper attempts an analysis of the earliest levels of human sensorimotor development from a cognitivist perspective. Following the observations and theoretical work by Piaget in the 1930s, research into cognition in the young infant underwent a decline. However, the last fifteen years have witnessed a vigorous revival of interest and perhaps we should take a close look at this new enthusiasm. In the final analysis it must be said that the proliferation of research in this area results to a large extent from the availability of new methods of acquiring data (habituation techniques, advances in technology, etc.). This preoccupation with the tools of investigation has brought with it a compartmentalization of research—research which often has as its sole object the analysis of the sensory system's capacity for discrimination, without having posed the problems of the elaboration of that capacity. One is left with the impression that the human infant reduces to a collection of 'abilities', unconnected with one another. Our aim is to try to present a view of the earliest levels of development which corrects this picture to some extent.

The paper is organized as follows: in the first section we give some definitions, and preliminaries to an analysis of development. Then we will present: our view of the initial state of the infant, distinguishing between organism and subject; our conception of the first levels of development; and finally, some factual observations where experimental examples are interpreted level by level. The paper ends with some remarks of more general significance.

Definitions

The analysis of the baby's development from the cognitivist viewpoint cannot avoid the problem of the theoretical place occupied by the indices used. With respect to these indices, we will make clear the framework within which we wish to consider them. Thus, we use the term *functioning* when we intend to refer to the ensemble of potentially observable material facts. We reserve the term *activity* to refer specifically to cognitive aspects that depend on some observable functioning. Thus, functioning will be the index, in certain situations, of a cognitive activity that is never directly visible.

The hypothesis of a link between activity and functioning allows the use of recorded indices of functioning as descriptions of an underlying activity.

Classically, the descriptive *value* of recorded indices, relative to the activity one wishes to describe, is regarded as stable. This *a priori* assumption, which depends on an epistomlogical choice, comes down in the end to postulating that the organism is identical with the 'subject'. In our view the organism is an object of the environment, and for cognitive activities at the sensorimotor level it is an object-to-be-known (objet à connaitre). Those cognitive elaborations which allow regulation of the baby's behaviour in a new way, will by this very fact bring about changes in the meaning of observed behavioural indices. They cannot have a constant value insofar as they relate to cognitive activity.

It is therefore, appropriate to specify the value and the meaning of recorded indices at each moment of development, otherwise incoherence and contradictions between results are inevitable. Given this perspective, a large part of the controversies between various authors (age at which particular behaviours appear, significance of variations in heart rate, etc.), might be by-passed if the point were not masked by a pseudo-consensus on this question.

One delicate point of theory and methodology is the question of 'making sense' (*prise de sens*) in relation to physiological signals (*indices physiologiques*). A good illustration of this problem is provided by the observations made some time ago by Turro (1920) on adults in skilled occupations: acrobat, printer, dancer, etc. Turro was concerned to show that a task new to the subject involves particular elaborations of the organism. In particular he points out, concerning tactile physiological signals, that:

. . . If therefore the [tactile] points vary according to the individuals' occupations even though the peripheral radiation of tactile nerves is observed to be uniform in everyone, these points are not congenital and do not depend on the number of tactile terminals distributed between them, but on the number of psychomotor coordinations which establish them. (*Ibid*).

'Points' here refers to the two-point tactile discrimination threshold of Weber.

In an experiment on tactile sensitivity in acrobats in training (learning to walk on a tightrope), the threshold for discrimination measured with Weber's compass in the interscapular region is found to be considerably reduced after training. The effect of this training largely depends on a process of cognitive elaboration of physiological signals. It is seen clearly in adults, where the maturational aspect is effectively absent, and it can be interpreted in terms of 'making sense', of a new elaboration of a previously existing configuration of physiological signals. For the infant the on-going processes of cognitive elaboration are often masked or confused with facts of maturation which are themselves not unaffected by practice. We believe that only the component relating to the aspect of 'making sense' is strictly psychological. This conception leads one to consider the human environment in its physical and social dimensions as a support whose importance is as great as that of biology: these dimensions direct activity and play an important role in the process of *equilibration*. In Piaget (1967) this process is essentially a property arising out of biology. In later levels of development, because it rests less directly on biology, it acquires teleonomic aspects. When the physical and relational (*relationelles*) dimensions of the human environment are considered, as well as biological ones, there is defined for the subject what might be called a task, which gives the process of equilibration some leverage on the situation itself.

The initial state

The new-born infant may be described as a polysensorial organism, a totality that is both active and acted upon by the environment. Its dominant characteristic in the cognitive domain may be summarized as follows: an interface, the mother's body, has been drastically lost at birth. By interface we mean the elaborated ensemble of properties of the organism; this elaboration does not reduce simply to the biological support but takes into account significations, representations of the surrounding world. The sensitivity of the foetus to external agencies through the mother's body is not simply proportional to the physical stimuli present: Féré (1887) points out that the foetus reacts to social and emotional properties of the environment as well as to physical ones: the motor response of the foetus is not proportional to the physical magnitude of the stimulus. Féré puts forward the idea that ' . . . all active movements of the foetus are in reality reflex movements following an excitation of which the mother may be unaware . . .'. Thus, active aspects start to be evident during life *in utero*, and as much in relation to social as to physical properties of the environment relayed by the mother's body. Wallon (1925, 1949) emphasizes the passage at birth from a physiological to an emotional symbiosis. The environment into which the new-born infant finds itself suddenly thrown is not only endowed with physical properties. The human environment affords (*recele des*) biological, physical and social properties (by social we mean emotional, relational, communicative, etc.), and it is the ensemble of these properties that will be the raw material for a cognitive elaboration. In the cognitive domain the infant's state at birth is therefore not that of a 'tabula rasa'. An ensemble of functionings *in utero* has allowed the formation of actions appropriate to this environment. Birth, as the drastic loss of this environment, makes necessary for survival a set of modifications in the physiological domain (respiration, temperature regulation, etc.) and a reorganization of the new interfaces available. The latter are constituted principally by sensorimotor loops—visual, tactile, kinaesthetic, postural, etc. These interfaces are phylogenetically determined and in this new environment are objects-to-be-known, like the rest of the world. The organism, however, is a privileged object, since all sensorimotor cognition will be supported by it in the course of cognitive activities, some aspects of which are reflected in the organism's functionings.

It is appropriate at this point to characterize what is commonly called 'the subject's point of view'. At birth there is no reason to attribute a subjectivity that is stable and centred on the organism. To do so would be to presuppose a represented organism: the subject's body. Wallon (1949) writes of a region of fusion, and an emotional symbiosis. Piaget (1936) shows that the organism and the environment constitute an indissociable whole; that consciousness, if it exists, is initially absence of differentiation. Piaget's interest goes beyond the description of a static state to the dynamic aspect: the activity of action schemes. Subjectivity is tied to these functionings, and objects are conceived as 'aliments' for the activity, raw materials for assimilation and accommodation by the action schemes.

Mounoud (1979) believes that 'there exist several levels of elaboration of reality . . . and that there exist partially adaptive behaviours unique to each level. . .'. We share this central concern with the dynamics of the processes. The cognitive activity which re-elaborates the interfaces of the organism takes the form of a 'making sense' of the organism's functionings and of the human environment. Successive levels of elaboration of certain properties of activity, of the body and of objects, will define stages in this development. The analysis will focus on processes of *action formation* rather than on description of the levels of subjectivity or consciousness, which would have the disadvantage of being a static, closed description of the baby's cognitive state. Sensorimotor functioning is the visible index of this construction, provided one carefully defines its lines with cognitive activity. It is also the instrument of this construction.

The first stages of development

At birth the new-born infant's reflex structures are in interaction with other objects of the environment. The situation is that of a functioning totality: the organism, as a *biological entity*, is a collection of phylogenetically determined adaptations. The baby, as an *element of the human environment*, is caught up in a network whose determinants have biological, physical and social origins. Stability of functioning is necessary to provide a basis for cognitive elaboration which takes into account both of these entities—biological and relational. Progress cannot be resolved into a simple effect of practice; it is necessary to postulate a support for which we have called 'making sense' (*prise de sens*). We define the latter thus: the repetitions and regularities manifested by the environment (which includes the organism) are reflected in the dynamic organization of neurophysiological signals arising from the interfaces of the organism. (Within biology the level of neurophysiology seems to us the best for characterizing the material support.) These signals constitute the support for 'sense-making', which in turn will regulate the activity. Such 'minimal representations' are only activated while the action is occurring, so they do not have the classical characteristics of representation (that is, the idea of something deferred, of evocation, etc.).

This definition allows us to describe behaviour at the first level of development. One of the features common to many recorded observations of the new-born infant when it is alert, is the total engagement of the organism in some task: its activity is polarized by a sensorimotor loop which orients and completely mobilizes the organism. We might say that the baby is 'all sucking' or 'all vision', in the sense that other peripheral stimulation results in an intensification of the on-going activity. Stimulation of the grasping reflex while nutritive sucking activity is in progress intensifies that activity; nurses are well aware of this and often make use of it.

The activation of various sensorimotor loops will successively bring into existence 'universes' formed by 'sense-making' provoked by regularities in the environment. Each universe will be predominatly visual, tactile/kinaesthetic, or oral etc. It is impossible at this level to postulate a subject—object dualism. Such universes constitute dynamic totalities which encompass the organism, the environment and the action, without distinction. What distinguishes this first level is the *exclusive* aspect of the organism's involvements, exclusive because the entire organism participates and is involved in a given activity.

The second level is characterized by the simultaneous stabilization of two 'sense-makings' grounded in patterns of physiological signals arising from different sensorimotor loops. This does not mean that at this level it is possible to have 'sense-makings' outside the current action, but that the action may jointly call upon two sensorimotor loops. Such temporal and spatial co-occurrences are tied to properties of the human environment. Visual and tactile properties of an object meet at the same place in physical space. This joint stabilization of 'sense-makings' marks the beginning of a segmentation in observable functionings and a decline in the infant's global reactions.

At the third level, co-ordination of the stabilized 'sense-makings' will bring into existence a 'subject', an 'object', and simultaneously an elementary 'space' supporting the co-ordinated properties. If the organism's interfaces are the instruments and the support of 'sense-makings' (*prises de sens*), the co-ordinations which create the object relation (*relation objectale*)—we use this term in a sense not far removed from Winnicot's—also have physical and social properties in the human environment. One of the fundamental material elements of this co-ordination is regularity which occurs throughout the tactile and visual universes for example. The co-ordinations will make the organism a site (*lieu*) where the co-ordinated visual and tactile instruments are supported.

The represented object must not be confused with the material object, which supports quite other physical and social properties that could be elaborated, just as the organism must not be confused with the elaboration that is made of its interfaces. And finally, the space that is constructed must not be confused with physical space. From this level on, subject, objects and space will grow richer and become re-elaborated as a function of new encounters and of regularities arising from an environment of which the organism is an integral part.

The first three stages are summarized in Fig. 7.1. We believe it is important to emphasize at the first level the aspect of globality, and of polarization of the activity. At the second level, the regularities and co-occurrences necessary for cognitive elaboration are present because the sensorimotor systems generally address multimodel objects. At the third level the dominant fact is the overturn in stratification; from a totality unifying the organism and the object in an activity, we pass to elementary 'representations' of the organism, the object and a space that links them.

From this level on, we may speak of *object relations* (*relation*

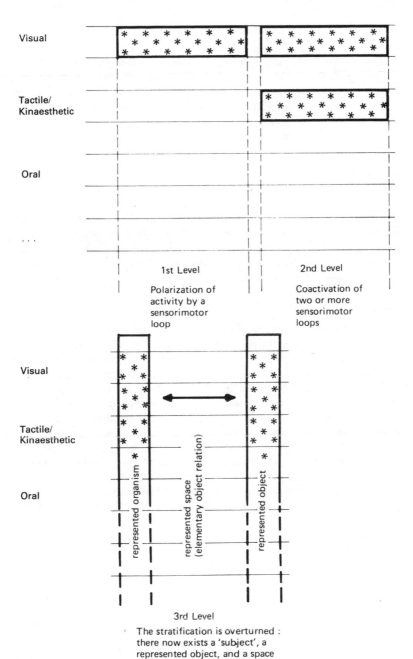

Fig. 7.1 The first three levels.

objectale) and describe functionings in terms of *purposive action* (*action finalisee*). The concept of *action formation (formation des actions*) might be used as a generic term covering the process of cognitive elaboration, since it includes both instrumenting (*instrumentation*) the organism and simultaneously elaborating the properties of the object in a space.

Examples from experimental observations

We have put forward the hypothesis that cognitive elaboration of a sensorimotor system necessarily takes place through co-ordinations manifested in the very functioning of the organism. Regularities, as properties of the environment, are the fundamental bases for this elaboration. To illustrate this view, we will address ourselves to an analysis of the problems posed by the infant's oculomotor activity in its connections with postural activity.

First level

The oculomotor system has been well described by physiologists. Let us simply recall that at the sensory level, the retina consists of a central zone and a peripheral zone, or of a gradient of receptor distribution which allows a more-or-less arbitrary division into different sectors. The eyeballs are moved by a powerful group of muscles; there is little obstruction of the movements and the conditions of functioning are relatively stable. In the course of its displacements the eye does not encounter material obstacles, and resistances due to friction are weak and constant. In the physiological domain what is important is the fact that the covariations between foveal stimulation and peripheral stimulation, to which movements of the retina give rise, are automatically inscribed on that surface, since the fovea occupies a determinate place on the retina. This is probably one of the most powerful regularities imposed upon cognition. Let us note that only movement is capable of revealing this property, thereby allowing its elaboration.

The reflex scheme[1] of ocular fixation, present at birth, puts the sensory aspects (the retina) into a reciprocal dependence with the motor ones (execution of the act which by covariation, reveals the anatomical dependence between the fovea and periphery). This reflex is thus a source of regularity provided that luminous stimuli are present. But this reflex is not only seen in connection with stimulation by light: Mendelson and Haith (1978) have shown that in darkness the new-born infant develops well-organized oculomotor patterns: the distribution of saccadic amplitudes, and the spatial distribution of fixations in the field, can be shifted by lateralized sound stimuli: there is displacement of the centre of gravity of the exploration towards the sound source and focalization of the pattern of exploration. The same babies placed in weak ambient illumination have 'disorganized' oculomotor patterns: the amount of nystagmus is increased. When they close their eyes the activity breaks off, is brought to a halt. The moment the eyes re-open, they are once more stationary and centred; the source of disturbance has been properly detected and the reaction adapted. These facts show that oculomotricity (*oculomotricité*) is operational at birth, but that it operates on bases that differ in part from those that are useful in the environment into which the baby is thrown at birth. Light arriving on the retina momentarily disorganises oculomotricity, although later on similar stimulation by light will be the support for regulations. These properties of the organism and of the physical environment will need to be elaborated in the cognitive domain in order to reorganize ocular motricity on new bases, by relying on properties acquired earlier. Here we must introduce, independently of maturational asects, the concept of 'making sense' of certain qualities of the retina and of ocular motricity. The plasticity of functioning which allows this adaptation is a far cry from the pure reflex, and the idea of a reflex scheme seems to us quite appropriate. We have here the formation of new actions which rely on stabilities of functioning. These stabilities are the source and foundation of functions which surpass them, which seems paradoxical if we try to do without cognitive elaboration of the material conditions of these behaviours.

In tasks involving large amplitude visual pursuit, in addition to the visual response, head movements are elicited which form part of a postural response of the new-born. We have shown (Bullinger, 1977) firstly that babies of sixty hours are capable of orienting themselves towards a source of visual stimulation, and moreover that they can follow a moving object by correctly orienting the head. The organization of these movements is part of a global postural form, where not only is the head mobilized, but the entire body takes part. The assymetrical, static posture at the start is comparable to a tonic neck reflex (Peiger, 1962). During the pursuit one may observe a lurching of the posture, from left to right or from right to left; if one analyses the portion of the pursuit relating to the mid-line position of the mobile, the baby appears to throw its arms forward in order to seize the object. This precocious prehension, described by Bower, Broughton and Moore (1970), among others, is to be understood as a participation of the entire organism in the activity of pursuit. These movements, determined by the situation as a whole, pre-figure the

Infancy and Epistemology

re-elaborations of prehension under visual control which are established around the third month.

Another index of this global participation of the organism in the
activity of pursuit is the variation in heart rate accompanying visual
pursuit in the new-born. In an unpublished study we recorded heart
rate at the same time as the orientation of the baby's head towards
the stimulus. Every 3s we noted whether or not the orientation of the
head and the stimulus coincided (plus or minus), and the direction of
change in heart rate (plus or minus); we thus obtained two sets of
results which may be expressed in Table 7.1.

Table 7.1. Change in heart rate in relation to appearance or disappearance of
a stimulus in the visual field. This table presents the results from twelve
babies (mean age: sixty hours). Taken individually, each baby gives significant results (correlation coefficient of (*points Phi*). The results presented
here show that an increase in heart rate is associated with loss of the mobile,
while a decrease corresponds to appearance of the mobile in the visual field.
These results, compatible with data already known, are interpreted in terms
of global participation by the organism engaged in a visual pursuit task.

Variation in instantaneous mean heart-rate	Head orientation		
	+	−	TOTAL
+	42	83	125
−	85	48	133
TOTAL	127	131	258

There is a massive effect: an acceleration in heart rate corresponds
to loss of the stimulus. At the moment when the baby finds the mobile
again, heart rate deceleration occurs., If one takes the results for each
individual, all subjects show the same effect, and it is significant
(correlation coifficient of point phi, Dasnelie, 1969). As with posture, one has here an index of global participation by the organism in
the activity. In interpreting these reactions we follow Graham and
Clifton (1966); an increase in heart rate is here a defensive reaction,
while a decrease is an orientation reaction. Detailed analysis of body
movements in the fifteen to thirty day old child, in situations
involving visual pursuit of a moving object, shows that at these ages
the possibility of visual pursuit depends on the baby's overall
posture. The latter is generally assymetrical (the position known as
'the fencer') and only rarely allows a pursuit movement to cross the
mid-line axis into the side opposite to the posture being held.

The sequence of pictures shown in Fig. 7.2 (pp. 184–5) was taken from a 16 mm film. The baby was filmed from in front (a mirror placed above the baby reflects the view from above, as well as the values of two counters: the time base on the left, and the angular position of the mobile on the right). The mobile moves automatically along a semicircular path in front of the baby. In this example the baby is twenty days old, and the mobile starts from the baby's right. The 'tonic neck reflex' position is typical, and the baby follows the mobile. When the mobile reaches a position a little way beyond the mid-line axis, the baby's posture cannot tip over into the other half-field; the baby loses the mobile and returns to a starting posture around which it develops intense ocular and postural activity, which might be thought of as activity aiming to bring back a sight (*spectacle*) now vanished.

Quantitative analysis by age groups (see Table 7.2) of amount of pursuit, its amplitude, the amount of segmentation (number of times that the baby, having visually captured the mobile and then lost it, manages to find it again) shows the dominance of posture in pursuit activity for the first group.

Table 7.2 Indices of visual pursuit activity grouped according to babies' ages. The amount of pursuit is an overall measure of the mean performance of the different age groups. It will be seen that the amount of full pursuit is increased for the second group, where there is strong domination by the mobile's trajectory. Correlatively, the amount of segmentation (number of interruptions during the same pursuit) is small. The amplitude of pursuits in group 1 shows that they only rarely exceed half the trajectory (160° maximum).

	Amount of pursuit	Full pursuit	Amount of Segmentation	Mean amplitude
	%	%	%	degrees
Group 1 20–49 days	50	13	34	87
Group 2 50–79 days	76	47	14	114
Group 3 80–150 days	5	12	61	113

a

b

d

e

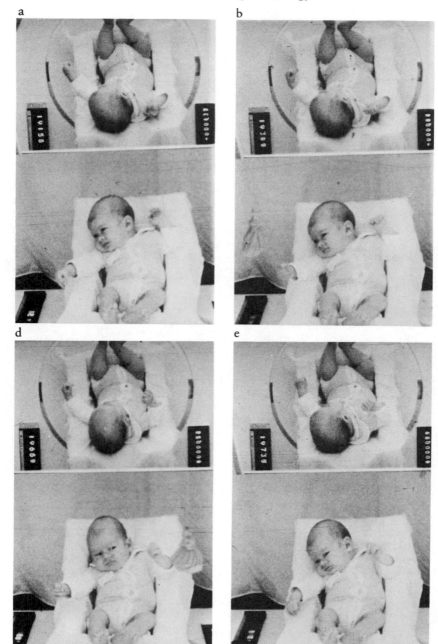

c

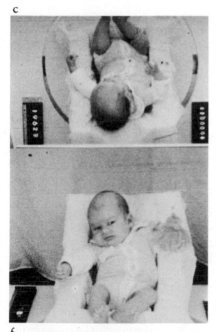

f

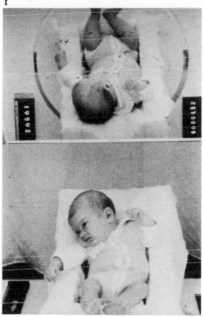

Fig. 7.2 Pictures taken from experimental films showing a baby aged twenty days engaged in visual pursuit of a mobile moving in a semicircle in front of him. A mirror above the baby reflects the view from above in which appear both the value of the time base (left) and the angular position of the mobile (right). The mobile in this case starts to the right of the baby and the starting posture is the typical tonic neck reflex (TNR). The baby follows the mobile. When the mobile passes the mid-line, the baby, its posture holding it back, still looks at the mobile (picture), then loses it (pictures 5 and 6) and returns to a posture identical to that at the start. At this moment intense activity is displayed. For this level, the possibility of pursuing an object is governed by the posture the baby adopts. The sequence is 7.2 abcdef

The mean amplitudes are of the order of one half-field since after the mobile is lost there is no search activity directed by properties of the object, but a return to the starting posture. Groups two and three will be discussed later.

If one analyses the quantity of movement produced by the babies during this pursuit activity, one finds a remarkable stability across the three age groups. By contrast, the spatial organization is different if one takes as reference points the nose, the two eyes and the two wrists, and treats a point on the chair as a fixed reference, the deformations of the triangles constituted respectively by the nose and the two eyes, and the nose and the two wrists, provide a picture which allows the specific character of the movements to become clear.

Fig. 7.3 (pp. 188–9) shows a baby of twenty days in this task. The mobile moves from left to right as seen by the observer. The time axis is vertical, and the configurations of points are taken twice a second; a criterion for the amount of movement allows us to keep only those pictures which show an important postural change. Fig. 7.3b and 7.3c are similar diagrams for babies aged sixty and 100 days, and will be discussed below.

These few results, taken from various studies, are useful here as observational data. They make clear the organism's global activity while it is engaged in a 'visual' task, for example. Such global participation is essential. There are no grounds for a dissociation of the object from the activity which accompanies it. It is this totality which gives rise to regularities and provides the raw materials for a 'making sense' which is supported by the activity itself.

Second level

This level is characterized by cognitive elaboration existing in a stable relationship with different sensorimotor loops. The concurrent elaborations initiate a process of dissociation of functionings, a dissociation which makes new co-ordinations possible. Ocular motricity can provide us with examples of this aspect of dissociation.

The motor functioning of the eye is characterized essentially by two types of motricity. The first of these produces a succession of fixations on a static scene, the second produces dynamic fixation of a moving object (whether it is the scene or the baby which moves). These two capacities set in motion the same oculomotor apparatus, but in distinct modes. These modes of functioning are well co-ordinated physiologically, but require elaboration in the cognitive domain. During the elaboration one may expect to see particular behaviours as evidence of this process.

We presented babies aged seven to eight weeks with a stable object (made of 'Lego' blocks) for twenty seconds (Bullinger, 1981a, 1981b). The object then moved for five seconds, and arrived at a different position where it remained for twenty seconds. Throughout the forty-five seconds eye-movements were recorded (see Fig. 7.4, p. 190). The analysis showed that during the final phase the gaze would return to the region where the object had been at the start of its movement and where there was no longer anything.

Since we know how attractive a salient object can be, and the difficulty a baby usually has in detaching itself from a scene, such returns of the gaze seem to us highly significant, especially since control experiments, in which changes of position were presented without a visible trajectory, do not produce similar behaviour. The lack of co-ordination of the saccadic and smooth pursuit systems in the cognitive domain, is reflected in the exploration of the scene; involved in the exploration are two instruments that are not yet co-ordinated and which seize on two different properties of the object. Dissociation appears at the moment the executive rules of the new-born's oculomotricity, described by Haith (1978), are superseded. Rules one and two describe oculomotor activity in darkness:

Rule 1: If awake and alert the light not too bright, open eyes.
Rule 2: If darkness is found, initiate an intensive controlled search.

Rules 3 and 4 provide the key to eye movements in an illuminated field:

Rule 3: If light is found, but no edges, engage in a broad, sometimes uncontrolled search.
Rule 4: If an edge is found, stay near the edge and attempt to cross it.

The transition from Rule 3 to Rule 4 is direct; but mastering the transition from Rule 4 to Rule 3, observed in our results, implies a new kind of control, one which allows disengagement from the 'visual grasping' (Rule 4) that is typical of the new born. Our results show that around seven to eight weeks the visual system begins to free itself from biological determination. The possibility of this happening necessitates taking into account properties of the oculomotor system's functioning that are not dissociated from the scene (spectacle). Seen in this light, the problem of the co-ordinations of properties of the spatial field is directly related to co-ordinations of the systems governing the various types of motricity.

In the domain of posture a similar development can be seen. In the

Fig. 7.3. These diagrams are the result of a computer analysis of film sequences showing pursuit of a moving object by the baby. Each frame from the film is represented here by five connected points; the small triangle represents the nose and the two eyes; the large triangle, the nose and the wrists. The diagonal line from left to right shows the trajectory of the mobile. The time axis is verticle and the sequence starts from the top. A criterion for quantity of movement is set for each subject, such that the diagram is not overloaded. (a) This shows a baby of twenty days. We see the start of a tilting of the posture, in which the entire body axis participates. From the middle of the trajectory, the baby loses the mobile and goes back to a posture close to that of the start. (b) This shows a baby of fifty-eight days. The changing posture, associated with the trajectory, is evident in the shortening of the nose–left wrist segment, and the correlative lengthening of the nose–right wrist segment. The deformation of the nose–left eye–right eye triangle shows the orientation of the head as it follows the mobile. (c) This shows a baby of 102 days. The head is oriented correctly towards the mobile, but no longer is there evidence of any relationship with arm movements.

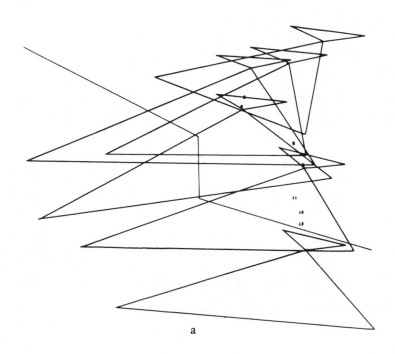

a

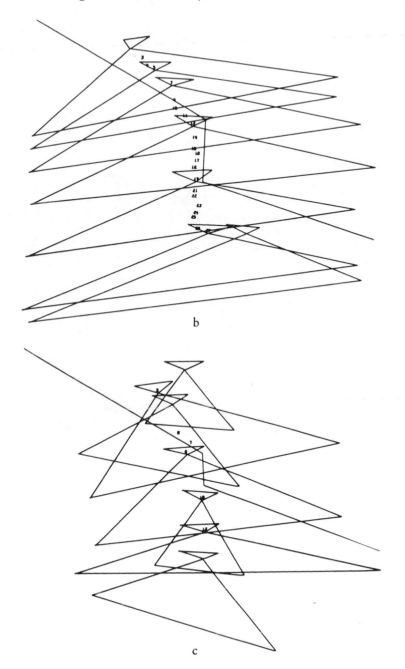

b

c

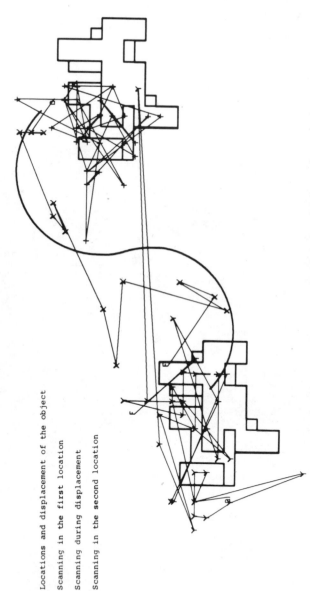

Locations and displacement of the object

+   Scanning in the first location

x   Scanning during displacement

y   Scanning in the second location

Fig. 7.4. This diagram shows the oculomotor activity of a baby of eight weeks exploring a three-dimensional object. During the first time period (marked +), the object is stationary in one part of the available field. Oculomotor activity gets well under way around the object; this exploration lasts for twenty seconds. The object then moves as shown by the curved line. Oculomotor activity during this period of five seconds (marked X) is associated with the object's movement. At the new location of the object, the baby explores for twenty seconds (marked Y). It is during this period that we find the gaze returning to the first location, now empty. This ability to leave the salient object is interpreted as a start in taking account of properties of the scene and properties of the oculomotor system.

study mentioned above, concerning pursuit of a moving visual object, the behaviour of the seven to ten week old baby shows that it is practically enslaved by the mobile. Pursuit is possible if the whole body participates in the movement. Crossing the mid-line axis is accompanied by a change of direction in the postural asymmetry, and is still the most precarious moment (see Fig. 7.5 pp. 192—3).

Quantitatively, the amount of full pursuit in this age group is very high (Table, 7.2, group 2); the baby seems entranced by the situation. By the same token, the amount of segmentation is very small and the mean pursuit amplitudes are greater. When the mobile is lost the activity which follows does not take account of spatial properties of the trajectory; posture dominates and the baby returns to an asymmetrical posture, which is often the starting one. Analysing the deformations of the triangles for subjects of this group shows the typical deformation of the triangle formed by the left and right wrists and the nose; rotation of the head on its axis is better than in the previous group, where the body axis tilted as a whole in order to orient the head correctly. Here the movements are less extensive. In situations where the mobile stops during its trajectory a stillness in the posture is also observed: corresponding to the stopping of the mobile is a suspension of the body movements associated with its displacement.

Here, as with the visual system, the dominant characteristic is the inseparability of properties of a sensory system and properties of a material object. It is specifically this totality which is elaborated, which 'makes sense' (*prend du sens*), thereby superseding a mode of control which depended exclusively on biologically determined structures. We may speak here of a pole of maximum accommodation, provided we are careful to say that it is activity as such which is so well tuned to the situation itself.

Third Level
This level is dominated by co-ordination of specific elaborations made at the previous level. From the point of view of the co-ordination of actions, the work of Piaget (1936) is an important reference for this level. Describing the stages of co-ordination between vision and prehension, Piaget says of the baby's hand '. . . the hand's principal activity is prehension . . .' (*Ibid.* p.84). He then describes the different stages, and at the last stage of interest to us he says, ' . . . as soon as coordination occurs the object tends to be assimilated to several schemes simultaneously: it thus acquires a set of significations and consequently a solidity (*consistance*), which makes it of interest in itself' (*Ibid.* p.112). The 'making sense' is here

a   b

e   f

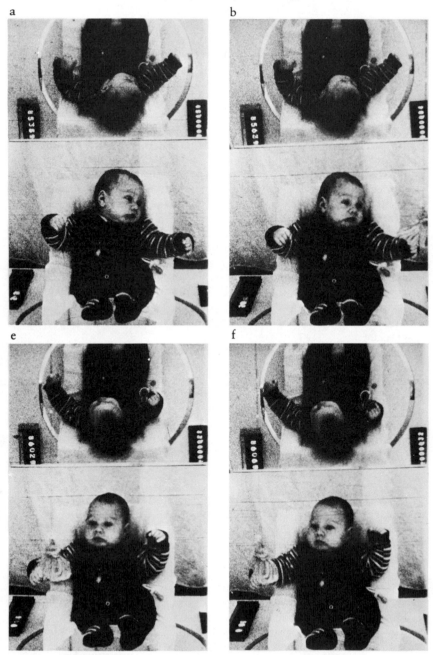

Fig. 7.5   These pictures were produced under the same technical conditions as the series presented in Fig. 7.2. Here the baby is aged fifty-eight days and the mobile starts from his left. The lifting of the right arm and forward extension of the left, as well as the orientation of the head, create a posture close to the TNR. The baby follows the

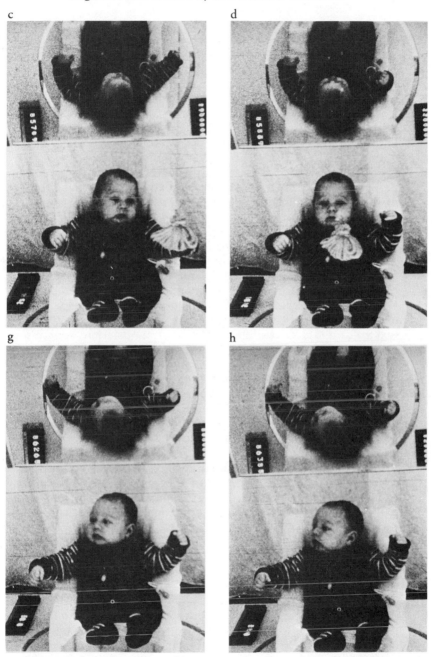

mobile, and when it is in front of him we see that the asymmetry of the posture is reversed; extension of the right arm and lifting of the left. The posture is associated with the spatial location of the mobile and is totally involved in the pursuit activity. We must point out the almost perfect symmetry between the first and last pictures. The sequence is 7.5 abcdefgh.

clearly the dominant aspect of the achievement of this stage, which brings into existence an object. However, Piaget's point of view obscures the whole question of those properties of the organism that are elaborated concurrently with the object. This is not to say that Piaget confuses subject with organism at earlier levels (he is always careful to speak of a 'scheme' and 'aliments for schemes'). However, from the level of co-ordinations the confusion sets in: it is 'the subject who grasps'. This coincides with the moment at which the hand becomes a tool; as an instrument mastered by cognition it is incorporated into the subject and its objective properties cease to be visible: it is the subject who manipulates an object. The elision of levels comes suddenly, and we must tread carefully; between subject and objects there are always more or less elaborated sensorimotor systems.

In our own research in the area of vision and posture we see that in group 3 (see Fig. 7.3c), the pursuit activity is of a very different nature from that in the other groups. In fact, relative to the preceding group, the amount of segmentation is greatly increased, while amplitude and amount of pursuit remain stable. This result is evidence that babies of this age are capable of taking their eyes off the mobile and finding it again. Exploration of the scene is directed by the spatial and temporal properties of the object's trajectory, and no longer by the search for a typical posture. At this level, the relations seen in the earlier groups between position of the arms, orientation of the head, and direction of the mobile, have disappeared. The head is an independent segment which can be oriented as a function of the task independently of the rest of the body. We will say that the cephalic segment has become instrumentalized. This is a preliminary and necessary condition for the co-ordination of vision and prehension described by Piaget (1936), whereby the hand in turn becomes a tool (see Fig. 7.6 pp. 196–7).

In the course of new co-ordinations there has taken place in the cognitive domain re-elaboration of the organism and the object, which brings into existence an instrumentalized body, an object which supports co-ordinated properties and a space which connects them both.

From this level on we must speak of purposive action, since there exist representations in which the action and the object are associated. Such a perspective allows us to conceive of this dialogue with the object as an object relation.

From this level on, oculomotor activity is likewise instrumentalized and all the studies in this area show the remarkable stability of the visual system. In effect, the recording of several parameters of ocular motricity reflects above all the functioning of the oculomotor system. The inference to the underlying cognitive activity is far from being direct (Mayer, Bullinger and Kaufmann, 1979). Outside an initial period of elaboration, which comes to an end very early in development, we think that only tasks which call upon the visual system in a new way can teach us about the connections between vision and cognitive processes.

Conclusions
The theoretical perspective we have outlined treats the cognitive elaboration of sensorimotricity (*sensori-motricite*) as a dominant function in the earliest levels of development. It is however, always present at later levels; throughout life there is always the possibility that a task will call upon the organism in a new way. Thus, problems relating to the acquisition of motor skills are not an isolated area, unconnected with the rest of the body of theory.

Taking account of sensorimotor systems as objects of knowledge, allows by extension an analysis of sensorimotor substitutes, whether we think of a tactile retina, an ultrasonic guide, or any other kind of active prosthesis. The mechanisms of appropriation are of the same kind as for sensorimotor loops arising from the organism. The analysis of results with such prostheses should be done both at the level of effects in relation to the surroundings (manual capture of objects, movements of the body itself, avoidance of obstacles, detection of moving objects, etc.) and at the level of effects on the body itself: analysis of postural and motor reorganizations, and of the reco-ordinations to which such aids give rise, (Pailhous and Bullinger, 1977).

The dominant view in the study of sensorimotor development treats the subject as an active pole which attributes properties to objects as a result of its actions. This perspective leaves unclarified the organism as an object of knowledge. We believe it is necessary to consider that between the 'knowing subject' and the world, there always intervene biologically determined sensorimotor systems. Their elaboration is correlative with the elaboration of the objects in the human environment with which these systems interact.

Acknowledgements
The author's research was carried out with the assistance of the FMS (Swiss National Science Foundation, grant no: 1–393–0–76, in the Psychology Laboratories of the University of Geneva, Brown University (Professor L. P. Lipsitt) and the University of Denver (Professor M. M. Haith). The follow-

a

b

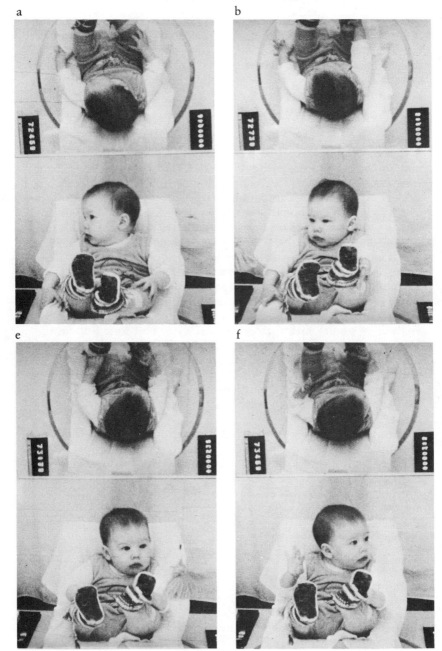

e

f

c

d

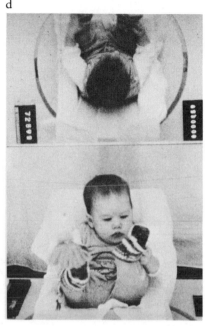

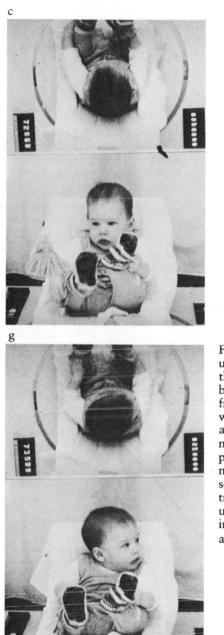

g

Fig. 7.6   These pictures were produced under the same technical conditions as the series presented in Fig. 7.2. Here the baby is aged 103 days. The mobile starts from the right of the baby, who pursues without involvement of the arms in the activity. In picture d, the baby leaves the mobile and looks at his feet. In the next picture (four seconds later) he immediately finds the mobile again. The search is related to properties of the trajectory, and no longer to a global posture. Only the cephalic segment takes part in the activity. The sequence is 7.6 abcdefg.

ing people took part in the research: J. L. Kaufmann, C. Lienert, J. Mayer, P. Rouget, A. Cassella, D. Page, J. Bloch, M. Sakellaropoulo, and K. Purcell. The photographs taken from films were produced by A. Perruchoud.

Note

The term 'reflex scheme' is borrowed from Piaget (1936, p.39), who uses it for other sensorimotor systems; this term clearly indicates the biologically determined nature of the functioning. The functioning is, as it were, constrained; on the strength of this stability it allows an interiorization, and thus in turn a modification, of the functioning itself.

References

Bullinger, A. (1977) 'Orientation de la tête du nouveau-né en présence d'un stimulus visuel', *L'Année Psychologique*, 2, 357–64.

Bullinger, A. (1981a) 'Variation du rythme cardiaque en concomitance avec un spectacle visuel chez le nouveau-né (in preparation).

Bullinger, A. (1981b) 'Activite oculomotrice chez le bébé en présence d'objets stables et en mouvement' (in preparation).

Bower, T. G. R., Broughton, J. M. and Moore, M. K. (1970) 'The coordination of visual and tactual input in infants', *Perception and Psychophysics*, 8 (1), 51–3.

Dagnelie, P. (1969). Théorie et méthodes statistiques: I. J. Ducolot (ed.) SA, Gembloux.

Féré, C. (1887) *Sensation et mouvement*, Alcan, Paris.

Graham, F. K., and Clifton, R. K. (1966) 'Heart-rate change as a component of the orienting response', *Psychological Bulletin*, 65, 305–20

Haith, M. M. (1978), 'Visual competence in early infancy', in Held, R. Leibowitz, H. W. and Teuber, H. L. (ed.) *Handbook of Sensory Physiology, Vol. VIII: Perception*, Springer Verlag, New York.

Mayer, E., Bullinger, A. and Kaufmann, J. L. 'Motricité oculaire et cognition dans une tâche spatiale', *Archives de Psychologie*, XLII, 183, 309–20.

Mendelson, M. J. and Haith, M. M. (1978) 'The relation between audition and vision in the human newborn', *Monographs of the Society for Research in Child Development*, 41 (4, serial No. 167).

Mounoud, P. (1979) 'L'utilisation du milieu et du corps propre par le bébé', in Piaget, J. Mounoud, P. and Bronckart, J.P. (ed.) *Encyclopédie de la Pléiade, La Psychologie*, Gallimard, Paris.

Pailhous, J. and Bullinger, A. (1978) 'The role of interiorisation of material properties of information-acquiring devices in exploratory activities', *Communication and Cognition*, 11 (2), 209–34.

Peiper, A. (1962) 'Réflexes de posture et de mouvement chez le nourrisson', *Revue de Neuropsychiatrie infantile*, 10, 511–30.

Piaget, J. (1936) *La naissance de l'intelligence chez l'enfant*, Delachaux and Niestlé, Paris.
Piaget, J. (1967) *Biologie et connaissance*, Gallimard, Paris.
Piaget, J. (1969) *The Mechanisms of Perception*, Routledge & Kegan Paul, London.
Turro, R. (1920) 'Les origines de la représentation de l'espace tactile', *Journal de Psychologie*, **1920**, 769–86.
Wallon, H. (1925) *L'enfant turbulent*, Alcan, Paris.
Wallon, H. (1947) *Les origines du caractère chez l'enfant*, PUF, Paris.

Translators' note
There are certain words and phrases of theoretical importance in the French original which cannot be translated comfortably into English. We believe this reflects differences in the conceptual heritage of psychologists writing in the two languages. In such cases we give the French in brackets immediately after the first occurrence of a word or phrase, and thereafter, only where it seems necessary for clarity.

The most difficult case is *prise de sens*: we translate it idiomatically as 'making sense', as when we say that some complex situation, not initially understood, eventually comes to 'make sense'. Unfortunately this seems to imply the existence of someone, a subject, to whom 'it makes sense', or who 'makes sense of' it; whereas in Bullinger's text this term, together with the more inclusive 'cognitive elaboration', is meant to refer to the very process by which subjectivity is engendered.

The word *relation*, in addition to its more abstract use sometimes has in French a specifically *social* connotation which has no English equivalent; it appears here as the adjective 'relational' (*relationel*), and means, approximately: pertaining to social relations particularly in their emotional aspect.

Motricite, which we simply transliterate as 'motricity', means *systematic* motor functioning; Thus 'ocular motricity' refers to a system of eye-movements (for example, saccades).

We translate *scheme* as 'scheme' rather than 'schema' following the clarification given by Piaget (1969) in the preface to *The Mechanisms of Perception* 'In our usage, these terms correspond to quite distinct realities, the one operative (a scheme of action in the sense of instrument of generalisation) and the other figurative (a figural or topographical schema)'.

8 Representation and Sensorimotor Development

PIERRE MOUNOUD AND ANNIE VINTER
(TRANSLATED BY RUTH BARNARD)

Statement of the Problem

Some problems raised by the notion of representation.
The notion of representation typically serves as a linking concept
between several disciplines. Touched on by sciences such as
mathematics, logic, and cybernetics, it assumes particular importance in the 'life sciences', like biology and physiology, ethology,
linguistics and psychology. In each of these areas, the notion of
representation is put forward to answer specific problems.

A foremost problem concerns mediation between subject and
object. Some psychological theories depict the subject–object relation as direct and immediate; others suggest intermediaries between
the individual and his environment. A second category of problems
relates to those of meaning, of translation (or coding), and these are
connected. We may ask, for example, if it is necessary to invoke the
notion of representation to account for the specific responses of the
subject (or of any other living thing) towards the particular form of
his environment. In ethology, the works of Tinbergen and Lorenz
show that the animal is born with the translation of certain directly
meaningful external realities already established and these trigger a
more or less stereotyped series of behaviours. In molecular biology,
the existence of information exchanges between molecules based on
the use of a precise genetic code has been demonstrated. The concept
of representation could be introduced here to explain the efficient
and straight forward linkage between a pre-established organization
of activity in the animal or molecule and certain dimensions of the
environment. The problem of constructing symbols and of conserving experiences also raises questions pertinent to representation. In
the latter case, the links between representation and memory are
studied.

Representation and mediation

Representation is a central notion in psychology whether one adopts a synchronic or diachronic[1] point of view towards the subject's conduct.

From the synchronic point of view, the notion of representation raises the problem of mediation in the relations of the subject to his environment. Bower (1976) sees development in terms of the specification and differentiation of representations which are at first abstract and he postulates the constant existence of mediations in the relation between the child and his environment. Some psychoanalytic theories like those of Klein, Heimann, Isaacs and Rivière (1966) conceive the link between the individual and his environment as always mediated by representations. In contrast classical behaviourist theories assert that it is pointless to resort to internal mediation, to representations in the broad sense, in order to understand the activity displayed by the individual in his environment. This principle of economy, frequently erected as a methodological principle, nonetheless reveals the general theoretical assumption that the subject's relation to the external world is direct. The contingencies of reinforcement present in the situation suffice to determine the organism's behaviour. Let us stress that this position is no longer characteristic of behaviourist theories as a whole, which allow—at least in an adult, and perhaps in the child—the necessity of introducing intervening variables between the stimuli provided by the environment (internal or external) and the activity of the subject.

There are, in psychology, theories which deny the existence of pure representation in the sensorimotor period. Wallon, for example, supports a contrast between 'situational intelligence' as in the sensorimotor period and 'discursive intelligence' by basing this contrast on absence of the capacity for representation in the sensorimotor stage, this appearing only towards the age of two years. Similarly, for Piaget, sensorimotor intelligence is characterized by the absence of the capacity for pure representation, which arises around eighteen months with the appearance of the semiotic function and constitutes a new representative form of intelligence. The break introduced between two forms of intelligence leads each of these authors to pose the problem of the relationship between thought and action, a problem discussed elsewhere (Mounoud, 1979; Mounoud and Hauert, 1981).

Representation and meaning

From the diachronic viewpoint, the notion of representation raises the problem of changes in the meaning which the individual attributes to his actions and to objects during development. Genetic psychology furnishes examples of this evolution, which we can illustrate with work carried out by one of us (Mounoud, 1970) on the child's construction and use of tools. One of the experimental situations consisted in extracting a plug surmounted by a ring from inside a narrow-necked bowl, with the aid of various instruments. The manner in which children justify their failures or successes shows how they progressively build different meanings relative to their action and to the tools. Children of four years retain only—as the sole pertinent property of the instrument—its length, to which they attribute the success or failure of the action. Towards five years the grasping aspects of instrument and action become significant. At six years the child exhibits a unified conception of the instrument and its intrinsic properties but does not fully understand the relationships which obtain between its different parts relating to the grasping situation, these relational properties will be elaborated between six and nine years.

The problem of constructing meanings necessarily leads back to that of elaborating representations which allow the translation, by means of a chosen code, of the properties of objects with which the subject is confronted, and of the characteristics of the actions he initiates. By code, we mean any transformation (or system of transformations) which allows the establishment of correspondences between the elements of two wholes. These transformations can vary greatly according to the properties of the elements they concern and the nature of the relations between the two wholes. By coding, we mean a particular use of the code. The activities of coding consist in sampling, analysis, organization of information, or in establishing relationships between coded information inputs. It is quite clear that no system can function without using a code which allows it to establish a correspondence between certain dimensions of the internal or external environments (and their variations), and certain internal states of the system. This type of function is particularly carried out by the sensory receptors, which have long been called analysers, and which function as signalling systems. It is through coding that the child (or the adult) manages to sample information about the world in order to give direction to his action. The coherence, completeness and objectivity of such information are proportionate to the degree to which representations have been established. Numerous questions arise here: how are these representations built up? Does the child elaborate several systems of meanings? If so, do the meaning systems carry out codings of the object which are compatible with each other or mutually exclusive?

We will approach these problems chiefly through the study of the sensorimotor period.

Representation and memory

The notion of representation considered from a diachronic view-point also raises the problem of the relationship between representation, memory and the conservation of experience. By memory, we mean any internal organization of content (or system of internal organizations of content) which act as internal models by reference to which realities acquire meaning for the subject. One might call a particular organization of a certain content a memory trace. It seems very difficult to understand the functioning of the individual without postulating the enduring existence of certain data which are relative both to perceptual input and motor input.

The problem of the relation between representation and memory leads one to ask whether recall of experience and the recognition of objects presuppose the existence of a system of traces, the trace being understood as an internal translation of external reality. Writers like Janet (1928), Bartlett (1932) and de Schonen (1974) have defended the thesis of memory based essentially, if not exclusively, on an activity of reconstruction, thus relegating any system of traces to a subsidiary or even non-existent role. Such a conception is tantamount either to denying the existence of memory as a mechanism for conserving experiences, or to assimilating memory to a system of rules for reconstruction (or coding) devoid of figurative elements. By contrast, a writer like Wulf (1922) reduces memory to a system of traces whose conservation may or may not lead to distortions in recall (Mounoud, 1977).

As far as the sensorimotor period is concerned, Watson (1981) distinguishes three types of memory: regenerative memory, which consists in transforming a current experience so that it shows characteristics in common with a past experience (this is almost an evocation); reactive memory, which allows recognition of a past in a current experience (this is close to a memory of recognition); and associative memory, which allows association between two or more experiences. Each of these is divided into short-. and long-term memory. For Watson, regenerative memory presupposes representation (we might also wonder if the other forms of memory don't also presuppose this).

It is now a matter of enquiring into the relationships which exist between representation, coding and memory. Can the notion of representation be assimilated to that of coding? If this is the case the role of representation would be to provide an interface between the perceptual and motor systems. In this view, memory consists in reconstruction since only the activities of information coding are pertinent to an account of how the interaction between subject and environment proceeds: formed representations of memory traces do not intervene as determinants of the subject's behaviour.

To give to representation the status of an interface between the afferential (perceptual) system, and the efferential (motor) system appears to be an original point of view in psychology, though this position is widely accepted in cybernetics. Most writers who study perception in psychology do not concern themselves with the use or integration of perception in the motor behaviours of a subject, and, conversely, writers concerned with the study of motor behaviour are largely uninterested in perception. Research carried out on prehension in the infant provides good examples of this: errors in grasping are attributed either to a defect in the motor system, or to a perceptual problem, but the coding relations between perceptions and actions are rarely investigated.

Another way of looking at the relations between representation, coding and memory is to enquire whether the systems of traces, or formed representations, must also play a part in coding the environment which the individual carries out in order to sift information from it. In this view, memory is no longer conceived of as essentially a reconstructing activity; the traces themselves, as the coded contents of reality, would also play a part in the memory processes.

Representation and programmes of action
In order not to dissociate the study of perception from that of action one must define processes which interconnect the two levels. Arbib (1980) adopts a theoretical orientation inspired by cybernetics, defining perception as a 'potential action' and he is necessarily led to postulate the existence of mediations, or intermediaries, 'perception of an object (activating appropriate perceptual schemas) involves gaining access to routines for interaction with it (motor schemas) . . . .' The introduction of the notion of routine as a mediator of relations between perception and action, a commonplace idea in cybernetics, is interesting. It is comparable in some ways to a programme of action, defined elsewhere (Mounoud, 1981; Hauert, 1978). As we know, a routine does not operate directly on the information provided by the programmer (data external to the machine); translations of such data in the machine language necessarily intervene. These play the part of representations or codings on which the functioning of the routine is based. In the same way, anticipation and execution of a programme of action depends

on the nature of the representation which the subject possesses of the objects, with which the programme is concerned. Thus programmes of action and representation are related notions.

In a cybernetic machine, any treatment of data is carried out by means of a double coding procedure: the first is related to the language of communication with the outside (the programme), the second consists of the machine language (or internal communication). We shall try to show how this 'double coding' is equally appropriate from the psychological viewpoint, and how it permits us to raise the problem of differentiation between the subject and the environment in the sensorimotor period which interests us here.

The aim of this chapter is on the one hand to show the pertinence of the notion of representation to understanding sensorimotor development; and on the other, to present a model for the development of representation. The first of these objectives requires a discussion of Piaget's theory of representation and of his concept of the relation between reference and referent. We will show how Piaget had difficulty with the problem of representation largely because he refused to consider the existence of intermediaries in the relations which unite the baby to the environment. This will be discussed in the next part of the chapter, then having considered Piaget's position from a theoretical point of view, we will see in the third section how the analysis of behaviours displayed from birth also brings some fundamental empirical data to our conception of the problem. Finally, in the fourth section, we will show how the development of representation takes place during the sensorimotor period.

Some Aspects of the Piagetian Concept of Representation

The notion of representation does not appear central to Piaget's work; on the contrary, Piaget has always tried to have little recourse to it, in order to concentrate on the transformations or operations which the subject performs on reality. Paradoxically, it is nonetheless one of the first concepts, along with those of assimilation, accommodation and co-ordination (Piaget, 1936, 1937, 1946) which he elaborated theoretically.

In *La naissance de L'intelligence chez l'enfant (The Origins of Intelligence in Children)* (1936) and *La construction du réel chez l'enfant (The Construction of Reality in the Child)* (1937), Piaget tried to show how the child manages, through his actions, to be placed in an organized world, where different spatial, causal and temporal relationships obtain between different objects. Sensorimotor constructions lead to establishment of invariants such as the permanence of the object and the 'group' structure of movements.

The former develops through six stages, the last being characterized by the child's ability to master an object's unseen movements.

Piaget, who, for the first five stages, had kept the notion of representation out of his explanatory theory, felt it necessary to introduce this idea to account for the new achievement of following the movements of an object which are not subject to direct perception. The infant must have constructed a mental representation to account for the permanence of the invisibly moving object. Thus, only in retrospect did Piaget trace the possible origin of representation in the development of imitation.

Differentiated signifiers

Piaget distinguishes between representation in the broad sense, assimilated to thought, and representation in the restricted sense, conceived of as 'the symbolic evocation of absent realities'.

In the restricted sense, representation of past events or absent objects is assured by the mental image, the symbol or the verbal sign. These devices of notation are the instruments of a memory of evocation, which appears around eighteen months according to Piaget. The substitutes or representatives have the status of signifiers.[2] The contents or structural forms which give them meanings have the status of signified.[3]

Piaget called the signifiers (with which it will be appropriate to integrate perceptual signs) 'figurative instruments', incumbent on knowledge of states-of-affairs. That is to say they carry out translations of certain dimensions of reality. Figurative instruments depend strictly upon operative instruments (schemes, operations . . .) which in turn deal with transformations and account precisely for the change from one state to another. They permit relationships to be established both between objects and their properties and between positions of the body and those of its parts.

Piaget has tried to trace the origin of these differentiated signifiers in the development of imitation. The status he accords to imitation in relation to representation always remains ambiguous as Bronckart and Ventouras-Spycher (1979) note: sometimes, imitation 'marks the junction of the sensorimotor and the representative' (Piaget, 1946) and 'is one of the possible terms between sensorimotor behaviours and representative behaviours' (*Ibid.*), at other times 'imitative accommodation accounts for the formation of signifiers necessary to representative activity' (*Ibid.*) Imitation develops in parallel with sensorimotor behaviours: the linked notions of co-ordination between schemes and of differentiation between assimilation and accommodation are invoked to explain the genesis of imitation. Deferred imitation will be considered as a valid indicator for judging the internalization of accommodation movements and thence the building of an internal image. If the development of imitation is described in relation to sensorimotor schematization, representation is conceived as a sort of 'picture-memory' which seems to represent states of reality.

It is not satisfactory to resort to imitation as a possible origin of the processes which lead to representation. In the first place, we will see that the infant is capable of imitation at a very early stage. So how can it be argued that imitation is constitutive of representation, although, as we shall stress, early imitation does not have the same status as later imitations? We take the opposite point of view from Piaget, that the presence of representation must necessary precede imitation: how could one otherwise explain the isomorphism which the subject introduces between the behaviour of the model and his own? Though we do not think it to be through imitation that the child constructs his representative ability seen as a coding process, we nonetheless believe that imitation of the self or others plays an important part insofar as the construction and organization of the content of representations is concerned.

Perceptual indices
Representation in the broad sense can be assimilated to thought, whose essential function, for Piaget, concerns knowledge of reality, that is to say, the attribution of meanings. During the sensorimotor stage, meanings are constructed through perception and action of the subject; they are taken from sensorimotor schematism. For Piaget, the signifiers of the sensorimotor stage are essentially perceptual indices. 'We call *index* any sensory impression or directly perceived quality whose meaning [the referent] is a sensorimotor scheme or object' (Piaget, 1936).

Indices provide knowledge of the object's qualities, that is to say of its particular properties, but in a direct manner, whilst this knowledge, obtained by means of differentiated signifiers, is mediated by representations. Indices show general characteristics of being undifferentiated from the signified, that is to say of constituting an aspect of the object or scheme and of only being actualizable in the presence of the object or the action.

It does not seem acceptable to us to argue that these indices form part of the object; they are translations which are necessarily internal to the subject, otherwise there would be no point in calling them signifiers. As we shall see, this position partly arises from the confusion Piaget introduces into the definition of the 'signified'; moreover it contradicts his thesis on the 'reading' of experience.[4] The indices' second characteristic, to be triggered only in the presence of the object or through the course of action, means that one acknowledges the existence only of a recognition memory in the sensorimotor period, memory of evocation appearing with the semiotic function. We mentioned in the introduction that Watson distinguished three types of sensorimotor memory: reactive, regenerative and associative memory. Regenerative memory is defined by the child's ability to modify a current experience in such a way that it presents characteristics in common or even identical with a past experience. As Watson stresses, this closely resembles a memory of evocation (and not of *'ressurgescence'* as Piaget (1981), would like to believe, the more so as we have difficulty in understanding the meaning of this term!). He interprets the vocal imitations of the infant of five to eight months in this way and the eight-month-old child's searching to find an object which has momentarily disappeared from his field of vision. There would thus exist, well before the age of eighteen months, facts which provide evidence for a memory of evocation. The characteristics of perceptual indices which Piaget lists (and whose pertinence we debate), together permit him to deny the existence of representation in the strict sense during the sensorimotor period, and to describe the infant as having a direct relation to his environment.

To understand the way in which Piaget manages to have little recourse to representation in the sensorimotor stage, it is necessary to remember one of his fundamental postulates. This is that the function of a scheme of action is to tend to incorporate the whole of reality. The baby tries to exercize action schemes on the whole collection of objects furnished by the environment. The properties of objects encountered will bring about modifications in the form of the infant's actions. Reciprocally, these differentiated forms of actions will reveal the different properties of objects. The same object will be able to give rise to different perceptual indices as a result of its assimilation to different motor schemes. By the reciprocal coordination of the schemes, these different indices of the same object will refer one to the other thanks to the infant's inferential activities. Thus the object acquires a more and more autonomous existence from the subject's point of view and parts of the object become sufficient to trigger a behaviour (or a scheme of assimilation). For some time the object's meaning remains dependent on the application of the assimilation scheme to that object: from a part, the infant does not reconstitute the whole. When from an index (or from several indices), the child reconstitutes the whole object, a first form of object permanence will appear (Piaget's stage four). A first form of permanence, but still lacking representation because the object seems to lose its existence when it is no longer directly visible. Finally, when the presence of indices is no longer necessary for the child to believe in the object's existence, Piaget will say that the child has constructed a representation of the object.

We, however, believe it is impossible to have scant recourse to the notion of representation in explaining sensorimotor development. For an index to trigger an assimilation scheme, it seems necessary that that index be attached to a particular meaning, and the representations which are at the infant's disposal provide this meaning.

The signified
The most debatable aspect of the Piagetian concept of representation lies in his manner of defining the signified. The signified may indicate the scheme of action itself, an event, an object (present or absent) or a concept. To allow that the signified can be defined equally by the object as by the scheme or by the concept raises very different epistemological options whose confusion shows the difficulty of transposing these linguistic ideas to the field of psychology.

We can try to illustrate with examples that show it is impossible to define the signified by the object. How does one manage to say 'this is a table' when we see a table? The signifier corresponds to an internal translation of this object-table. If we say that the signified is the table itself, this object-table possesses all the meanings we know about it (for example, it has weight, a colour, it serves different uses, we can work or eat at the table). Thus, all these meanings belong to the table and are not dependent on a subject who uses or sees the table.

Let us take another example, of a person who interprets a footprint in the snow as an indication of an individual's passage. How does the person manage to elaborate this meaning? The signifier is elaborated from the indentation in the snow, it corresponds to an internal translation of this object-footprint. All signifiers result from the subject's internal elaborations but some can be externalized or materialized (for example, drawings, words) which confers a special status on them. To see an individual as an object possibly signified by the indentation in the snow is to recognize that the signified object possesses the particular property of leaving footprints. Again the object signified would exist independently of any subject who perceived or acted upon it.

Now we all know that this realist, materialist position is contrary to Piaget's fundamental epistemological stance. A possible alternative to this first solution is to assert the internal nature of the signified and thus assimilate it to systems of relations or processing of reality. Piaget adopts this viewpoint when he accords to the scheme or the concept the status of signified, conceived as processing instruments, insofar as they organize themselves in whole structures. Piaget's thinking still seems slightly uncertain for he defined the scheme 'as a completed whole of perceptions and movements' (Piaget, 1936), that is to say as an instrument of exchange or relation between the subject and the environment and no longer as a structure of the subject's action defined independently of the contents on which the action bears. Nonetheless it cannot be denied that the signified, from this viewpoint, is confused with [the] cognitive structures or processing instruments at the subject's disposal. This option, which considers that the object has no existence of its own outside the system of structuring that the subject applied to it, belongs to an idealist thesis which has also been criticized, though perhaps less strongly, by Piaget. When Piaget defines the signified in this way, he tends to confuse the instrument of representation itself with the result of applying this instrument to a given reality. In other words, he does not distinguish the figurative instruments themselves from the results of their application in the form of particular representation. Of the signified, he only retains a structure whose function is to allow the attribution of meaning.

These notions of signifier/signified were proposed by de Saussure (1916) who attempted to establish a definition of the verbal sign. When Piaget took up these notions, he simplified them considerably (Bronckart and Ventouras-Spycher, 1979). According to de Saussure, two types of material reality have to be processed by the subject to establish a verbal sign: on the one hand, an acoustic substance; on the other, a material substance which corresponds to the content to be expressed. These two realities give rise to two images, the auditory image and the concept, which arise from individual constructions; they are not to be confused with the signifier/signified pair. Language constitutes the signifier and signified by establishing a system of relationships and differences between signifiers on the one hand and signified on the other. For de Saussure, signifiers and signified are reducible to forms constructed on the basis of relationships and of differences established between themselves.

Though for de Saussure as for Piaget, the signifier is assimilated to a form, Piaget does not distinguish levels equivalent to those of substances (acoustic or material), images (the acoustic image or concept) and meanings (signifier and signified). Piaget does not declare himself on the link between the signified and the substances or contents, except when, in a far too realist manner, he defines the signified as the object itself, which as we have just seen is incompatible with his epistemological position. On the other hand, Piaget introduces these two levels of form and content into the signifier/signified pair itself: in some way the signifier becomes a substance with regard to the signified, a conception which differs radically from de Saussure's. However, when Piaget studies signifiers as mental images, he doesn't treat them at all as organizations of contents, but once again as figurative instruments. Now, we think it is particularly important to link these notions with the contents of reality with which individuals are presented. Piaget has studied the development of representation from the angle of the construction of a code, but he has never concerned himself with the representations built up from applying this code to various realities.

One of the writers of this paper has proposed defining signifiers by means of the sensory messages and different levels of elaboration which they can reach, and signified by the internal organizations capable of interpreting them (Mounoud, 1976). Defined like this, it is clear that signifiers and signified are two inseparable aspects of any representation. In the fourth part of this chapter we shall propose a model for the development of representation without further attention to this distinction between signifiers and signified, which in many ways is arbitrary. We shall nonetheless show how the three levels distinguished by de Saussure in the constitution of a verbal sign can be related to the stages in the construction of a representation.

The Initial Organisation of the Infant's Behaviour

Before setting out in detail our own model of the construction of representation, we intend to describe and anlyse two types of activity shown by the baby very early in life; namely behaviours that illustrate the capacity for auditory–visual co-ordination and precocious imitation.

Psychology, in recent years, has been marked by a considerable change in position on the infant. Certain empirical facts clearly point to a contradiction in the conception, at one time generally widespread, of an immature infant without any real capacity to organize his relations with his environment. Most psychologists now regard the neonate as possessing complex abilities for handling information. These abilities should not be compared with those of the adult in terms of greater or lesser complexity. The neonate, just like the adult, carries out performances that presuppose extremely complex and sophisticated handling of a vast amount of data.

The abilities that the neonate exhibits are quite varied: ability to discriminate visually (Fantz, 1964; Bower, 1974; Carpenter 1973) olfactory and taste discrimination (Lipsitt, Engen and Kagan 1963), and auditory discrimination (Wertheimer, 1961; Eimas, 1975; Hammond, 1970). The ability to co-ordinate seems even more astonishing: co-ordination of vision and reaching (Bower, Broughton and Moore, 1970a), audio-visual co-ordination (Aronson and Rosenbloom, 1971; MacGurk and Lewis, 1974), audiomotor system co-ordination (Wertheimer, 1961; Butterworth and Castillo, 1976; Alegria and Noirot, 1978) and visuo-motor co-ordination, as research on early imitation shows.

We shall concentrate particularly on two types of co-ordination that still give rise to certain controversies: audio-visual co-ordination and early imitation. At the outset, we should like to stress the scant regard generally paid by writers to the ages of the infants they are studying. It is not unusual to find that results obtained from infants a few days old are directly compared with those obtained from infants aged two to three months. Such an attitude denotes a failure, that we strongly criticize, to take into account developmental hypotheses. We consider that only a developmental model permits understanding of some apparent contradictions thrown up by experimental research.

The initial state of audio-visual co-ordination
Research on the problem of audio-visual co-ordination raises three main types of question about our knowledge of the sensorimotor period: do there exist, from birth, initial co-ordination among sensory systems and between sensory systems and motor systems. If they exist, do these co-ordinations imply a plurimodal representation of the object? And finally, how do we reconcile the existence of early representations with the idea that the neonate is subjectively undifferentiated from its environment?

Wertheimer (1961) has shown that a few minutes after birth a neonate produces a preponderance of ipsilateral eye movements when a sound arises in its environment. He interprets this data in terms of an initial co-ordination between auditory and visuo-motor space in the neonate, which he believes arises from a reflex function. Replication of this research has revealed more precisely the conditions under which these co-ordinations can be demonstrated (Turkewitz, Birch, Moreau, Levy and Cornwell, 1966).

Butterworth and Castillo (1976) have recorded spatially co-ordinated eye movements in infants a few days old in response to a tone which followed a series of 'clicks'. Sounds were presented at random to left and right of the subject or in blocks of trials to the left or right. When the sounds had a fixed origin, they noted eye movements contralateral to the direction of the sound. They therefore infer the presence of an innate audio-visual co-ordination, but as Butterworth (1981) later stressed, this hypothesis is not sufficient to account for the development of subsequent forms of co-ordination. Following Jones and Kabanoff (1975), he suggests that the eye movements might coincide with the stabilization of an auditory memory relating to the position of the sound.

The research of Alegria and Noirot (1978) is concerned with infants of six days old. From three loudspeakers situated respectively opposite, on the left, and on the right of the infant, the word 'baby' was emitted once every two seconds for a total of twenty trials. The infants in the experimental group turned their heads in the direction of the loudspeaker, with their eyes open, often vocalizing, much more frequently than the infants in the control group. The findings of Alegria and Noirot permit two conclusions: on the one hand they affirm the ability of the neonate to refer an auditory input to a spatially oriented motor programme, on the other this may imply an ability to locate a sound in space.

In fact, neither Wertheimer (1961) nor Butterworth and Castillo (1976) arrive at such a conclusion, which poses problems about the abilities of the neonate. The possibility of locating a sound in space necessarily implies the definition of two spaces in relation to each other, the space occupied by the subject's body and the space from which the sound originates. What is more, the latter is presumed to be organized according to a geometry calculable by the subject, so that the infant manages to determine the orientation of his head with respect to the spatial co-ordinates of the point from which the sound issues.

Butterworth adopts a position opposed to the one developed by Alegria and Noirot when he doubts that neonates 'expect that a sight be accompanied by a sound', even if spatially organized connections between the oculomotor system and the auditory system exist. One would have to show that the neonate reacted with surprise towards unexpected or surprising placings of the sound. Here we can refer to research by Aronson and Rosenbloom (1971), McGurk and Lewis (1974), and Lewis and Hurowitz (1977) although this evidence must be treated carefully, since it was undertaken with infants older than those already discussed.

Aronson and Rosenbloom (1971) tested seven infants aged between thirty and fifty-five days in two types of situation: a normal one where the mother's voice was spatially congruent with her face, and an audio-visually discordant one where this spatial congruence did not exist. Infants of thirty days appear perturbed by the audio-visual discordance; they react to it by increasing the frequency of tongue protrusions and mouth movements. According to Aronson and Rosenbloom these reactions show the infant's ability to perceive stimuli across several modalities in combination.

McGurk and Lewis (1974) tried to replicate this research, with some methodological controls (in particular the order of presentation of the tasks and subject sampling). They show that at four and seven months, the number of head movements in the direction of the sound increases significantly in the discordant situation, a tendency which also appears in infants aged one month. The writers consider that 'these data, therefore, afford no support for the hypothesis that the very young human infant lives in a perceptually unified audio-visual world', given that no reaction of surprise or distress arises during the experiment. They conclude, however, that at these ages the ability to locate a sound is relatively efficient. Such conclusions seem contradictory to us; as we have already stressed, locating a sound in space necessarily implies a pluralist representation of the sound's source.

Lewis and Hurowitz (1978) suggest another interpretation of head movements shown by infants in situations characterized by audio-visual spatial dissociation: these could be exploratory reactions provoked by a situation which 'violates' the 'integrated audio-visual person schema', this being an intersensory organization already present at birth. In their study infants aged between one and four months were tested. The frequency of lateral head movements increased significantly in situations where the voice was displaced from the face, and where the voice and face were not matched (for example, the mother's face with a stranger's voice). The authors believe the results support their hypothesis, since the greatest frequency of head movements was found in discordant situations. However, their data are difficult to interpret because, firstly, age groups are not separated and secondly, no distinction is drawn between conditions with the mother or with a stranger, nor between control conditions.

Even if they seem contradictory in some respects, taken as a whole, the above mentioned pieces of research help to show the existence of initial sensorimotor co-ordinations (co-ordination of the auditory and motor systems). The demonstration of these initial co-ordinations raises questions concerning the Piagetian conception of the infant's initial state. For Piaget, the sensory and motor systems would initially define heterogeneous or non-co-ordinated spaces, functioning in isolation. The infant's perceptions would thus consist of different 'perceptual tableaux without substantial substratum' (Piaget, 1947) which would trigger each other in the course of the infant's activity. The spaces would only come to co-ordinate with each other subsequently, depending on the construction of mobile and differentiated sensorimotor schemes. The existence of early co-ordinations, to which *we* accord the status of adaptive behaviour showing a certain level of elaboration of reality, gives by contrast an important empirical basis to the conception of a neonate characterised by a complex, co-ordinated sensorimotor organization.

Aronson and Rosenbloom's experiment, and the other experiments mentioned, could be interpreted in terms of the existence of very early audio-visual intersensory co-ordinations, as if hearing a sound implied the expectation of seeing an object. The research of Bower, Broughton and Moore, (1970a) on reaching for virtual objects by neonates could, in the same way, lend support to the presence of an intersensory sight–touch co-ordination. As far as the infant is concerned it is a matter of asking whether this bimodal specification belongs to an external object or whether it is determined by the functioning of the infant's sensory systems. In the first case the infant will be said to possess perceptual representations of the external objects from which he would then be partially differentiated. The experiments mentioned could thus be interpreted as evidence for perceptual anticipation: the detection of an auditory input would be sufficient for the infant to anticipate the presence of an object in his vicinity. With such a conception it becomes difficult, not to say impossible, to maintain simultaneously the idea of an initial unitary framework. Butterworth on the other hand opts for the second alternative. According to him, the different pieces of research prove the existence:

of an innate functional relationship between audition and vision that provides a unitary spatial framework in relation to which patterned information can be detected [but] this is not the same as an ability to anticipate visual consequences on auditory stimulation. (1981 p.54).

Even though we also do not think that the neonate possesses objectified perceptual representations of his universe, we would nonetheless like to modify Butterworth's point of view. We propose to describe the infant's aforementioned performances in terms of sensory anticipation. It is then possible to conceive of these performances as illustrating 'an ability to anticipate visual consequences on auditory stimulation'. This anticipation is determined and controlled by intersensory motor co-ordinations and not at all, as will subsequently be the case, by an ability in the infant to make inferences. Inference necessarily presupposes a distinction between premise and conclusion, which is translated, in our example of audio-visual co-ordinations, by a subject–object differentiation. On the contrary, a visual anticipation (an expectancy of the visual system) may exist without the subject having in any way constructed a representation of the object as an object to be seen. One might nevertheless say that the organism 'carries out' an inference of this nature. Such a position leads us naturally to modify the notion of undifferentiation: one can only assert the existence of an initially undifferentiated state relative to the perceptual elaborations of reality that the infant subsequently carries out. It will also be said that the child of about two years lives simultaneously in a dualist position as regards his ability for perceptuo-motor experience of reality and in an adualist position as regards his new abilities (of a conceptual nature) for interaction with his environment. From our point of view, the notion of adualism is not pertinent when one considers the neonate in terms of its initial abilities for handling information, which we assume to be based on intersensorimotor co-ordinations. By contrast, it becomes pertinent as soon as the infant's new coding abilities, of a perceptuomotor nature, appear.

Early Imitation
The theoretical propositions on which we have based our review of research on auditory–visual co-ordination suggests the existence of distinct levels of translation of reality by the new-born and by the baby of several months. At birth the baby would possess representations of a different kind than those constructed by the baby several months old. We will qualify the first group as 'sensory' and the second as 'perceptual' representations.

We must now ask about the nature of these initial representations. In particular, if representations of external objects exist, does it mean that the infant also possesses representations of his own body? Do such initial representations give rise to reconstructions? Research work on early imitation provides a substantial empirical basis for enquiring into the existence of initial representations.

Recently an important controversy has developed about the presence of imitative abilities in the neonate. Some writers (Maratos, 1973; Meltzoff, 1976; Meltzoff and Moore, 1977; Dunkeld, 1979), have argued in favour of the existence of imitation other writers (Lewis and Hurowitz' 1977; Hayes and Watson, 1979; Jacobson and Kagan, 1979) attempt to show that the phenomena observed can be explained by experimental artifacts of various kinds.

We shall try to centre this review around the following problems. Does the presence of early imitation necessarily imply representation of the self's body and that of others? More generally, does representation precede imitation? We have already seen which solution calls Piagetian theory into question. How do we account for these imitations if they exist? Do they spring from a reflex function or from an innate schema of recognition of the 'fixed action pattern' type, do they result from a social apprenticeship or from contingent reinforcements, or do they depend upon the child's cognitive development? Finally, we will have to enquire into the status of early imitation in the development of the child's imitative abilities and into the links between early and subsequent imitation.

Maratos (1973) carried out a longitudinal study of twelve infants aged one to six months, tested every fifteen days and centred her research around two hypotheses. The first concerns the genesis of imitative abilities. Maratos subscribes to the developmental model elaborated by Mounoud (1970, 1976) that postulates the existence of initial sensorimotor co-ordinations that are subsequently dissociated and reconstructed. In this view the infant of a few weeks would show imitative abilities, which would then temporarily disappear whilst the baby was developing. The second hypothesis concerns the status of the models the infant can imitate. According to Maratos, the only models imitated by the very young infant involve parts of the body with which he would have experimented during the intra-uterine and perinatal periods. She presented infants three types of model: visual, kinesthetic and auditory. At one month the only models imitated are tongue protrusions and mouth movements (visual models), and these imitations then disappear. In a general sense Maratos' hypotheses are confirmed by these results.

Meltzoff (1981, this volume Ch4) describes several experiments on early imitation, trying to introduce the necessary methodological controls (particularly regarding control of the 'arousal effect' and coding of the infant's behaviours). He studied immediate and deferred imitation (with or without a lapse of time between presentation of the model and occurrence of the response) and carried out an analysis which allowed differentiation between qualitatively distinct degrees of imitation. Models included tongue and lip protrusion, opening the mouth, and sequential movements of the fingers. Between two and three weeks the infants showed themselves capable of imitation, even when imitation was deferred. Meltzoff and Moore (1977) conclude 'infants have the ability to act on the basis of a centrally stored internal 'model' or representation of a perceptually absent gesture to-be-imitated'. What we find interesting in this conclusion is that it associates the presence of representations with that of a memory trace.

Each of Dunkeld's (1979) pieces of research aims to test one of Piaget's (1946) hypotheses on the age-level at which various imitative abilities appear. It is not easy to compare Dunkeld's data with those already mentioned, because she groups infants of quite different ages (three and thirteen weeks for example). She presented a large variety of models and used criteria for judging imitative behaviour similar to Meltzoff and Moore's and she also demonstrated that three-week-old infants imitate tongue protrusions, though these behaviours subsequently undergo a regression (around eight to eleven weeks). From six to seven weeks, the infant imitates mouth opening movements (three weeks in Meltzoff), but imitation of finger movements is not apparent. Dunkeld discusses her data (regarding imitating and smiling) in relation to alternative theories (Piaget, Watson, Trevarthen, Bower) and offers the following explanation: 'Early imitation may be an epiphenomenon of social intercourse, but it may develop into a real vehicle of learning, through social reinforcement'. For Dunkeld therefore, the development of imitation would have no relationship with that of representation.

The controversy that has recently surrounded the question of early imitation places the debate essentially on a methodological level. Lewis (1979), Lewis and Hurowitz (1977) and Hayes and Watson (1979), have attempted to show that Meltzoff's methodological controls are inadequate. Lewis (1979) attempts to define the act of imitation and to specify the parameters pertinent to it (the degree of similarity of actions between the model and the subject, the temporal parameters, the nature of the actions to be imitated . . .). He insists, as do others, on the necessity for controls over arousal and the baseline response level. Lewis' and Hurowitz, and (1977) experiment, undertaken with infants aged one, three and six months, respected these controls. Whatever the age of the infants, they found that tongue-protrusion occurred whether the model was a tongue-protrusion or a movement of the fingers, or even some other model. It is surprising that these authors found no evidence for imitation between one and six months. This contradicts many other studies (including Piaget's own) and cannot be due to anything other than faults in experimental procedure.

The criticism of Meltzoff' and Moore's research put forward by Hayes and Watson (1979) concerns the use of the pacifier control in deferred imitation (see Meltzoff, 1981, this volume page 96). According to these writers, imitations were a 'function of the experimenter's unintentional monitoring of the infant's mouthing activities on a pacifier immediately before the response period, rather than of the model presented to the infant'. That is, Meltzoff was said to have presented the 'tongue protrusion' model immediately after he had unconsciously observed the infant make mouthing movements.

They suggested two situations in which tongue protrusions could be experimental artifacts. In the first, the experimenter withdraws the pacifiier from the infant's mouth when the infant sucks on it with his tongue; in the second the experimenter takes out the pacifiier when the infant shows no sucking or pushing activity. Naturally the number of tongue protrusions is shown to be significantly higher in the first situation than in the second. It must be stressed that this criticism, if it is acceptable, is only applicable to part of Meltzoff's researches and is not applicable to those of Maratos and Dunkeld. The interpretation of early imitation proposed by Watson (1966) is formulated in terms of contingent reinforcement. The child may detect a contingency between his action and the appreciative reinforcement behaviours of the mother (or of the experimenter).

Jacobson and Kagan's (1979) criticisms of Meltzoff' and Moore's work are more theoretical. They show that tongue protrusion responses can also be released by inanimate stimuli (a pen, a golf ball); they are not specific, selective imitations of the model. We refer the reader to the article by Meltzoff and Moore (1979) for their reply to these criticisms.

At first sight, demonstrations like these might cast doubt upon the scientific value of research showing neonatal imitation. But however convinced we are of the pertinence of arousal and baseline controls, the last two criticisms mentioned reveal a vital flaw. Unlike Maratos, Meltzoff or Dunkeld, these researchers seem to have carried out no qualitative analysis of responses. It seems evident to us that a tongue-protrusion imitation is qualitatively different from a spontaneous protrusion and the confusion of these two categories of response would be enough to explain the results of Hurowitz and Lewis, and of Hayes and Watson. In spite of these controversies, we think that research shows with consistency, the existence of early imitation, particularly with respect to the face. Only Meltzoff seems to have put forward evidence for imitation of finger movements.

These early imitations give rise to a double paradox. The first concerns the differentiated aspect of the infant's behaviours: how does one explain the infant's ability to differentiate tongue-protrusions from, for example, mouth-opening movements, when at the same time his imitative abilities seem limited to a few models? But the existence of this paradox is not quite proven. None of the research mentioned has really investigated the neonate's imitative ability with parts of the body like the hands, the arms or the legs. In any case, several hypotheses could be advanced to explain the limitations discovered in the infant's imitative abilities. For example, different speeds of maturation of proximal and distal parts of the body could be responsible. Thus the neuron circuits leading to the proximal parts (like the mouth) could be mobilized more rapidly than those which end in the distal parts (such as the arms or legs). A second hypothesis concerns intrauterine experience (see, for example, Maratos). The infant may only be performing movements analogous to those already excercised so that various mouth movements could effectively give rise to more intense responses than those of the arms or hands.

The second paradox raises more interesting issues. It arises from putting together data on imitation with research on the discrimination of facial expressions. Gibson (1969) showed that the ability to discriminate facial expressions is limited in the infant and Spitz' (1952) findings also have a bearing upon this question. The mouth is only distinguished as a feature of the face quite late, around four to five months yet the infant appears able to discriminate at three weeks between a tongue protrusion and an opening of the mouth. We believe that to resolve this paradox, reference must be made to different, previously ordered levels of coding of reality. The three-week-old infant carries out a coding procedure of a qualitatively different type from that carried out by the infant of several months. We have called the first sensory and the second perceptual coding.

Various other attempts have been made to explain early imitation. Watson (1966), for example, introduces the notion of contingent reinforcement but we do not believe this can account for the isomorphism between the model's behaviours and those of the subject. How, by detecting a contingency, does the infant manage to match his movements to those of the model? What is more this cannot explain the decrease in imitative abilities observed by Maratos or Dunkeld.

Eiblesteldt (1979) proposes that imitation could be considered a fixed action pattern. The model would trigger a more or less stereotyped response in the infant. Several facts seem to us to run counter to this explanation including the temporary disappearance of certain imitation behaviours after birth (see also Meltzoff 1981 this volume Ch4).

Dunkeld rejects the notion of a link between the development of imitation and representation. If they evolve in parallel how does one explain why the child first imitates the movements of non-visible parts of the body (tongue-protrusions) and then the movements of visible parts (hands), when, in the Piagetian theory, the 'representation' of visible parts of the body precedes that of non-visible parts? We feel that this question is wrongly formulated; it takes no account of different levels of understanding reality; early imitations are not directly comparable with later imitations. Piaget described the development of imitation during the sensorimotor period and omitted early imitations, just as in his description of the development of sensorimotor co-ordinations, he neglected initial co-ordinations.

We are more inclined towards the proposition of Trevarthen, Hubley and Sheeran (1975) or Meltzoff (1976) according to which the neonate would possess an innate body schema which would authorize matchings between parts of his own body and corresponding parts of others' bodies. Only the presence of a representation of the body of the self, which we have termed sensory, can explain early imitation. Thus we believe the presence of representation to be necessary in order for the child to be able to imitate, for otherwise it is impossible to account for the isomorphism which the subject introduces between his own movements and those of the model.

Imitation at birth and later imitation translates different levels of understanding reality. We therefore refuse to consider early imitation as pseudo-imitation (Piaget) or as pre-behaviours, unrelated to later behaviours. The link between these two types of imitation poses the problem of the relation between different levels of representation: are we to believe, for example, that perceptuomotor representations are built up from sensorimotor representations? Would there be an integration of the lower-level coding in the higher or a control of the first by the second? Or would the different types of coding which the child possesses co-exist with no relation to each other? Hauert (1978), discussing the relationship between conceptual and perceptual representation (or coding) defends the hypothesis that perceptual representations would be progressively modified by conceptual representations whilst the latter were being built up; however, transformed perceptual representations can still be evoked as such, under certain conditions.

Towards a Model of the Development of Representation
The study of auditory-visual co-ordination and early imitation have shown (in our view), the necessity of the notion of representation to explain the sensorimotor period. Each of these behaviours undergoes a momentary disappearance to reappear later, around three to four months in the case of audio-visual co-ordination, and eight to nine

months for the imitation of tongue-protrusions. We have proposed that by introducing different levels of coding of reality (internal or external), these two sets of co-ordinations (the first present at birth, the second appearing later) can be accounted for. It is now a question of deciding on the later genesis of these initial intersensorimotor co-ordinations, that is to say on the development of representations established by the subject. The problem of the origin of representations can only be suitably posed within a global conception of behaviour considered as transactions between an organism and its surroundings. From this viewpoint, the development of grasping visually perceived objects is one of the best ways of illustrating stages in the construction of new representations.

General considerations
The notion of representation has strict links with the notions of code and memory for which we gave very general definitions in the introduction. It can be considered from its two aspects. First, representation as internal organization of contents, or traces, or memory. Whether these are formed or in process of formation, they bring about mediations or interfaces between the subject's perceptions and actions. Second representation as a coding process, a translation operating between internal realities or between internal and external realities, by means of coding instruments. This latter approach enables full consideration to be taken of the transactions which occur between the subject and environment. It seems clear that any separation of these two aspects of representation must be partially arbitrary. A memory carries out a certain codification of experience; it is therefore not independent of the codes at the subject's disposal. On the contrary, it seems important to us to distinguish carefully between instruments of representation (or coding) and representations which are formed or in process of construction and which result from applying these instruments to various realities. As we have already seen, Piaget is only interested in the *development* of instruments of representation (figurative instruments) without distinguishing the development (if it does occur) from the results of applying these instruments. For our part, we postulate the pre-formation of coding instruments: at birth, around eighteen months, and towards nine to ten years the child acquires new coding abilities in a programmed manner. The results of applying these new abilities, or representations, gives rise to new development. Representations are constructed through transactions which take place between the subject and his environment.

The distinction established between the two aspects of representation acquires particular importance when the notion of representation is related to that of programmes of action. Whilst he is developing, the child constructs different programmes of action which govern the modalities of his transactions with the environment. We consider the programming of a behaviour to be directly related to the degree of elaboration of the properties of both organism and environment. Thus, one can study how the infant manages to adapt his actions to such physical properties of the object as for example its weight (Mounoud, 1973). The programme will be satisfactory when the infant has built up complete representations of the object concerned. The activity of coding, or sampling information, predominates the more these representations (as organizations of content) are still partial or incomplete. Conversely, it is reduced to an absolute minimum when complete, global representations are available.

In such a view, representations cannot be understood as static configurations of reality states. In fact, apart from their close connections with programmes of action, it would be more correct to talk of the building of a perceptuo-motor organization (integrating representations and programmes of action) during the sensorimotor period from an initial sensorimotor organization, than of the development of perceptual representations from initial sensory representations.

Representations are built up within programmes of action (or strategies). Already formed representations, which play a support role from which new meanings can be elaborated, intervene in the building up of new representations. The nature of the translations or codings of his environment or of his own body which the infant carries out, must also be taken into consideration when characterizing the construction of representations. We distinguish four types of code: sensory, perceptual, conceptual, and semiotic code; which correspond to four successive levels in this construction:

(i)   the sensory level, correlated with the perinatal period;
(ii)   the perceptual level, reached around eighteen months;
(iii) the conceptual level; which gives rise to
(iv)   the semiotic level around nine to ten years.

During development the child reorganizes his transactions with the surrounding world several times; these upheavals mark phases or stages of development, just as they take place within a single stage. Each of these stages begins with a homogeneous organization of behaviours which contains within it the programme for subsequent reorganizations (Mounoud, 1976).

Having made these general points, we can attempt to trace the manner in which representations develop during a given stage, in this case the sensorimotor stage.

The initial organization of the infant's behaviour
The infant's activity at birth is governed by a set of reflexes which will determine his reactions to stimuli which reach him. These reflexes are neither isolated nor heterogeneous but define an organized comprehensive structure, within which they appear differentiated and co-ordinated.

Audio-visual co-ordination and early imitations provide good examples of the complexity of the organization which connects the infant to his environment. At this level the problem of intentionality in the infant's behaviours does not arise, as we have already indicated. The infant is connected to the environment by an intersensorimotor organization internal or external which determines that certain actions follow certain stimuli. The organism is able to programme particular behaviours when particular configurations of stimuli present themselves. It reveals a completely anticipatory functioning; the behaviours could be described as triggered, or needing no active organization on the subject's part. With the example of audio-visual co-ordination we saw an illustration of the organism's anticipatory abilities; on hearing a sound the visual system expects and prepares itself to receive visual stimulation. The organism's abilities for control seem on the other hand to be minimal. At birth we can identify an elementary form of control which consists simply in registering the result of carrying out an action as a failure or success, an all-or-nothing classification. If the action has succeeded, it is not useful to initiate it again; if not, a new action is programmed. But the infant cannot make use of the information provided by carrying out a first action (by taking account of the transformation process or of the divergence (between the target and the effect achieved) in order to carry out the second. If, for example, he fails to take hold of an object, he will have no extra chances of success when he makes the second attempt. Thus, contrary to what is generally agreed in psychology, we consider that the neonate initially possesses a memory of evocation, built up by the repertory of his actions and of their consequences, and that this permits him to anticipate his behaviours, but that he does not have a recognition memory which would allow him to correct his behaviours on the basis of previously initiated behaviours. This could be expressed by saying that the neonate functions like an open loop, with minimal retroaction.

The grasping behaviours of the neonate illustrate this description well. The findings of Bower (1970a, 1970b) show that, during the first days of life, the infant is capable of a very surprising type of prehension: he can stretch out his arm in the direction of a moving object, opening his hand while so doing, and in some instances closing it around the object. The infant's grasping behaviours show that account is taken of certain categories of information, relative to his situation (distance, orientation), to his actions (scope, speed . . .), and to the objects (speed). These dimensions are specified by the intersensorimotor organization with which the infant is equipped at birth, owing to formed sensory representations. It is these which establish the links between complex configurations of sensory messages (giving information on the distance, size, shape . . . of the object) and motor programmes (specifying the action with regard to direction, scope, speed . . .). They permit an explanation of how the infant can exhibit complex grasping movements triggered by visual information when these are not accompanied by visual control. Remarkable co-ordinations are thus present between visuo-motor, tactuo-motor and postural activities.

The complexity of initial co-ordinations is further borne out by the fact that they involve a set of parts of the body or a set of infant's postures. For example, following something visually does not merely involve moving the eyes and the head, but also necessitates finely orchestrated postural modifications of the trunk, arms and legs (Bullinger, 1981 this volume Ch7). One might say that at birth everything varies in relation to everything else. Development can be described as a progressive selection of certain initial sensorimotor liaisons.

The particular mode of transaction that exists between the infant and his environment is brought about by biunivocal linkages based on sensory translations of internal and external realities. If the neonate reacts well to visual, tactile stimulations etc., these still do not have meanings comparable to those built up by the infant of some months who will be able to refer them to perceptible external objects. The existence of initial intersensorimotor co-ordinations confirms that of representations of totalities, where a distinction between representations of the body of the self and representations of external objects is difficult, or even impossible, to establish. Initial representations are necessary to the functioning of early co-ordinations that indeed require the construction of mediations between perceptions and motor behaviours. We term these representations sensory, in order to distinguish them from others, of a different type, established subsequently by the infant. As we have already stressed, these internal initial representations cannot be referred to a universe of objects. There is a strict correspondence between the internal status and transformations of the subject and the external status and transformations of the environment, but none of the neonate's internal states or transformations can be referred, attributed or connected by him to anything which might be an element of reality or a part of himself.

The sensorimotor dependencies or connections which the sensorimotor organization exhibits are not under the infant's active control. Development can be seen as the infant's progressively taking control of his behaviours. We distinguish different forms of control of behaviours in the course of the development of representations.

Initial representations are the result of phylogenesis (on this level, it would be possible to draw analogies with fixed action patterns) just as they arise from the infant's intrauterine experience. In our view, it is not admissible to describe the infant's initial behaviours as exhibiting knowledge in the strict sense. They only consitute one of the necessary conditions for the establishment of knowledge. Another necessary condition is provided by the human being's capacity for building new internal representations that can be referred to a universe of objects. New representations concern the respective states of the organism and of the environment as well as the transformations that allow the change from one state to another. We speak of knowledge in the strict sense when these representations are constructed. What status should be accorded then to the infant's initial behaviours? They show knowledge or meanings which are only experienced or actualized by the organism and constitute the matter and substance which form the basis for objectivization, for the developing awareness of reality and of the self (that is to say the construction of a new system of meanings).

The new born's acquisition of a new coding ability will permit new representations to be established. It will overturn the initial relationship in comparison with which he will find himself in an adualist position. Adualism arises from the infant's inability to pick out in an interaction that which arises from his own action, from that which arises from other physical or social objects. In our view, the construction of a distinction between the self and others (subject—object) is made possible by the infant's double coding of realities: sensory coding and perceptual coding. The problem of consciousness, and of the subject's intentionality will spring from the initial existence of an internal duality, which allows the progressive establishment of the subject—object duality.

The construction of partial or multiple representations

How will the system constituted by the infant and his environment be modified? By means of the perceptual code the infant will bring about a new sampling, a new analysis of sensory messages relative both to his actions and to objects. Whilst the meanings of these messages were initially determined by sensory representations, they will be progressively redefined by means of the perceptual code and give rise to perceptual representations. Certain initial sensorimotor connections will thus be re-established; they escape from the control of the initial sensorimotor organization which then appears dissociated.

Reaching behaviour undergoes a considerable change between the fourth and eighth weeks. The tactuo-motor and visuo-motor activities of the arm and hand become progressively dissociated. The phases of approach and seizure are now only partially co-ordinated. At birth the grasping reflex correlates synergic flexions of the elbow, wrist and fingers with tactile and proprioceptive information from the hand and arm (Twitchell, 1965, 1970). Some tactile information provided by the hand thus forms the subject of a new coding and gives birth to partial perceptual representation. These establish relationships between certain tactile information and the flexing movements of the fingers. During this stage we are thus witnessing the selection of this sensorimotor connection, and its re-establishment on the perceptual level. As for proprioceptive information, this is always coupled with synergic flexions of the wrist and elbow, just as the activities of the head and eyes are coupled with those of the arm and hand (tonic neck reflex). These sensorimotor connexions as a whole remain determined by the initial sensory representations. As the perceptual coding is applied to the sensorimotor information, sensory representations are thus rendered inoperative. Other tactile information is then coupled with other movements, with the help of perceptual representations in process of construction. Thus movements of opening and closing the hand, initially controlled by sensory representations, find themselves redefined by perceptual representations. The infant thus builds a representation of his hand as a reaching instrument.

The phase of approach to the object also undergoes a reorganization on the perceptual level and appears momentarily dissociated from the phase of capture. Between nine and twelve weeks, White, Castle and Held (1964) describe a 'swiping' response which consists in projecting the closed hand towards the visually perceived object. This response is later (around thirteen to sixteen weeks) changed to a 'raising' response, where the infant stretches his arm to the object by a target controlled visually and tactually the nearer it gets. Among other things, each of these reactions shows how the infant manages to integrate the 'distance from the object' dimension into his new perceptual representation, in order to initiate his movement. Field (1976a, 1976b, 1977) has studied how infants progressively take distance from the object into consideration in their reaching behaviour. Visuo-motor activities, initially determined by sensory representations, will also undergo new coding. White, Castle and Held (1964) show how the change comes about from 'peripheral following', where information inputs trigger following movements only when they reach the periphery of the retina, to a so-called 'central following', where the peripheral and foveal parts of the retina are co-ordinated, which thus allows the visuo-motor subsystem to anticipate the successive positions of moving objects.

The infant thus builds up, principally during the first three months, partial perceptual representations both of his own body and of external objects. Some dimensions of internal and external reality are objectified by the infant, and he can then act on them in a controlled manner. We have termed this type of representation 'multiple representations' (Mounoud and Guyon-Vinter, 1979), in order to make clear that, from the infant's point of view, they do not refer to an object endowed simultaneously with a set of properties. In a way, understanding an object through one of its properties makes it a new object each time for the infant. For example, the object which the infant follows visually cannot seem to him the same as the one which he grasps.

As he has not built up representations of the whole (of himself or of the external world) the infant's anticipatory ability now proves itself restricted. He must attain control step by step and recognition memory is gradually established. At this stage we can say that the infant's functional world is of the 'respondent' type (Mayer, 1978). We should add that the sensorimotor connections which have still not undergone a re-establishment on the perceptual level, remain under the control of the sensorimotor organization. Thus, a state of partial co-ordination remains.

The construction of total or unique representations
During the second stage, ranging between three to four months and seven to eight months, representations previously broken up form new co-ordinations and give birth to global, 'total representations'.

For the infant, objects, like his actions, are singularized or individualized. In the same way, the infant can comprehend himself as one object among others. The identification of the object (or of others) is only carried out when it appears with the whole of the properties the infant has been able to objectify. Any divergence from this rigid pattern breaks the identity. At this stage, representations are of the 'unique' type. Sensorimotor connections, objectified during the preceding stage, become once again co-ordinated with each other. At this level, perceptuo-motor organization, in constitution, has completely supplanted sensorimotor organization as the control-centre for the infant's behaviours. The child's behaviours simultaneously take into consideration the object's various properties (size, distance, weight . . .).'

At this stage, reaching behaviours are once again well defined with regard to the distance, direction, speed and size of the objects. The whole of the reaching behaviour (approach and capture) is carried out in a rapid and direct movement. The arm and hand are stretched in the object's direction without being visually controlled. Thus the trajectory has been anticipated, as has been the opening and closing of the hand. The movement is pre-programmed before it is carried out, whereas it was formally elaborated step by step, during the preceding stage. The advance organization of actions is made possible by the existence of these total representations which furnish *a priori*, relatively strict definitions of the properties of the object with which the infant is interacting. The infant's functioning corresponds to an 'operant' functioning, which can anticipate, but is rigid and adapts with great difficulty to variations in situations. At this level the child's behaviours always show limited possibilities for correction or control. These limitations are direct consequences of the nature of the perceptual representations available at this stage of development.

These representations are rigid and cannot be broken down or analysed. We might talk here of representation-stimulation. Indeed there is a one-for-one correspondence between the information acquired by the subject about his actions or about objects, and the representations built up about his actions or those objects. The object loses its identity if it is transformed, the action cannot be modified whilst it is being executed. The control present at this level consists in carrying out the action, then evaluating the difference between the state-of-affairs expected and the state-of-affairs achieved so that a correction can be introduced in the organization of the subsequent action.

The construction of synthetic or typical representations
The first two stages in the construction of representations mark the end of a first phase which brings about unique representations. This

first phase will be succeeded by a second phase during which these representations can be modulated or broken down. Between six to nine months and sixteen to eighteen months, the infant will construct representations which will allow his activity to be modulated or adapted as a function of the variations in the characteristics of the objects he encounters. The new coding of information received from objects or actions consists in establishing relationships between parts of the action or between parts of the action and situational variations, or between parts of the object, or between different objects. This phase can thus be described as a period of establishing the relational properties of the object and the action. The infant will be able to master the variation in an object's dimensions as well as the variations which obtain in the relations between it and other objects. In the Piagetian sense, the object becomes permanent: its momentary disappearance is attributed to the establishment of a new system of relations (spatial, temporal or causal) between the subject and the object. Representations which characterise this phase are called 'typical', that is to say, adaptable to a class of objects, situations or actions.

At the level of action, the infant will take into consideration the particular values of the dimensions of the object to which they apply. Such a functioning, called 'mixed', entails both a pre-programming of initial parameters of action, and an adaptation of these, by external control, to the current data of the situations. Corrections will be introduced in the course of executing the actions.

Many experimental findings bear witness to the reorganization of reaching behaviour around seven to eight months. We must first recall the important break which Halverson (1931) noticed between behaviours prior and subsequent to thirty-two weeks. For him, it is as if during a first stage, the hand was passively moved towards the objects, whereas from thirty-two weeks it is the movements of the hand which determine the complex articulations (finger movements and reaching) of the arm. Results obtained by McDonnel (1975) on the behaviour of reaching for objects visually perceived through prisms with infants aged from sixteen to forty-three weeks, also show a split on thirty weeks. From sixteen to thirty weeks, infants succeed in grasping the object in the same proportion of attempts, with or without a prism; on the other hand, between thirty and forty-three weeks, successes are proportionately more frequent without the prism.

Finally, mention should be made of work carried out by Wishart, Bower and Dunkeld (1978) on the comparative evolution of reaching for objects perceived either visually or auditorily in infants aged seventeen to fifty-two weeks. For objects perceived auditorily, there is a marked improvement in performance from seventeen to twenty-two weeks, then a fall-off up to thirty-nine weeks, which then picks up again from forty-three to fifty-two weeks, without, however, achieving again the level of performance reached at twenty-two weeks. The evolution of these performances for visually perceived objects is the same in general terms, but much less marked. We consider that these results emphatically confirm the reconstruction which reaching behaviours undergo during the second half of the first year, and which is a consequence of the different stages in the establishment of perceptual representations.

Conclusion
In the second section of this chapter we mentioned the possibility of establishing relationships between the concept of development and representation which we have put forward, and that of de Saussure regarding the constitution of a verbal sign. Initial sensorimotor connections bring about 'substances', the contents from which the system of perceptual meanings will be built. 'Unique' representations constitute 'images', translations of these initial connections in a new code. Finally, 'typical' representations provide a new system of meanings, called perceptual meanings. They result from the establishment of various relational systems (intra- and inter-object) issuing from 'unique' representations. But from our genetic perspective, we must modify this point of view: the initial substances can be seen as a system of meanings (sensory meanings), in the same way as the system of perceptual meanings provides the substances from which the system of conceptual meanings will be elaborated.

In this article we have tried to interpret sensorimotor development through the construction of internal representations (or memory) conceived of as structuring or organization of content. The appearance of new coding abilities makes the establishment of new representations possible. This is subject to a genetic regulation and it would thus depend very little upon particular interactions which take place between the child and his environment, unless interaction were meant in a very broad, non-specific sense. Formed representations are directly dependent on the experiments which the child has been able to carry out (specific role of the environment).

Notes

1 These terms contrast contemporaneous or 'steady states' (synchronic) with changing or evolving (diachronic) processes in development (Editor's Note).
2 The French *signifiant/signifié* is sometimes translated by the words 'term/referent' or 'term/meaning' (Editor's Note).
3 See Note 2 above.
4 The phrase 'reading of experience' corresponds to the Piagetian expression *lecture de l'experience*. This is a difficult concept to translate succinctly but it implies that the subject *necessarily* requires appropriate cognitive structures to understand reality. Properties of objects in and of themselves are insufficient to explain children's difficulties in comprehension. (Editor's Note).

References

Alegria, J. and Noirot, E. (1978) 'Neonate orientation behavior towards human voice', *International Journal of Behavioral Development*, 1 (2)
Arbib, M. A. (1980) 'Perceptual structures and distributed motor control', in Brooks, V. B. (ed.) *Handbook of Physiology, Vol. III*. American Physiological Society
Aronson, E. and Rosenbloom, S. (1971) 'Space perception in early infancy: perception within a common auditory–visual space', *Science*, 172, 1161–3.
Bartlett, F. C. (1932) *Remembering: A Study in Experimental and Social Psychology*, Cambridge University, reprinted 1977.
Bower, T. G. R. (1974) *Development in Infancy*, W. H. Freeman, San Francisco.
Bower, T. G. R. (1976) 'Concepts of development', in *Actes du XXI Congrès international de Psychologie*, PUF, Paris, pp.79–97
Bower, T. G. R., Broughton, J. M. and Moore, M. K. (1970a) 'Demonstration of intention in the reaching behavior of neonate humans', *Nature*, 228, 679–81
Bower, T. G. R., Broughton, J. M. and Moore, M. K. (1970b) 'The coordinations of visual and tactual inputs in infants', *Perception and Psychophysics*, 8, (1), 51–3
Bronckart, J. P. and Ventouras-Spycher, M. (1979) 'Le concept piagéti en de représéntation et la conception soviétique d'autorégulation', in Zivin, G. (ed.) *Development of Self Regulation Through Speech*, Wiley, New York.
Bullinger, A. (1981) 'Cognitive elaboration of sensorimotor behaviour, in Butterworth, G. (ed.) *Infancy and Epistemology*, Harvester Press, Brighton, this volume pp.173–91.

Butterworth, G. (1981) 'The origins of auditory visual perception and visual proprioception in human development', in Walk R. and Pick H. (eds) *Perception and Perceptual Development*, Vol II, Plenum, New York.

Butterworth, G. and Castillo, M. (1976) 'Coordination of auditory and visual space in newborn infants', *Perception*, 2, 155–60

Carpenter, G. C. (1973) 'Mother–stranger discrimination in the early weeks of life', paper presented at the Biennial Meeting of SRCD, Philadelphia, 1973.

Dunkeld, J. (1979) 'The function of imitation in infancy', PhD thesis University of Edinburgh.

Eibl-Eiblesfeldt, I. (1979) 'Human ethology—concepts and implications for the Sciences of man', in *The Behavioral and Brain Sciences*, Vol. 2. 1–57

Eimas, P. D. (1975) 'Speech perception in early infancy', in Cohen, L. B. and Salapatek, P. (eds) *Infant Perception from Sensation to Cognition*, Vol. 2, Academic Press, New York, pp.193–231

Fantz, R. L. (1964) 'Visual experience in infants: decreased attention to familiar patterns relative to novel ones', *Science*, 146, 668–70

Field, J. (1976a) 'The adjustment of reaching behavior to object distance in early infancy', *Child Development*, 47, 304–8

Field, J. (1976b) 'Relation of young infants' reaching behavior to stimulus distance and solidity', *Developmental Psychology*, 12 (5), 444–8.

Field, J. (1977) 'Coordination of vision and prehension in young infants', *Child Development*, 48, 97–103

Gibson, E. J. (1969) *Principles of Perceptual Learning and Development*, Appleton Century Crafts, New York.

Halverson, J. (1931) 'An experimental study of prehension in infants by means of systematic cinema records', *Genetic Psychology Monographs*, 10, 107–286

Hammond, J. (1970) 'Hearing and response in the newborn', *Development Med. Child. Neurol.*, 12, 3–5.

Hauert, C. A. (1978) 'Propriétés des objets et propriétés des actions chez l'enfant de 2 à 5 ans', postgraduate thesis, University of Geneva.

Hayes, L. and Watson, J. S. (1979) 'Neonatal imitation: fact or artifact?' paper presented at the Biennal Meeting of the SRCD, San Francisco, 1979.

Jacobson, S. W. and Kagan, J. (1978) 'Released responses in early infancy: evidence contradicting selective imitation', paper presented at the International Conference on Infant Studies, Providence, R. I., 1978.

Jacobson, S. W. and Kagan, J. 1979) 'Interpreting "imitative" responses in early infancy', *Science*, 205, 215–7.

Janet, P. (1928) *L'évolution de la mémoire et de la notion de temps*, A. Chahine, Paris.

Jones, B. and Kabanoff, B. (1975) 'Eyes movements in auditory space perception', *Perception and Psychophysics*, 17 (3), 241–5.

Klein, M., Heimann, P., Isaacs, S. and Rivière, J. (1966) *Développements de la psychanalyse*. PUF, Paris.

Lewis, M. (1979) 'Issues in the study of imitation', paper presented at the Meeting of the SRCD, San Francisco, 1979.

Lewis, M. and Hurowitz, L. (1977) 'Intermodal person schema in infancy: perception within a common auditory–visual space', paper presented at the Eastern Psychological Association Meetings, Boston, 1977.

Lipsitt, L. P., Engen, T. R. and Kagan, H. (1963) 'Developmental changes in the olfactory threshold of the neonate', *Child Development*, 34, 371–76

McDonnel, P. M. (1975) 'The development of visually guided reaching', *Perception and Pscyhophysics*, 18 (3), 181–5

McGurk, H. and Lewis, M. (1974) 'Space perception in early infancy: perception within a common auditory visual space?' *Science*, 186, 649–50.

Maratos, O. (1973) 'The origin and development of imitation in the first six months of life', postgraduate thesis, University of Geneva.

Mayer, E. (1978) 'Acquisition d'habitudes motrices chez le jeune enfant', thesis project, University of Geneva.

Meltzoff, A. N. (1976) 'Imitation in early infancy', DPhil thesis, University of Oxford.

Meltzoff A. N. (1981) Imitation, intermodal coordination and representations in early infancy. In Butterworth G. E. (ed) Infancy and Epistemology, Harvester Press, Brighton, pp.85–114.

Meltzoff, A. N. and Moore, M. K. (1977) 'Imitation of facial and manual gestures by human neonates', *Science*, 198, 75–8

Meltzoff, A. N. and Moore, M. K. (1979) 'Interpreting "imitative" responses in early infancy', *Science*, 205, 217–9

Mounoud, P. (1970) *Structuration de l'instrument chez l'enfant*, Delachaux and Niestlé,

Mounoud, P. (1971) 'Développement des systèmes de représentation et de traitement chez l'enfant', *Bulletin de Psychologie*, 296 (XXV), 5–7, 261–72.

Mounoud, P. (1973) 'Les conservations physiques chez le bébé', *Bulletin de Psychologie*, 312 (XXVII) 13–4, 722–8

Mounoud, P. (1976) 'Les révolutions psychologiques de l'enfant', *Archives de Psychologie*, XLIV, 171, 103–114.

Mounoud. P. (1977) 'Gedächtnis und Intelligenz', in *Die Psychologie des 20. Jahrhunderts, Band 7, 3. Teil*, Kindler Verlag, Zurich.

Mounoud, P. (1981) 'L'utilisation du milieu et du corps propre par le bébé', in Piaget, J., Mounoud, P. and Bronckart, J.–P. (eds). *La Psychologie, Encyclopédie*, Gallimard, Paris (in press).

Mounoud, P. (1977) 'Cognitive development: construction of new structures or construction of internal organizations?' paper presented at the Seventh Symposium of Piaget Society, Philadelphia, 1977.

Mounoud, P. (1979) 'Importance de l'action dans le développement cognitif de l'enfant', paper presented at the Congrès de Psychomotricité, Lugano, 1979.

Mounoud, P. and Vinter, A. (1979) 'Recherches expérimentales sur l'image do soi chez l'enfant et l'adolescent', paper Présenté au Congrès International 'Production et Affirmation de l'Identité', Toulouse, 1979.

Mounoud, P. and Hauert, C. A. (1981) 'Sensori-motor and postural behavior: its relation to cognitive development', in Hartup, W. W. (ed.) *Review of Child Development Research*, Vol. 6, The University of Chicago Press, Chicago (in press).

Piaget, J. (1936) *La naissance de l'intelligence chez l'enfant*, Delachaux & Niestlé, Paris.

Piaget, J. (1937) *La construction du réel chez l'enfant*, Delachaux & Niestlé, Paris.

Piaget, J. (1946) *La formation du symbole chez l'enfant*, Delachaux & Niestlé, Paris.

Piaget, J. (1947) *La psychologie de l'intelligence*, Armand Colin, Paris.

Piaget, J. (1981) 'Les conduites sensori-motrices', in Piaget, J. Mounoud, P. and Bronckart, J. P. (eds) *La Psychologie, Encyclopédie de la Pléiade*, Gallimard, Paris, (in press).

Saussure, F. de. (1974) *Cours de linguistique générale*, Mouton, Paris.

Schonen, S. de. (1974) *Organisation et Recherche des informations: Contribution à une théorie de la mémoire*, Mouton, Paris.

Spitz, R. (1952) *La première année de la vie de l'enfant*, PUF, Paris.

Trevarthen, C., Hubley, P. and Sheeran, L. (1975) 'Les activités innées du nourrisson', *La Recherche*, 56, 447–58

Turkewitz, G., Birch, H. G., Moreau, T., Levy, L. and Cornwell, A. L. (1966) 'Effect of intensity of auditory stimulation on directional eye movements in the human neonate', *Animal Behavior*, 14, 93–101

Twitchell, T. E. (1965) 'The automatic grasping responses of infants', *Neuropsychologia*, 3, 247–259.

Twitchell, T. E. (1970) 'Reflex mechanisms and the development of prehension', in Connolly, K. (ed.) *Mechanisms of Motor Skill Development*, Academic Press, London.

Waite, L. H. and Lewis, M. (1979) 'Early imitation with several models: An example of socio-affective development', paper presented at the Society of Research in Child Development meetings, San Francisco, 1979.

Watson, J. S. (1966) The development and generalization of 'contingency awareness' in early infancy: some hypotheses. *Merril Palmer Quarterly of Behaviour and Development* 12, 2.

Watson, J. S. (1981) 'La mémoire dans la petite enfance', in Piaget, J. Mounoud, P. and Bronckart, J. P., (eds) *La Psychologie, Encyclopédie de la Pléiade*, Gallimard, Paris (in press).

Wertheimer, M. (1961) 'Psychomotor coordination of auditory and visual space at birth', *Science*, 1961, 34

White, B. L., Castle, P. and Held, R. (1964) 'Observation on the development of visually-directed reaching', *Child Development*, 35, 349–64.

Wishart, J. G., Bower, T. G. R. and Dunkeld, J. (1978) 'Reaching in the dark' *Perception*, 7 507–12.

Wulf, F. (1922) 'Ueber die Veränderung von Vorstellungen (Gedächtnis und Gestalt)', *Psychol. Forschungen*, 1, 33–373.

9 Perspectives on Early Communications

ANDREW LOCK AND MATTHEW BROWN

Piaget and Pre-linguistic Communication

The recent concern with semantic and pragmatic aspects of language development has led to renewed interest in the relationship between linguistic and cognitive development. Slobin (1973) for example argues for the primacy of cognitive over linguistic development: the child must be able to cognize the physical and social events encoded in language, and he must be able to process and store linguistic information; in other words, there are cognitive pre-requisites for language on the one hand, to do with meanings, and on the other, to do with forms and structures. As evidence for this position, he cites studies of bilingual language development (Mikěs, 1967; Mikěs and Vlahovíc, 1966) where children develop means of expressing locative notions in Hungarian before they do in Serbo-Croatian, suggesting that their ability to recognize semantic relations is in advance of their linguistic expressive abilities. Again, Bloom (1970), suggests that an ideal account of linguistic development would specify at least three inter-related components—linguistic experience, non-linguistic experience, and cognitive-perceptual organization—and provide an account of the ways in which their interaction governs the development of linguistic competence. McNamara (1972) and Schlesinger (1971) suggest that the child is aided in learning syntax by being able to infer the meanings of sentences from their non-linguistic contexts, while Brown (1973) explicitly suggests that the child's ability to grasp semantic concepts is a function of his sensori-motor development:

... the first sentences express the construction of reality which is the terminal achievement of sensorimotor intelligence. What has been acquired on the plane of motor intelligence (the permanence of form and substance of immediate objects) and the structure of immediate space and time does not need to be formed all over again on the plane of representation. Representation starts with just those meanings that are most available to it, propositions about action schemas involving agents and objects, assertions of non-existence, recurrence, location and so on. . . . (*Ibid*, p.200)

As often as not, and quite naturally so, Piagetian theory is turned to by developmental psycholinguists for their insights into cognitive development. Yet this is a form of cognitive theory in which language is relegated to a very secondary role in development. The primary emphasis in Piaget's theory is, by contrast, on 'thought', or cognition.

It is Piaget's contention that the representative function is not present at birth, but develops slowly throughout the pre-representational, sensorimotor period, first through imitation and later via a much broader semiotic ability which allows the child to decentre from the immediate spatio-temporal environment to which his sensorimotor knowledge restricts him. Language arises through a gradual development of imitative ability to the level at which it begins to provide the footing for the construction of signifiers which mediate the transition from the sensorimotor to the semiotic period.

Throughout Piaget's theory, language plays the part of representing thought processes, but in doing so, always follows on *after* advances have been made in the cognitive field: 'language is not considered to be dynamic in provoking changes in thought structures' (Karmiloff-Smith, 1979, p.7). Piaget's position on language is most apparent when he draws on Furth's work (1966) with deaf children to bolster his view that language is not necessary for cognitive growth—since deaf children can attain certain abilities without the use of language.

Sinclair has been the major developer of Piaget's theory with regard to language development. She stresses a line between early language and sensorimotor intelligence. She notes (Sinclair, 1937a) that very early in infancy there is no differentiation made between action, object and agent: 'an action or reflex pattern during the first months constitutes an unanalysable entity' (*Ibid*. p.411). These notions only become differentiated very gradually. Similarly at the level of language, it too shows an unanalysed beginning: 'Holophrases form unanalysable entities. They are followed by two and three word utterances . . . indicative of two differentiations: between action and object, and between the child himself as actor and another acting subject' (*Ibid*.). What language accomplishes is a linguistic reconstruction of the child's knowledge at a new level of representation:

at first the child expresses a [possible] action pattern related to himself, in which agent, action and eventual patient are inextricably entwined. Second, he either expresses the result of an action done by somebody else, . . . or an action he performs or is going to perform himself. In this way, the capacity for representing reality follows at a later stage the same evolution which took place when the child was still dealing directly with reality without representation. (Sinclair, 1973b, p.23)

Piagetian theory, then, does not see language development as a major problem, being more interested in the child's logico-mathematical development; and in the theory of genetic epistemology being advanced, language is treated more as a symptom than a cause of intellectual development.

It may seem surprising from the above that Piaget should attract so much recent attention from those interested in the development of language itself, having relegated language to a minor role. But a recent statement shows his relevance in a post-Chomsky era, and an agreement with Brown's position cited above:

the formation of language is certainly a later development than sensorimotor intelligence, the remarkable functioning of which can be observed in, among others, the chimpanzee and the human baby before any semiotic function. This type of intelligence includes precisely everything that Chomsky needs to furnish his so-called innate fixed nucleus with a logic of actions. (Piaget, 1977, p.3)

Thus, in principle at least, Piagetian theory offers a general account of cognitive development within which linguistic development can be situated, without needing to refer to any form of innate linguistic development. Firstly, the syntactic structures of language have been argued as showing isomorphisms with the logical structures described by Piaget (see Sinclair, 1967, 1969, 1973a, 1973b). The invocation of innate mechanisms is thus not required, a cheering point to a developmentalist, who by trade not only falls back on innateness if totally perplexed and left with no other option. And secondly, it becomes possible to link the semantic content of early utterances to pre-verbal sensorimotor schemas (Brown, 1973, p.200; Edwards, 1973; Nelson, 1974).

Recent Studies Linking Language Development and Cognitive Development

Ingram (1978) has examined Piaget's work on the sensorimotor period (Piaget, 1952, 1954, 1962) in an attempt to draw out a specific account of language development. This is a necessary task because, as noted above, Piaget does not directly address this subject, so that pertinent observations occur scattered throughout sets of observations on his children relating to more general patterns of their cognitive development. Ingram seeks to show how the attainment of linguistic milestones compares with that of cognitive milestones, the specific linguistic milestones being these:

Period 1 0;10–1;5
One word at a time, words are used in a variety of functions, e.g. as wish, request, etc. Small vocabulary.
Period 2 1;6–2;0, or later
One word at a time at onset; use of single words in semantic roles such as Agent, Object; use of sequences of one word utterances; rapid growth of vocabulary; (month or two later) vocabulary up to 50 words; onset of multi-word utterances; (several months later) onset of information function; onset of references to absent situations.
Period 3 2;0 onwards
One-word utterances no longer used; onset of ideational and textual functions (c.f. Halliday, 1975). (Ingram, 1978, pp.281–2)

While there may not be much disagreement over Ingram's characterizations, his list is arguably incomplete. Dore, Franklin, Miller and Ramer (1976) suggest that there are other prior and intervening stages of vocalization; and Carter (1974), Bates (1976), Greenfield and Smith (1976), Sugarman-Bell (1978) and Lock (1980) emphasize that the child also has gestural means of communication at his disposal. But Ingram's reorganization of Piaget's observations, along with observations from early diary studies of Shinn (1900), Hogan (1898) and Preyer (1895), and work by Menn (1976), does suggest the following correspondences.

In sensorimotor stage five, the first words will appear, highly variable in usage although context-bound at the very start, and not usually more than ten or so in number. This corresponds to stage one in language development. In sensorimotor stage six, there is an increase in vocabulary although utterances are still single words. With the onset of representation, one finds the first reference to past events, the occurrence of linguistic play, appearance of multiword utterances, and the use of 'what is it?' questions to ask the names of things.

However, it is not easy to clearly correlate Piaget's sensorimotor stage six, and the onset of the semiotic function, with what Ingram calls periods 2 and 3 of language development. The second period is a long one with several sub-stages, and its later sub-stages overlap with the onset of the semiotic function. There is also some ambiguity about the distinction between sensorimotor stage six and the semiotic function: while in Piaget (1954) stage six is said to be marked by the early development of representation, Piaget and Inhelder (1969) suggest that stage six is simply an interface between the end of the sensorimotor period and the beginning of the semiotic period. It is difficult to be certain therefore whether representational abilities should be taken to mark sensorimotor stage six or the onset of the semiotic function. Ingram's conclusions from this preliminary investigation are cautious: firstly, that we may need to redefine stage six in the light of language development (but this is surely circular); and secondly, that specific aspects of sensorimotor development, stage five means–end relations imitation might have a relationship to the appearance of pragmatic and syntactic forms of language.

Piaget's stage five is also seen as crucial by Bates (1976). Her approach is more concerned with pragmatic aspects of language development, setting them within a more general framework of communicative ability, and emphasizing the gradual transition from pre-linguistic communication to language. After Austin (1962) she distinguishes perlocutionary, illocutionary and locutionary aspects of speech acts. While perlocutionary effects are those unintended by the speaker, illocutionary effects are the result of deliberate intention, but may be accomplished non-verbally as well as verbally. When words are used in the service of illocutionary ends, then one may speak of the locutionary aspects of a communicative act. Bates' use of Austin's terminology is perhaps illegitimate: arguably Austin never meant to suggest that the different aspects of speech acts could be treated as autonomous aspects of communication, as Bates implies (c.f. Dore, 1978), and there is no need to look to speech act theory for terms describing the different kinds of intentional and unintentional communication (c.f. Lyons, 1972; Mackay, 1972). But be that as it may, it would still appear that Piaget's stage five closely corresponds to the onset of pre-verbal, intentional communication. Stage five involves the invention of new means to particular ends, and tertiary circular reactions, where secondary circular reactions are recombined on a higher level. In particular, there is the development of tool–use, or means–end relations, where the child uses one object to obtain, or act on, another. Bates suggests that this is a pre-requisite for the development of gestural performatives: the protodeclarative, when a child uses an object to gain the attention of an adult and the protoimperative, when the child invokes an adult's help in obtaining an object. These in turn are communicative schemas into which in stage six words can be fitted.

A similar approach is taken by Sugarman-Bell (1973) who suggests that in stage five the child becomes capable of combining object-oriented and person-oriented schemes developed in stages three and four. In these latter two stages, the child can progressively sustain more complex interactions, with objects or persons, but the various repertoires of behaviour involved remain separate. A similar pattern of development is also described by Trevarthen and Hubley (1978), but Trevarthen offers a different non-Piagetian interpretation (see later).

A point stressed by Bates is that communicative development should be seen as a continuous process, where transitions between stages or phases are very gradual. This is born out by the work of Dore (1978) and Carter (1974). Dore, Franklin, Miller and Ramer (1976) report that before the first recognition words appear, there is the development of phonetically consistent forms, which are unclassifiable as either babbling or words, being idiosyncratic, easily isolable, and frequently occurring, usually in conjunction with particular situations or actions. Carter (1974, 1979) also reports such a development, but in stressing the co-occurrence of vocalizations with gestures, suggests they be termed 'sensorimotor morphemes', a term designed to capture both their basis in the actions of the child, and their nature as the smallest units of significance within the child's early communication system. While not concerned particularly with demonstrating a correspondence between individual sensorimotor stages and stages of sensorimotor morpheme development, Carter's use of Piagetian terminology does reflect a general preference for a Piagetian rather than a nativist account of language development, the fundamental precursors of speech being found in sensorimotor action patterns, and their subsequent development being a function of progress in the development of representational abilities, and the progressive freeing of the structural organization of communicative functions from particular action schemes.

An immanent criticism of the preceding studies is that they assume the concept of sensorimotor stage to be a unitary one, so that correspondences between cognitive and communicative development can be made simply at a level of stage attainment. This assumption is, however, problematic: Piaget's sensorimotor stages are defined in terms of performance on tasks involving various clusters of behaviours, and although Piaget would in general argue for a unitary concept of stage, it is also true that he acknowledges that performance on one set of tasks may not be at the same level as in other tasks. The allocation of a child to a particular level of development is, therefore, not very straightforward, and as a result, some attempts have been made to produce ordinal scales of development, the best-known probably being that of Uzgiris and Hunt (1975). Corrigan (1976, 1978, 1979) in particular has looked at the correlations between object permanence and language development. Various hypotheses have been put forward regarding the relevance of object permanence, the most frequent being that children need a permanent notion of an object before they can talk about it, or name it. For example, Bloom (1973) suggested that her daughter Alison produced two main classes of words, functors such as *more, there*, or *allgone*, referring across classes of objects and events, and substantives referring to specific classes of objects. Functors were produced earlier than substantives, and lasted longer, while substantives at first were not generalized, but remained tied to particular action-schemes. Only with the presumed onset of object permanence was there an increase in Alison's naming behaviour at one-and-a-half years. Corrigan's study explicitly tested for these hypothesized relationships, using a modified version of the Uzgiris-Hunt object permanence scale, and her results suggest that the hypotheses be viewed with caution. Firstly, she found that when age was partialled out, there was only a very low rank correlation between object permanence and language complexity, although at the onset of stage six, and of the pre-operational period, there were increases in vocabulary. Secondly, no differences in usage of functors and substantives were found.

A further hypothesis, that syntax should not appear before the representational capacity complied by the attainment of stage six object permanence, is questioned by Corrigan (1976) and Ingram (1978), who both report finding children who produce multiword utterances before object permanence attainment.

These criticisms need not be substantial, however. Lock (1978) notes the occurrence of an ability to combine gestures, for example crying to attract attention and raising the arms in order to be picked up. This ability is probably attained before stage six is consolidated, and may bear a relation to early word combinations (c.f. Lock, 1980). Further, Gopnik (1978, 1979) has argued that many early words are used by the child for furthering the sorts of plans of action that appear in stage five of the sensorimotor stage: words such as 'more', 'allgone', 'oh dear', 'down' etc. It is unclear how the extension of this use of words, from saying 'more' to 'more apple' for example, would require the attainment of object permanence as a pre-requisite. Lock (1980) has argued that much of early language use is technically non-propositional, this including some early word combinations. True propositional speech appears later. It may well be that stage six corresponds to the attainment of a propositional ability, it being more obvious how this latter ability may be predicated upon the attainment of object permanence.

The Adequacy of Piagetian Theory as a General Framework for Language Development.

There have, though, been a number of more substantial criticisms of the adequacy of Piagetian theory as a general framework for language development. These fall under the following main headings:

1 the question of representation and its reliance on the semiotic function;
2 the role of social factors in development;
3 the conception of the child implicit in Piagetian theory.

We will for convenience deal with each of these issues separately. But it is important to remember that a number of common topics cut across these different themes.

Representation and Language
Piaget assumed that the neonate is equipped with only a few basic action structures, such as the sucking reflex or the palmar grasp, etc. It is the elaboration of these during the sensorimotor stages that provides an initial basis for the internal representation of the external world; but this in itself does not explain how internal representations become detached from the 'here and now'. To explain this Piaget looks to the development of imitation. In particular the development of the child's ability to imitate gestures which he cannot see himself perform is a problem, explained by Piaget as a function of the child's exploration of his own face or body, and of the faces and bodies of others. Both types of exploration produce similar patterns of accommodation, and at the same time, the child is forming correspondences between what he sees and what he feels: thus the child learns that if his face feels the same as another's face, then it must look the same also. Piaget's theory predicts that this sort of imitation will not occur until the period of co-ordination of secondary circular reactions, between eight and twelve months. There is, however, mounting evidence of the ability of very young infants to produce facial imitations. [see Meltzoff 1981, this volume Ch4 and Mounoud and Vinter 1981, this volume Ch8]. These results are taken to be evidence that the child already possesses at birth a supramodal representational system, such that the infant is able to form a common representation of gestures he visually perceives, and gestures he feels himself perform. Hence, Moore and Meltzoff suggest

'The capacity for acting on the basis of an internal representation of the external world may not be the culmination of psychological development in infancy as Piaget conceived—but merely its starting point' (Moore and Meltzoff, 1978, p.157). This does not imply that a Piagetian position on the relationship between language and cognition is incorrect. Rather, Moore and Meltzoff argue, it is misconceived, in that the relations between object permanence, imitation, and language development must be revised in the light of new findings about the infant's innate competence. In particular, they argue that object permanence is a function of the development and elaboration of rules bearing on invariant transformations of the infant's perceptual field, and that while the development of object permanence is crucial to language development in that it provides a basis for intersubjectivity between infant and adult, similar processes to those governing object permanence development are also at work in the infant's perception of language, enabling him to detect invariant relationships between events and aspects of adult speech.

Social Interaction and Language Acquisition
One of the questions which can be asked about infants is whether their responses to persons are different from their responses to objects. Bower (1979) suggests that infants are born sociable, with a natural ability to distinguish what Buber (1958) calls I–Thou and I–It relations. To support such a view, we need evidence that there are different repertoires of responses to persons and objects, and that infants' responses to persons are interactive and communicative. An immediate argument against such a position is provided by Watson (1973). He suggests that smiling arises as a response to the detection of a contingency between infant behaviour and rewarding environmental responses, and that because such contingencies are most usually provided by adults, in the playing of games ('the Game', which sets up an ideal conditioning situation) with a full-front upright face presentation, that this is why infant smiling is elicited by faces. In other words, 'the Game' is *not* important to the infant because people play it, but rather people become important to the infant because they play 'the Game'. However, infant smiling begins to appear in the first weeks of life, before adults have begun to engage the child in games, and usually appears in situations of repose rather than stimulation. Also, it seems that very young infants show preferential responsiveness to the human face. Goren, Sarty and Wu (1975) claim to have demonstrated this with neonates whose average age was nine minutes! This evidence suggests that people are important to the infant in their own right.

Further evidence that infants respond differentially to persons and to objects is provided by Brazelton, Tronick, Adamson, Als and Wise (1975) and Trevarthen (1977). They both suggest the infant reacts to objects with rapt attention, alternating with abrupt and brief turning away, and with jerky bursts of movements and swipes. When reacting to a person, there are smooth and rhythmical cycles of attention accelerating through imitations and greetings and decelerating through disengagement. Brazelton, Tronick, Adamson, Als and Wise (1975) suggest that such behaviour establishes an effective synchrony between adult and infant, while Trevarthen refers to it as primary intersubjectivity. Both these terms seem to imply the sort of interpersonal phatic communion talked of by Malinowski (1923), or the dialogue of reciprocity talked of by Spitz (1963). Perhaps the best known research on synchrony is that carried out by Condon (1979). Early work on the micro-analysis of filmed adult-adult interaction revealed that changes in the pattern and direction of body movements occurred synchronously with changes at the phonic level of speech, both for the speaker—self-synchrony, and for the hearer—interpersonal synchrony (Condon, 1979). This has been shown to occur in infants also: whether presented with English or Chinese speech, infants at two weeks moved synchronously with the patterns of speech (Condon and Sander, 1974). That infants should respond in this way suggests there is a specific biological basis for early interaction with persons, rather than particularly satisfying objects as Watson suggests.

Condon's research has no particular bearing on the issue of whether infants are active or passive participants in interaction: he suggests that interactional synchrony occurs as a function of the essential organizational integrity of the central nervous system, in that the structure of incoming signals sets up resonances throughout the system. However, Brazelton, Tronick, Adamson, Als and Wise (1975) cite evidence that infants are sensitive to perturbations of normal interactions: an infant presented with his mother's deliberately motionless and expressionless face for several minutes will at first try to initiate interaction several times, but eventually lapse into a state of withdrawal. Trevarthen (1977) claims that by two to three months, infants are engaging in conversation-like exchanges with their mothers, led by the infant, who also shows 'pre-speech' movements: movements of the lips and tongue not necessarily accompanied by vocalization. That these early exchanges are conversation-like is confirmed by Bateson (1975), who calls them proto-conversations, and argues that they have all the characteristics of typical adult conversations: they are marked by turn-taking, the mutual orientation of posture and gaze, and they are 'about' something, even if in the case of infant–adult interaction what they are about is the mutual regulation of affect, as in phatic communion. Bateson does not demonstrate however that the infant is the main initiator of exchanges, but what she does show is that there is a pattern of mutual influence such that the conversation-like appearance of the interaction is not an illusion created by the simultaneous occurrence of two sets of periodically organized behaviours: that an infant vocalization was followed by a maternal vocalization, and *vice versa*, occurred more frequently than would be predicted by chance. While there was good evidence that the mother would wait for a reply from her child, it was not possible to conclusively show the infant would do the same. What appears to be the case is that the infant is active in the sense of providing rhythmic patterns of activity which the mother slots into rather than being active in the sense of slotting into the mother's patterns of activity.

While what has been discussed so far suggests that infants are socially precocious, one could argue that this merely serves to establish an emotional bond between an infant and its major caretaker, and this only has implications for personality development and theories of attachment, such as those put forward by Bowlby (1969). However, Bateson suggests that these early proto-conversations provide a basis for later participation in complex, sequentially organized interactions, such as games, and most importantly, linguistic dialogues. Such a view has been most explicitly espoused by Bruner in several papers (Bruner, 1975, 1976) in which he suggests that these early exchanges provide frames into which other activities can be fitted. Bruner confirms the analyses of Trevarthen and Hubley (1978) and Sugarman-Bell (1978) that at first a child can only attend either to objects or to persons, and that with the combination of the two, at around nine months, the foundations of joint reference are laid (Ninio and Bruner, 1978).

What is most noticeable about the development of communication is the extent to which the mother's behaviour, both verbal and non-verbal, is structured around the infant's activity. The mutuality of gaze in face-to-face interaction is reflected in the mother's continuous visual monitoring of the infant's line of regard (Collis, 1977). Mothers tend to name those objects at which a child is looking, and which she is looking at also (Collis, 1977). Similar findings can be cited for pointing: mothers point in the direction in which their children are looking, or point and gaze at the same time, and also tend to name objects at which they are pointing. (Murphy and Messer, 1977)

Drawing on such investigations, Newson and Newson (1976) argue that the social approach necessitates 'a shift of emphasis rather than an absolute disagreement with Piaget's philosophical standpoint'. What is needed for this shift of emphasis is 'to enlarge the concept of object to include human beings'. Where Piaget argues that knowledge has its origin in the interaction between the subject and object—initially at the sensorimotor level—and later attains the level of symbolic functioning, he maintains a non-social perspective, emphasizing the infant's manipulation of inanimate objects with representation functioning later for the uses of the individual. Newson and Newson, on the other hand, wish to change the focus. Their argument is that, rather than the symbolic function arising through an individual's developing abilities becoming capable of representing his direct actions upon the inanimate world:

> knowledge itself originates within an interaction process . . . between the infant . . . and other, more mature, human individuals who already possess shared understandings with other communicating beings. Furthermore, these shared understandings are embedded in a uniquely human way of conceptualising the world in spatial and temporal terms. In short, the child only achieves a fully articulated knowledge of this world, in a cognitive sense, as he becomes involved in social transactions with other communicating human beings. Knowing, and being able to communicate what it is that we know, need to be viewed as opposite sides of the same coin. (*Ibid.* p.85)

Taking this argument:

> that the origin of symbolic functioning should be sought, not in the child's activities with inanimate objects, but rather in those idiosyncratic but shared understandings which he evolves during his earliest social encounters with familiar human beings who are themselves already steeped in human culture. (*Ibid.* p.96)

it is possible to see how the correlations between stages in the development of communication, language and cognition, as outlined earlier, could hold true, since it is only the emphasis, not the essence, of Piagetian theory that is being shifted.

Conceptions of the Child Implicit in Piaget's Theory

There are, however, more radical views of the relation between social process and intellectual development. A number of writers appear to take the line that once one has admitted such a change in emphasis within Piagetian theory one has, in fact, totally changed its essential character. Piaget's theorizing is inherently individualistic in its emphasis—and perhaps necessarily so, since it *is* the individual who must in some way acquire and come to possess knowledge. Yet, in the views of many theorists, this assumption begs in an *a priori* fashion, the whole nature of our individuality. Rather than taking the view that we are individuals—full stop, the question of where our individuality comes from must be addressed. Shotter (1974), for example, points to this dilemma. An infant cannot live without thought, given his neotenous lack of ability to execute what biological directives he is endowed with, and yet he cannot think for himself. 'Until he has constructed his own thought mechanisms, I shall propose that he *uses* his mother as a 'mechanism' to do the thinking required in the realisation of his intentions' (*Ibid.* p.226). Ignoring questions of how exactly an infant might 'use' his mother—the nature of his influence, its intentionality, etc.—there can be discerned a very different conception of human development here: development as the wresting of individuality from what Spitz (1965) has termed a state of 'psychological symbiosis' between the infant and his adult caretakers. We are not *born* as psychological individuals in this view: we *attain* that state through development.

To contrast these views: for Piaget language arises through a gradual development of the imitative ability to the level at which it begins to provide the footing for the construction of signifiers which mediate the transition from the sensorimotor to the semiotic period:

The advantages of representative thought over the sensorimotor scheme are in reality due to the semiotic function . . . [which] detaches thought from action and is the source of representation. Language plays a particularly important role in formative process. Unlike images and other semiotic instruments, which are created by the individual as the need arises, language has already been elaborated socially and contains a notation for an entire system of cognitive instruments (relationships, classifications, etc.) for use in the service of thought. The individual learns this system and then proceeds to enrich it (Piaget and Inhelder, 1969, pp. 86–7).

The stress on the individual is obvious, the child 'standing over against the world which it knows' (MacMurray, 1961, p.11). Language is an ability an individual can acquire for the purpose of *thinking* more efficiently: 'language is the vehicle par excellence of symbolisation, without which thought could never become really socialised' (Piaget, 1954, p.54).

MacMurray (1957, 1961), on the other hand, sees language in relation to *action*, not thought, with the result of ending the 'solitariness of the thinking self' and placing the individual 'firmly in the world which he knows' (MacMurray, 1961, p.12):

Language is the major vehicle of human communication.
    Communication is the sharing of experience. (*Ibid.* p.12)
    . . . human experience is, in principle, shared experience; human life, even in its most individual elements, is a common life; and human behaviour carries always, in its inherent structure, a reference to the personal other . . . the unit of personal existence is not the individual, but two persons in personal relation . . . The personal is constituted by personal relatedness. The unit of the personal is not the 'I', but the 'You and I'. (*Ibid.* p.61)

MacMurray's reasoning behind this conclusion is that an infant's activities are not merely motivated, but that their motivation is regulated by intention, where the motives are the baby's and the intentions the mother's: 'The satisfaction of his motives is governed by his mother's intention' (*Ibid.* p. 51). The infant cannot think but he cannot live without thought; he cannot act intentionally, yet if no-one intends his survival and acts with the intention of securing it, he again cannot live: 'He can live only through other people and in dynamic relation with them . . . His rationality is already present, though only germinally, in the fact that he lives and can only live by communication' (*Ibid.* p.51). The field of social interaction thus becomes essential to the developmental perspective. The child functions as a part of the adult world from birth, and his development is one in which he wrests his mental operations away from adults to *become* an individual. It is through communication that his mental abilities are appropriated.

Whilst there may be echoes here of the views of Newson and Newson (1976) it is noticeable that it is not a change *in emphasis* that is being proposed, but a change *in essence*. It follows from MacMurray's view that:

if language [and hence communication] is fundamental to human existence, [then] the human sphere, the field of the personal, cannot be understood through organic categories, in functional or evolutionary terms. It means . . . that men are not organisms, that the human world is as distinct from the organic as the organic is from the material, though it is built upon the organic as the organic is upon the material. (MacMurray, 1961, p.12)

Then, as Gauld and Shotter have argued:

there is no hope of our being able to exhibit the nascent intentions, actions, concepts, communicative endeavours, etc., of the young infant as arising from some synthesis of behavioural or mental elements that are not intentional, conceptual, etc. (Gauld and Shotter, 1977, p.200)

It follows, in other words, that the conceptual system into which Piaget has moulded a formless world to yield compartmentalized coherence does not need to be tampered with: it requires fundamental recompartmentalization. Such arguments show it as necessarily following from MacMurray's position that the major concepts of what is essentially an hermeneutic explanation of action (as implied by MacMurray's, but not Piaget's position) are not translatable *au fond* into the terms of a theory formulated at a different level—Waismann's views regarding 'levels of discourse' notwithstanding (see Gauld and Shotter, 1977, p.11). Basically, where Piaget sees the *origins* of knowledge residing in the interaction between the subject and object, this more radical approach sees the *growth* of knowledge as located in the interactions between agents who share the locus of responsibility for the outcomes of 'their' actions: the origins of knowledge are to be sought elsewhere in the *indivisible* dialectic of biology and history, individual and culture: subject and object do not exist as *a prioris*.

Trevarthen has reviewed many of these Janus-faced stances in the course of redirecting our attention to the often overlooked empirical phenomena of this early phase of child development. He notes that 'there is undoubtedly considerable agreement about what infants do in communication during the first year . . . But none of the published accounts satisfactorily explain the consistent changes' (Trevarthen, 1978, p.223). His survey of the evidence leads him to conclude, with respect to the Piagetian position, that:

developments of personality and of communication in infancy cannot be explained by attending only to the cognitive achievements of the infant as an isolated perceiver and intender. They are probably not dependent on explorations with objects and requisition of schemata for constant properties of objects. (*Ibid.* p.226)

The social interactionist approach falls down because of the widespread agreement on the number of new achievements emerging at about nine months in the field of communication—irrespective of the time or place of the reported achievement, and thus in independence of social input. He concludes that the almost 'endless list of new achievements at nine months' could not be mastered unless there is an innate social aspect in the human's endowments whose flowering is regulated by processes of maturation.

We thus have three main positions. Firstly, there is the Piagetian, which may be criticized for its lack of a social perspective and its consequent supposed inadequacy in explaining the development of communicative abilities. Secondly, there is the social approach, attempting to rectify the shortcomings of the Piagetian in this context, by focussing on the development of rule-governed activities through social interaction. This approach, though, is bedevilled by the problems of the extraordinary regularity of infant development, and that raised by Harré (1974); that if human social behaviour is rule-governed one is still faced with the problem of explaining 'the universality of certain social types and presentation styles'. Finally, there is Trevarthen's solution: that the infant is innately endowed with two forms of intentionality, one directed at objects, the other at people; and that the unfolding of these abilities, and their subsequent interaction with each other is controlled by processes of maturation. From the epistemological position, this solution begs the questions of how these abilities gained their innate status, and how these properties are elaborated during their maturation in a social world by the individual.

A Fourth Theory
We believe that the above three approaches all contain an element of truth. That ultimately intellectual structures are located within an individual (Piaget); that the origin of many of these structures is to be found in the child's communicative interaction with his social world; and finally that there are innate components of intentionality (Mac-Murray) and their maturation (Trevarthen) involved in the development of both communicative and intellectual abilities. Further, we would argue that there is a common ground to be found in all these approaches in the concept of *implication*. Here, then, we wish to outline a synthetic approach to this stage of development.

Implication in the individual perspective
Although Piaget does not make emphatic usage of the notion of implication it has a central locus within the more general epistemological position he develops out of his developmental studies. The concepts of *consciousness* and *implication* go hand in hand, setting up and following paths whose realisation in consciousness constitutes development:

Consciousness sets up a system of interpretations whose basic notions are designation and 'implication' as between meanings: for example, 2 is not the 'cause' of 4, but its meaning 'implies' that $2 + 2 = 4$, which is not at all the same thing. These implications may be naive or simple, but they may also be elaborated by a scientific type of reasoning such as produces the 'pure' sciences of logic and mathematics . . . . Consciousness cannot be left out of account, since it is the very basis of the formal systems on which our comprehension of matter depends. (Piaget, 1971, p.49)

Consciousness is essential in order to judge truth and value, i.e., to reach the implications which specifically characterise them. (Piaget, 1963)

The other great contemporary philosopher whose major concern is with the growth of objective knowledge, Sir Karl Popper (1972), takes quite a similar line. Popper notes how human constructions, such as the number system, bring into being new consequences, but ones which were unintended by their creators: examples in this case being prime and perfect, odd and even numbers. Such *objective facts* as these are implicit in the number system, yet obviously it is possible for an individual to be able to count whilst remaining oblivious to these *hard facts* implied in the system he counts with. Cognitive development then becomes the progressive equilibration of cognitive structures to the point at which the logical necessity of such implied phenomena 'is recognized not only by some inner feeling, which cannot be proved, but by the intellectual behaviour of the subject' (Piaget, 1971, p.316).

Implication in the social perspective
Views very similar to those of Piaget (1971) are put forward by a major social protagonist, George Herbert Mead: 'nature has meaning and implication' (Mead, 1934, p.78fn). Mead, however, develops this point in the context of social rather than individual cognition:

Meaning can be described, accounted for, or stated in terms of symbols or language at its highest and most complex stage of development ... but language simply lifts out of the social process a situation which is logically or implicitly there already. (*Ibid*. p. 79)

As adults we are continuously coming face-to-face with ambiguous social situations in which we wonder 'does he mean *this* or *that*', or often unconsciously miss *that* and perceive only *this*, so setting in motion a train of unfortunate events. (This phenomenon is obvious in, for example, Tom Sharpe's novels, where the 'plot' is established through a tangled web of misunderstanding and its subsequent 'rectification'). As adults we are adept at picking up the implications of the social process. In Mead's view, so is the child, and his abilities develop through his coming to a perception of the implications of his acts, and his subsequent use of them to guide his future acts: these acts being necessarily social in character.

Though often apparently contradictory to Piaget concerning the relationship of consciousness and implication (for example Piaget, 1934, pp.17–8). Mead's views again have many similarities. The essential difference in emphasis is that he sees consciousness as initially an *emergent* out of the social process, and so ultimately the implications whose realisation constitute development are also to be located there. Once language-dependent consciousness emerges it engenders a reflective form of intelligence (that is, Piaget's 'consciousness') which can make explicit the implications it is presented with and presents to itself. Bar differences, then, in the connotations of the term 'consciousness', there is a marked congruity between the views of Mead and Piaget.

Further, as Mead, 1934, p. 335, notes the pre-condition of reflective intelligence is 'the development of the nervous system, which enables the individual to take the attitude of the others' (that is, make social implications explicit). Thus we also have a direct link between such formulations and those of Trevarthen (1977), and not an exclusion of them by the empirical data as Trevarthen himself implies. (*Ibid*. p.220) There is, then, an underlying congruity between both the individual and social (and probably also the maturational) approaches: that of the apprehension and realisation of implications.

Implication in communicative development
Within this synthetic perspective Lock (1980) has argued the communicative development (and hence also cognitive development, c.f. Newson and Newson, 1976) occurs through the child's coming to grasp a hierarchically ordered set of implications which arise out of his biological existence in a social world. This starting point is similar to that taken by Piaget, but here 'reflexes' or physiologically motivated actions are seen as having a social component—crying, for example, cannot be effective in a social vacuum. Thus the child is seen as initially reacting to the bodily discomforts he experiences, and the value one may anthropomorphically ascribe to such reactions is something like 'I do not want that', where 'that' is the source of discomfort. It is here that we come to the notion of a hierarchically ordered set of implications, for the value of the child's activity necessarily implies that there is some state of affairs which the child *does* want. However, until his needs and their objects become known to him, he can only reflexly express a negative attitude to his current state. Generally when he does so his mother will intervene to alleviate his discomfort—something she *must* do, for the infant is in many spheres incapable of doing this for himself (c.f. MacMurray, 1957,

1961). Through this intervention, and given the child is endowed with some form of memory, his needs and their objects will become determinate to him, and provide the basis from which his knowledge may grow. So as a result of being immersed in continued interactions the child will begin to cry with a knowledge of his goal—what he is crying for. His activity now has the anthropomorphic value 'I want that'. At first he gives little evidence in his actions of appreciating the next necessary implication in the hierarchy: while 'that' is provided only by the intervention of another agent, it is not until about nine months of age that crying and similar actions appear to be aimed *at* the other. Only at this time does he begin to use actions with the anthropomorphic value 'You do that'.

Anthropomorphic values have been ascribed to his actions for obviously the child himself cannot represent his knowledge to himself in a linguistic manner. However, when he does attain a representation ability through the semiotic function, language functions emerge in line with the above hierarchically ordered set of implications with some complications added by the phenomenon of reference: a decentration from comments on present self-events, to the expression of intent, to a linguistically staged appreciation of the actions of others (Lock, 1978). Pre-linguistic communication and language both follow along similar lines, being predicated upon a hierarchically ordered set of implications which are sequentially discovered by the child.

Bar the fact that Lock (1978) characterizes this process of discovery as socially, rather than individually, based and guided; and appears to use a different terminology; there seems to be an affinity between this and the Piagetian perspective espoused by Sinclair (1967, 1969, 1973a, 1973b): that language accomplishes a linguistic reconstruction of the child's knowledge at a new level, and does so in ways that almost recapitulate developments at the older level. While that affinity is there it should not be allowed to obscure the important differences in emphasis. We have already discussed the spheres of the individual and the social: here we will finish by looking at two other areas in conjunction: the nature and reality of pre-linguistic cognitive structures; and the relation of language to the development of the representational ability.

Our disagreement with Piaget here is rather abstract. Piaget regards the schemas of sensorimotor intelligence as cognitive structures constituting 'a sort of sensorimotor concept, or more broadly, the motor equivalent of a system of relations and classes' (Piaget, 1952, p.385). Whilst schemas come in all shapes and sizes, they share all the common characteristic of the constituent behaviour sequence being an organized totality: schemas are 'an ensemble of sensorimotor elements mutually dependent or unable to function without each other' (*Ibid.* p.244). As Karmiloff-Smith (1979, p.10) notes, Piaget argues that such cognitive structures 'are implicit *in the child's behaviour* rather than merely part of the observer's model'.

By contrast, while we would agree that sensorimotor schemas or action strategies are *implicit* in the child's behaviour, we regard cognitive structures as only potential, and one in fact more a part of the observer's model. We are saying something like this: the child possesses strategies to deal with the world in respect of the immediate problems it sets him. He may possess, say, a strategy for attracting another's attention to obtain food. That other is known, then, as a means to obtaining the bodily end of physiological satisfaction. This is different from saying that the other is known as an independent agent existing in objective space and time and detached from the child. And, in our view, it is only when independent cognitive elements come into being that it is legitimate to talk of cognitive structures. Prior to that the 'elements' of cognition are, as Piaget himself notes, structure-dependent totalities comprised of no structure-independent entities. Cognitive structures are part of the observer's model, and are present in the sensorimotor child's intellect rather in the manner that an oak tree is present in an acorn.

Thus we see the child's prelinguistic knowledge of agency say, as comprised of action schemes implicit in his behaviour, with notions such as agency etc. implied by this knowledge, but only potential in it. Thus the cognitive structure is implied by the action strategies, stands behind them, and is not called upon to inform action. Rather, action functions to inform the implied and potential cognitive structure, and bring it, through development, more to the forefront of the child's knowledge.

The above stems from our view of the relation of language, cognition and social reality differing from that proposed by Piaget. When Piaget sees cognition as the dominant factor, with language following on behind it, to represent knowledge preformed on the cognitive plane, our view is much closer to that of Karmiloff-Smith (1979, pp.13–4):

It could be argued that it is through language that children can best detach their actions from objects. Words are handy building blocks and can be used positively before they are fully comprehended. Language does not merely serve *post factum* as a tool for presenting what is already understood. Language is not only a symbolic representation of reality, but is a very essential part of that reality. It could be maintained, therefore, that language is not just the outcome of the need to detach objects from the child's sensorimotor action schemes: language can actually be considered as being constructive in the detachment process.

Prior to language knowledge is subjectively organized in a structure-dependent manner. Post-language it becomes objectively organized around isolable, structure independent units through the agency of language's symbolic power. The major cognitive event that language is responsible for is that of the propositional mode. Early language appears as a way of communicating an undifferentiated subjective relationship with the world in which action and object are necessarily not differentiated. It decentres slowly and in this process creates the propositional ability to objectively relate objects in the world (human and physical) to other objects. This process is one whereby objective form is given to those previously potential cognitive structures standing behind the child's strategies, and gives them an explicit existence (see Lock, 1980, Chapters 5 and 8 for a further discussion). However, while these structures are now created as actual, it should not be thought that they now come totally to the fore and guide the child's actions in the world. The contemplative mode is still a step back from the involved, so that while we may say that objective structures now exist, they do so in an *actually* implicit, as opposed to *potentially* implicit, fashion.

We say this because it is important to remember both Karmiloff-Smith's (1979) point that words are building blocks, and that young children rarely use language to philosophize about the world: they use it to act in the world—to be given things, share laughter about them, say 'hello' or 'goodbye' and so on. Language primarily deals with demands and regulating social interaction; only later, as these structures are flushed out more and more, do they begin to prompt activities such as questioning, seeking explanations and so on about the physical world.

Structures, then, are implicit in the child's behaviour at a second remove, and only become actualized through social interaction slowly drawing out these implications and injecting into them at a later stage the symbolic building blocks whereby they can become actual. By placing structures at this further remove, and crediting them as having a profoundly important existence in part of the observer's model—the observer really being a participant in the child's development—we are able to preserve the undoubted insights Piaget has provided by welding them to the social perspective encapsulated in MacMurray's view (MacMurray, 1957, 1961), that the child is necessarily part of a rational world at birth, the unit of personal existence being not the 'I' but the 'You and I'.

References

Austin, J. (1962) *How to do Things with Words*, Oxford University Press, London.

Bates, E. (1976) *Language and Context: The Acquisition of Pragmatics*, Academic Press, London.

Bateson, M. C. (1975) 'Mother-infant exchanges : the epigenesis of conversational interaction', in Aaronson, D. and Rieber, W. (eds) *Developmental Psycholinguistics and Communication Disorders*, New York Academy of Sciences, New York.

Bloom, L. (1970) *Language Development: Form and Function in Emerging Grammars*, MIT Press, Cambridge, Mass.

Bloom, L. (1973) *One Word at a Time*, The Hague, Monton.

Bower, T. G. R. (1979) *Human Development*, W. H. Freeman and Co., San Francisco.

Bowlby, J. (1969) *Attachment and Loss*, Vol. 1 *Attachment*, The Hogarth Press, London.

Brazelton, T. B., Tronick, E., Adamson, L., Als, M. and Wise, S. (1975) 'Early mother/infant reciprocity', in Porter, R. and O'Connor, M. (eds) *Mother–Infant Interaction*; *CIBA Foundation Symposium 33 New Series*, Elsevier, Amsterdam.

Brown, R. (1973) *A First Language : the Early Stages*, Harvard University Press, Cambridge, Mass.

Bruner, J. S. (1975) 'The ontogenesis of speech acts', *Journal of Child Language*, 2, 1–19

Bruner, J. S. (1976) 'From communication to language : a psychological perspective', *Cognition*, 3, 255–87

Buber, M. (1958) *I and Thou*, Charles Scribner, New York.

Carter, A. L. (1974) 'The development of communication in the sensorimotor period : a case study', doctoral dissertation, University of California, Berkeley.

Carter, A. L. (1979) 'Pre-speech meaning relations: an outline of one infant's sensorimotor morpheme development', in Fletcher, P. and Garman, M. (eds) *Studies in Language Acquisition*, Cambridge University Press.

Collis, G. M. (1977) 'Visual co-orientation and maternal speech', in Schaffer, H. R. (ed.) *Studies in Mother–Infant Interaction*, Academic Press, London.

Condon, W. S. (1979) 'Neonatal entrainment and enculturation', in Bullowa, M. (ed.) *Before Speech*, Cambridge University Press.

Condon, W. S. and Sander, L. W. (1974) 'Neonate movement is synchronised with adult speech : interactional participation and language acquisition', *Science*, 183, 99–101.

Corrigan, R. (1976) 'The relationship between object permanence and language development: How much and how strong?' paper presented to the Child Language Research Forum, Stanford University.

Corrigan, R. (1978) 'Language development as related to stage 6 object permanence development', *Journal of Child Language*, 5, 173–89.

Corrigan, R. (1979) 'Cognitive correlates of language : differential criteria yield differential results', *Child Development*, 50, 617–631.

Dore, J. (1978) 'Conditions for the acquisition of speech acts', in Markova, I. (ed.) *The Social Context of Language*, John Wiley, Chichester.

Dore, J., Franklin, M. B., Miller, R. T. and Ramer, A. L. H. (1976) 'Transitional phenomena in early language acquisition', *Journal of Child Language*, 3, 13–27.

Edwards, D. (1973) 'Sensori-motor intelligence and semantic relations in early child grammar', *Cognition*, 2, 395–434.

Furth, H. G. (1966) *Piaget and Knowledge*, Prentice Hall, New Jersey.

Gauld, A. and Shotter, J. (1977) *Human Action and its Psychological Investigation*, Routledge & Kegan Paul, London.

Gopnik, A. (1978) 'No, there, more and allgone : why the first words aren't about things', paper presented at International Symposium on First Language Acquisition, Japan.

Gopnik, A. (1979) 'Words and plans : the relationship of early language and intelligent action', paper given at The Child Language Seminar, Reading, England.

Goren, C. C., Sarty, M. and Wu, P. (1975) 'Visual following and pattern discrimination of face-like stimuli by newborn infants', *Pediatrics*, 56(4), 544–9.

Greenfield, P. M. and Smith, J. (1976) *The Structures of Communication in Early Language Development*, Academic Press, London.

Halliday, M. A. K. (1975) *Learning How to Mean*, Edward Arnold, London.

Harré, R. (1974) 'Some remarks on "rule" as a scientific concept', in Mischel, T. (ed.) *Understanding Other Persons*, Basil Blackwell, Oxford.

Hogan, L. (1898) *A Study of a Child*, Harper, New York.

Ingram, D. (1978) 'Sensorimotor intelligence and language development', in Lock, A. (ed.) *Action, Gesture and Symbol: The Emergence of Language*, Academic Press, London.

Karmiloff-Smith, A. (1979) *A Functional Approach to Child Language*, Cambridge University Press.

Lock, A. J. (1978) 'The emergence of language', in Lock, A. J. (ed.) *Action, Gesture and Symbol : the Emergence of Language*, Academic Press, London.

Lock, A. J. (1980) *The Guided Reinvention of Language*, Academic Press, London.

Lyons, J. (1972) 'Human Language', in Hinde, R. A. (ed.) *Non-Verbal Communication*, Cambridge University Press.

MacKay, D. M. (1972) 'Formal analysis of communicative processes', in Hinde, R. A. (ed.) *Non-Verbal Communication*, Cambridge University Press.

MacMurray, J. (1957) *The Self as Agent*, Faber, London.

MacMurray, J. (1961) *Persons in Relation*, Faber, London.

MacNamara, J. (1972) 'Cognitive basis of language learning in infants', *Psychological Review*, 79, 1–13.

Malinowski, B. (1923) 'The problem of meaning in primitive languages', supplement to Ogden, C. K. and Richards, I. A. *The Meaning of Meaning*, Routledge & Kegan Paul, London.

Mead, G. H. (1934) *Mind, Self and Society*, Chicago University Press.

Meltzoff, A. N. (1981) 'Imitation, intermodal coordination and representation in early infancy', in Butterworth G. E. (ed.) *Infancy and Epistemology*, Harvester Press, Brighton. pp.85–114.

Menn, L. (1976) 'Pattern, control and contrast in beginning speech: a case study in the development of word form and function', unpublished doctoral dissertation, University of Illinois

Mikeš, M. (1967) 'Acquisition des catégoires grammaticales dans le langage de l'ènfant', *Enfance*, 20, 289–98

Mikeš, M. and Vlahovıc, P. (1966) 'Razvoj gramatickih kategorija u decjem govoru', *Prilozi proucavanju jezika, II*. Novi Sad, Yugoslavia.

Moore, M. K. and A. N. Meltzoff (1978) 'Object permanence, imitation and language development : toward a neo-Piagetian perspective on communication and cognitive development', in Minifie, F. D. and Lloyd, L. L. (ed.) *Communicative and Cognitive Abilities: Early Behavioural Assessment*, University Park Press, Baltimore.

Mounoud, P. and Vinter, A. (1981) 'Representation and Sensorimotor development', in Butterworth G. E. (ed.) *Infancy and Epistemology*, Harvester Press, Brighton. pp.201–235.

Murphy, C. M. and Messer, D. J. (1977) 'Mothers, infants and pointing : a study of gesture', in Schaffer, M. R. (ed.) *Studies in Mother/infant interaction*, Academic Press, London.

Nelson, K. (1974) 'Concept, word and sentence : interrelations in acquisition and development', *Psychological Review*, 81, 267–85

Newson, J. and Newson, E. (1976) 'On the social origins of symbolic functioning', in Varma, V. P. and Williams, P. (eds) *Piaget, Psychology and Education*, Hodder & Stoughton, London.

Ninio, A. and Bruner, J. S. (1978) 'The achievement and antecedents of labelling', *Journal of Child Language*, 5, 1–15

Piaget, J. (1952) *The Origins of Intelligence in Children*, Norton, New York.

Piaget, J. (1954) *The Child's Construction of Reality*, Basic Books, New York.

Piaget, J. (1962) *Play, Dreams and Imitation in Childhood*, Routledge and Kegan Paul, London.

Piaget, J. (1963) 'The multiplicity of forms of psychological explanations', in Fraissé, P. and Piaget, J. (eds) *Traité de Psychologie Experimentale, Vol. I*, Presses Universitaires de France, Paris. English translation (1968) *Experimental Psychology : Its Scope and Method*, Routledge & Kegan Paul, London. Quoted in Gruber, H. E. and Vonéche, J. J. (eds) (1977) *The Essential Piaget*, Routledge & Kegan Paul, London. pp. 746–66.

Piaget, J. (1971) *Biology and Knowledge*, Edinburgh University Press.

Piaget, J. (1977) 'Chance and dialectic in biological epistemology: a critical analysis of Jacques Monod's theories', in Overton, W. F. and Gallagher, J. M. (eds) *Knowledge and Development, Vol. I*, Plenum Press, London.

Piaget, J. and Inhelder, B. (1969) *The Psychology of the Child*, Routledge & Kegan Paul, London.

Popper, K. (1972) *Objective Knowledge : An Evolutionary Approach*, Clarendon Press, Oxford.

Preyer, W. (1895) *The Mind of the Child*, Appleton, New York.

Schlesinger, I. M. (1971) 'Production of utterances and language acquisition', in Slobin, D. I. (ed.) *The Ontogenesis of Grammar*, Academic Press, London.

Shotter, J. (1974) 'The development of personal powers', in Richards, M. P. M. (ed.) *The Integration of a Child into a Social World*, Cambridge University Press, London.

Sinclair, H. (1967) *Langage et opérations: sous-systèmes linguistiques et opérations concrètes*, Dunod, Paris.

Sinclair, H. (1969) 'Developmental psycholinguistics', in Elkind, D. and Flavell, J. H. (eds.) *Studies in Cognitive Development : Essays in Honour of Jean Piaget*, Oxford University Press, London.

Sinclair, H. (1973a) 'Some remarks on the Genevan point of view on learning with special reference to language', in Hinde, R. A. and Stevenson-Hinde, J. (eds) *Constraints on Learning*, Academic Press, New York.

Sinclair, H. (1973b) 'Language acquisition and cognitive development', in Moore, T. E. (ed.) *Cognitive Development and the Acquisition of Language*, Academic Press, New York.

Slobin, D. I. (1973) 'Cognitive prerequisites for the development of grammar', in Ferguson, C. A. and Slobin, D. I. (eds) *Studies of Child Language Development*, Holt, Rinehart and Winston, Inc, New York.

Spitz, R. A. (1963) 'Life and the dialogue', in Gaskill, H. S. (ed.) *Counterpoint : Libidinal Object and Subject*, International University Press, New York.

Spitz, R. A. (1965) *The First Year of Life*, International Universities Press, New York.

Sugarman-Bell, S. (1973) 'A description of communicative development in the pre-language child', honours thesis, Hampshire College.

Sugarman-Bell, S. (1978) 'Some organisational aspects of pre-verbal communication', in Markova, I. (ed.) *The Social Context of Language*, John Wiley, Chichester.

Trevarthen, C. (1977) 'Descriptive studies of infant behaviour', in Schaffer, M. R. (ed.) *Studies in Mother–Infant Interaction*, Academic Press, London.

Trevarthen, C. and Hubley, P. (1978) 'Secondary intersubjectivity: confidence, confiding, and acts of meaning in the first year', in Lock, A. (ed.) *Action, Gesture and Symbol : The Emergence of Language*, Academic Press, London.

Uzgiris, I. C. and Hunt, J. McV. (1975) *Assessment in Infancy: Ordinal Scales of Psychological Development*, University of Illinois Press, Chicago.

Watson, J. S. (1973) 'Smiling, cooing and "the Game",' *Merrill-Palmer Quarterly*, **18**, 323–39.

List of Contributors

William A. Ball
Department of Psychology, Swarthmore College, USA.

Matthew Brown
Department of Psychology, University of Lancaster, England.

André Bullinger
Faculté de Psychologie et Des Sciences de l'Education, University of Geneva, Switzerland.

George Butterworth
Department of Psychology, University of Southampton, England.

Alan Costall
Department of Psychology, University of Southampton, England.

Kathleen R. Gibson
Department of Anatomy, University of Texas Dental Branch, Houston, Texas, USA.

Annie Vinter
Faculté de Psychologie et Des Science de l'Education, University of Geneva, Switzerland.

Andrew Lock
Department of Psychology, University of Lancaster, England.

Andrew N. Meltzoff
Child Development and Mental Retardation Center and Department of Psychiatry and Behavioural Sciences, University of Washington, Seattle, USA.

Pierre Mounoud
Faculté de Psychologie et Des Sciences de l'Education, University of
    Geneva, Switzerland.

James Russell
Department of Psychology, University of Liverpool, England.

Eliane Vurpillot
Laboratoire de Psychologie Experimentale, Université René
    Descartes, Paris, France.

Translation By:
Ruth Barnard
Nene College, Leicester, England (Chapter 8).

John Churcher
Department of Psychology, University of Manchester (Chapter 7).

Karen Clarke
Birkbeck College, London, England (Chapter 7).

Lesley Grover
Department of Psychology, University of Southampton, England
    (Parts of Chapter 8).

Index